Frances Donaldson,  rote
these letters to her hu   War.
The story they tell is   ave
been used to form the   me
biography. Much of th   is
already available throu   of *the*
Twenties, Freddy Lonsdale, A Twentieth Century Life).

Letters from Jack are occasionally included. He cannot tell much of the serious story of the war because of censorship. Sometimes his letters give more the impression of one long party and lots of friends – a contrast to the isolation and loneliness of Frankie, left behind to the grey skies and rationing of England.

Rose Deakin the daughter of Frankie and Jack was aged 2-7 years old during the war. She has put together the letters to form the life story of 1939-45 with comments and explanations where relevant.

Books by Frances Donaldson

Approach to Farming

Four Years Harvest

Milk Without Tears

Actor Managers

Freddy Lonsdale

Child of the Twenties

The Marconi Scandal

Evelyn Waugh

Edward VIII

P.G. Wodehouse

Yours Plum

History of the British Council

The Royal Opera House

A Twentieth Century Life

Books by Rose Deakin

Microcomputing: Everything you ever wanted to know
Women and Computing: The Golden Opportunity
Database primer
DbaseII explored

Books published by EVE

Someone Like Me by Emily Smith

Radiant Illusion by Nicholas Deakin

East Prawle through the Ages by Kate Jennings

Frances Donaldson:
A Woman's War

Letters to a soldier in the Second World War

Rose Deakin

Rose Deakin
Published by: EVE – Eden Valley Editions
1 Fircroft Way
Edenbridge,
Kent TN8 6EL
Tel: +44 01732 863 939
www.eveeditions.com
Email: eve@topfoto.co.uk

Printed by Createspace

Book Layout © 2015 BookDesignTemplates.com and Kate Jennings, using Garamond font and Palatino for italics

Cover Design by Fred Deakin

ISBN 978-0-9929723-4-9

Website: womanswar.com

Email: rosedeakin@gmail.com

Contents

Pictures: Thanks to the Healey family for permission to use Denis's photographs and drawing.

Thanks to Derry Moore for the photograph of them in old age

Thanks to Ellen Deakin for the tractor drawing.

Thanks to NPG for portrait of Freddy Lonsdale

The 2 photographs of Coventry are provided by Topfoto.co.uk

People mentioned: There is a Who's Who at the end which identifies the most important people mentioned in the letters.

Names: Most people are referred to by their own names, with one or two exceptions.

Timeline for WW2: There are several excellent internet sites with detailed timelines for the war, for example Wikipedia or http://www.historyplace.com/worldwar2/timeline/ww2time.htm

Thanks to everyone who has helped me with reading, comments, proof-reading and advice. I shall not mention names as there are many and you know who you are.

Foreword: Who was she?

She was my mother, Frankie, daughter of Frederick Lonsdale and married to my father, Jack Donaldson. Later in life she was a well-known biographer. As her literary executor I felt the responsibility, to history as well as to them both, to make available the fascinating letters written almost daily over the 6 years of the Second World War. My comments are partly reflecting my own childish view of events described and partly setting the historical context of war.

Frankie was not at all demonstrative and I never realized how much she loved us children, possibly especially me in the early days, until I was almost middle-aged. Had I had access to these letters earlier I would have realized, and I think the love she bore me filled me with confidence for the rest of my life. My brother Thomas was less confident because as the firstborn, with a heart problem as well, her anxiety about him was very great. Also he had a different personality – more anxious himself and given to tears.

The stress, loneliness and anxiety of the war made Frankie less flexible with Thomas and their relationship deteriorated over the years. She loved me mostly because of my frightfulness, saying on one occasion: 'Rose is a vile child. I could eat her'. She herself was a strange mixture of toughness and the nervous anxiety which she had inherited from her father.

Jack and Frankie before the war

Jack and Frankie were both born in 1907 and they married in 1935. Frankie was lucky to meet Jack, who adored her till death and could cope easily with her erratic temperament. She inherited this temperament from her father, Frederick Lonsdale, a leading playwright of his period in both London and New York. She had accompanied him everywhere, having dancing lessons with Fred Astaire, on close terms with people like Irving Berlin and the Gershwins and some members of the British aristocracy, who always opened their doors to welcome amusing and entertaining guests.

Jack came of public-service intellectual stock. His grandfather had been first Premier of New South Wales, his father was Vice-Chancellor of Cambridge University; one uncle was Bishop of Salisbury; the other, head of munitions in the First World War.

Although Jack went to Eton and Cambridge he became a socialist at the time of the General Strike (1926, when he was 19 and still at university) while many of his friends were driving buses to beat the strikers. From then on he devoted

2

himself to good works, gave away half his inheritance to finance the Peckham Pioneer Health Centre – an experiment in community health; resigned his city job to work there; and came very close to communism like many young intellectuals of the time.

His passion for music was a dominating part of his life and character. He founded the Eton Jazz band and later played in the Cambridge jazz band. The conductor was Fred Elizalde of the Savoy Orpheans. After the war Jack was on the board of the Royal Opera House for many years.

Jack worked for prison reform nearly all his life and was made a Life peer in 1967 and went on to be Minister of State for Northern Ireland, (he was offered either something in consumer affairs or Northern Ireland and, being him, chose Northern Ireland. This was in Harold Wilson's government in 1974) and afterwards Minister for the Arts (James Callaghan's government). He was 66 and my mother rang me and said, "Don't laugh, but your father has just been made a junior minister".

Frankie became a well-known writer and biographer. Her most successful work was a biography of Edward VIII for which she won the Wolfson History prize. Her book, The Marconi Scandal, was also highly regarded and quoted in parliament on several occasions.

During the war, Jack worked in logistics and troop supplies. He was 31 at the outbreak of war and served in the Royal Engineers. He was more than once chosen to sort out special problems, including liaising with the Russians in Teheran and being summoned to Cairo to help prepare the invasion of Sicily – the beginning of the victorious march through Europe.

Before the war shattered everyone's lives my parents' life together was idyllic. Without being really rich, they were not short of money, and had the pleasure of building their own house, for which they commissioned the famous architect Walter Gropius, then in England. Influenced by the Peckham health Centre philosophy they had planned how they would live and bring up children – until the advent of the war seemed to crush any such plans.

I visited the Wood House recently for the first time since I was 5 years old. I was stunned, not just by what a nice house it is, but the comparative opulence, set in a large garden and grounds, a biggish house with a servants' bell box in the kitchen. I had a sense of privilege and was astonished, as although in the childhood that I remember, both during and after the war, we had property, as in the farm, nonetheless my parents were always cash-poor. Extravagance was rarely allowed and there was always considerable difficulty in meeting the expenses of our education. We lived in a small farmhouse and ate in the kitchen. It was embarrassing when they came to visit us at school in our broken down shabby-looking car – or even sometimes a van.

The story hinges on Frankie's decision to buy a farm and farm it herself. She and Jack felt that this was the only way that they could provide the childhood that they had envisioned for us children and would also be part of a war effort for her. They always farmed in earnest, depending on it as their only source of income. We children learnt to somewhat despise 'gentlemen (or women) farmers' as cushioned by their other assets from facing the real challenge.

She buys a farm and at first she has to hire a bailiff, as she is too ignorant about farming to take charge. He lives in the farmhouse and she lives in the nearby village, feeling cut off from events. The man resists her efforts to learn as he knows it will be the end of his job if she succeeds. She becomes more angry and determined. At the same time she writes a book *about it and becomes celebrated in the farming world, being invited to broadcast for the BBC to England and America. She feels a fraud as she cannot really run a farm. This, with her nervous temperament, spells trouble.*

Later she breaks free, gets rid of the bailiff and takes over the farm. She does well at first but problems appear. Only by her ruthless perfectionism, determination and hard work does she finally solve the problems. The farm becomes highly rated by the government statistics and her milk yield tops the county records. She is supported throughout by Jack, away at war, who backs her actions in everything. His love is absolute.

There are few collections of women's letters written in the war. Women, especially if they had children to bring up or were too old to join the services, do not feature much in the history of the time – or indeed any time. Their letters were mainly lost, I suppose, because many of the troops would not have had the possibility to save them, travel with them and finally return them to home. Jack was able to do this.

The letters give a description of English life in rural conditions in World War II, an important piece of social history. They wrote almost daily to each other. There were 4 methods of post in the war, 1. Letter post. 2. Airgraph. 3. Postcard. 4. Cable/telegram. All were unreliable, so Frankie used them all, sometimes in duplicate for important letters.

Frankie fought a woman's war, not just bringing up children and doing her bit on the home-front, but fighting a battle to become a proficient farmer providing food for the nation, and taking on the hostility and obstruction of farm workers towards a woman entering a traditionally male-dominated sphere of work.

1: 1939

Phoney War & Buying a Farm

War was declared on 3 September 1939; the life of Jack and Frankie Donaldson, like so many others, was abruptly transformed. The shock was tremendous, although war had been expected. Jack had already enlisted in the army. Frankie had a fragile temperament and spent several days in tears. Old Nan, Jack's nanny from childhood who used to come and help with the children, said to her, "Well, you won't be much use to the children if you cry all the time."

Coney, left, Frankie, right, in despair at the announcement of war

As it happened, the war got off to a slow start. Before Dunkirk in May/June 1940, it was known as the 'Phoney War' and life was not very stressful. Nobody expected the war to last long.

They had discussed the possible future and considered farming as a life that would provide the childhood which they had envisioned for us children, and a good way of life after the war ended.

Frankie decided to buy a farm, although she was not brought up on the land and knew nothing about farming. So in early 1940 she signed up for the Northamptonshire Institute of Agriculture at Moulton, to take lessons. Two of her friends, Mary Dunn and Coney Jarvis, did the same and all three lived during this period at Mary's house, Castle Farm, Lavendon from where they went to Moulton daily. My brother and I with Mary's children, Serena and Nell were also there.

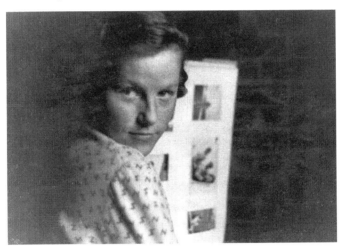

Mary Dunn

We were always told that Mary was the most attractive woman of her generation, as much for her personal magnetism as her beauty.

18 September, 1939

The more I think about things, the more I think, if we ever get back again and settled down, we'd better seriously try to take up farming. I know that I don't really want anything from life but to be with you and the children and work together at home, and I can't see what else we can work at. Think about it seriously.

January 15, 1940

When I arrived at Lavendon Mary had been the proud owner of a farm for about two weeks and had been attending the Farm Institute for about the same time. Her conversation was so lavishly sprinkled with references to stores, foddering, lime efficiency, soil analyses, and so on that I was in despair of ever catching up. However, she admitted that she had already made one or two bloomers in class, and when pressed for details said that on one occasion when the lecturer had been emphasizing the necessity of making sure, when buying a dairy bull, that it had a good milk record, she had remarked that she failed to see how a bull could have a good milk record.

Mary in her farmyard with Serena (right) and Nell

Coney and I enrolled without difficulty at the Farm Institute which we try to attend every morning. The snow lies so thickly and so frozen on the ground that one can walk round Mary's farm crossing from one field to another over the top of the hedges. Moulton is about ten miles away. Nine days out of ten when we have driven a few miles the car begins to boil and we wait until, by alternately running it until it boils and then turning it off and waiting, we gradually thaw out the water. We are almost invariably late.

17 April , 1940:
Do you know that Plummy and Ethel were caught at Le Touquet. I can't conceive what this can mean or whether they can emerge alive. I have not spoken to Leonora yet.

Plummy is P.G. Wodehouse, stepfather of her great friend Leonora. Ethel is his wife and Leonora's mother. He was my godfather, though, I think, oblivious of the fact.

(about the farming lecture:) O boy, there is only another ¼ hr of this lecture and seriously once I get out I don't believe I shall ever come in again.... When you think of what is going on all over the world I don't think I can stand sitting listening to this rubbish every day. For the last two months I have come entirely and only with the idea of being polite to Mr Stewart.

Frankie immediately understood the advantage of being on good terms with the teachers and people of influence in the world of farming. This acted to counterbalance the malignance of the working men.

Jack meanwhile was settling in France, managing trains and the logistics of troop movements supplying a part of the front line wherever it went.

6 December, 1939
We all went to lunch with the station master's, M. &

Mme Racine. This was a true epic. We started with 2 glasses of byrrh as aperitif, (a deux jambes!) and some pleasant hors-d'oeuvres. Then Coquille St.Jacques, which is a sort of scallop and very good. With this a very dry white Burgundy. Then the most delicious pigeon, roast with butter and a little brandy, one of the finest flavours I've tasted, and with it some excellent red Chateau neuf du Pape 1934. Then an old Norman custom i.e. a glass of Calvados all round "pour faire couler" so that you can start the next course without feeling jaded. Then roast chicken and the most beautiful stuffing, and a separate course of roast tiny potatoes. With this, some lovely red Moulin a Vent Burgundy 1933, then cheese and more Chateauneuf, then an exquisite apple tart, with a sweet Grave, then coffee and Cognac and more Calvados.

I was fascinated recently to read a novel called **To Bed with Grand Music**, *written at the end of the war by Marghanita Laski. This is a book, based on a true story, about a woman in almost exactly the same circumstances as Frankie, with a husband who, like him, 'seemed to be having a marvellous time. Moonlight picnics in the desert and sherry parties and dances and what-not'.*

Many of Jack's letters read as if he were attending one long party. For soldiers there was a lot of waiting around in the war and also any details of interesting topics, such as action or whereabouts, were censored. In that book the heroine failed to find a solution for her loneliness over 6 years and ended up serially unfaithful, embittered and heading for a broken marriage. Frankie solved the problem by hard physical work which always helped her cope with depression, as did Jack's unquestioning love and support. How lucky we were to have such parents. Frankie bought Gypsy Hall Farm, Wilmcote, nr Stratford-Upon-Avon, Warwickshire in March 1940.

I found the menus below when going through his papers recently. There were several more, from dates all through the war and in the Italian campaign towards the end.

The menu above, of a different feast but with the station master again – see drawing of train on the left. It says at the bottom: "a l'arriere de l'avant de l'arriere". (At the rear of the front of the rear.)

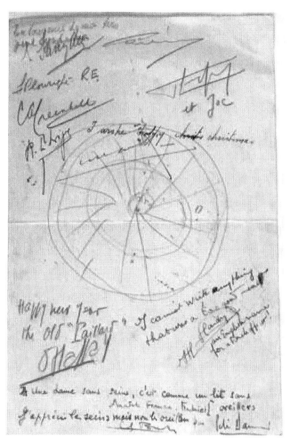

And here, the seating plan and signatures. Jack has not signed it so this must have been his copy. Someone has written: "Une dame sans seins, c'est comme un lit sans oreillers."And the reply is "J'apprecis les seins mais non le oreiller." Another says "I cannot write anything – that was too good meal". With signatures, mostly illegible.

5 April, 1940

The farm itself I still think is a good buy in many ways. No one will ever say the Donaldsons have bought a lovely farm but you know it wouldn't help us much if they did and we were losing a package on it.

12

This farm is so near the borderline of unattractiveness and that is what worries me about your not having seen it. To me it is not unattractive. I like its workmanlikeness. *There was another problem. Jack had some capital from the sale of a house.* However, partly because money was in some way unreal to him he gave nearly half of it to found an experiment in community health: the Peckham Health Centre.

The farm cost £10,000 and that left a capital float of £5,000 but there was no more. Unfortunately he lent this £5,000 to a friend called Julian Sorsbie, who now failed to repay it. This left Frankie short of money and capital that she had expected to have and to invest in stocking the farm. She always had a worrying overdraft to live with. A few months later she wrote:

20 July, 1940
About money: It is enough to throw it about, and quite seriously I do think you have got to stop ... and take up a feeling of more responsibility about the children. I take up quite definitely the line that you are being kind to Julian at the expense of the children.

2: 1940

Dunkirk and fear of invasion

The war took a turn for the worse. This was the end of the 'Phoney War' which is considered to have lasted from September 3rd, 1939 to May 10th, 1940. On that day German troops marched into Belgium, the Netherlands and Luxembourg. Jack was in a part of Normandy south of Dunkirk and thus not part of the retreat. He did not return to England until a little later. I have no information about how or exactly when he got back, except that it was later than Dunkirk.

9 April, 1940
Well, bang goes Denmark and most of Norway. The 6 o'clock news says a naval battle is in progress. I hope to God we swipe the buggers….I can't help feeling rather pleased that things are moving. It must bring it nearer to an end and will infuriate Americans and all neutrals.

14 April, 1940
A letter today, finally clinching the farm. You've been terrific in snap and decision. It's always right to go against the strong opinion of an expert. And if it's wrong, we can probably sell at no loss. I do think you're doing well.

10 May, 1940 Lavendon

Well now it's begun and it's difficult to know what to say. We have said it all so often and you will know quite well how I am feeling. The only thing we can do is to try to believe in our luck and go on attempting an ordinary life. Today I am simply shrivelled with nerves and misery but I suppose I will sooner or later get used to living in a real war. O dear it still seems unbelievable that this could happen to us. Try to write to me if only a p.c. with nothing on it.

I spend most of the day on my knees looking up places on a large map of France which lies on the floor.

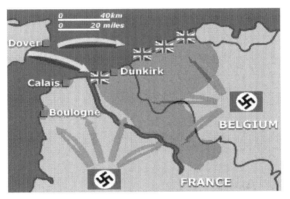

Battle positions, Dunkirk

25 May, 1940

I can't really write to you because I daren't even think of you. I don't know where you are or what has happened to you. But just in case the posts still work, this is just to tell you we are all right.

She wrote in a letter later in the war, in 1942:

"I was going thro' a drawer yesterday and found some letters of mine during the last weeks you were in France in May/June 1940. They were all incredible and I wouldn't have believed them except they were in my own handwriting, but there was one which was without

15

exception the most awful letter I have ever read. Sweat poured down my back and even tho' it was your property and not mine I burnt it. I would have liked to have burnt them all but I thought you might be cross. I think I must have altered. I can't imagine, under any stress of emotion, writing those letters today. But I suppose it was the most awful time of my life."

29 May, 1940 Lavendon
I got a letter from you today dated 22nd and posted on the 24th. I leave for the Institute before the post arrives and it will give you some idea of what I have been feeling during the last 10 days if I tell you that Mary put through 3 telephone calls to try and get hold of me to tell me the letter was there, though she knew I would be back at lunch time. The days I feared most for you were the 20th and 21st so the fact that this was written on the 24th …..Your letter is a very funny one and I could not resist reading most of it to Mary and we both shrieked with laughter. It is so immensely casual and says so fearfully little and, received in this devastating tension, unrelieved by having a job to do which has some bearing on the present events, it reads exactly like a letter from someone who is having a rather exciting holiday, say in the Pyrenees or sailing. You are immensely matter of fact and apparently at that time anyway have absolutely no idea of the sort of scenes which one's imagination creates for one when one is sitting impotently in England.

Of course it is quite different for you, but here an announcer on the wireless says in parenthesis and quite casually that the Germans have dropped bombs and parachutists on hundreds of railway junctions.

Jack was working at railways moving troops and supplies.

The subject is never referred to again and no more light is shed on it. But one knows one will hear no news of any

16

sort, possibly for a month. What was rather heavenly about your letter was your casual attitude that as you were very tired you would write me all details the next day – exactly as though one could count on a normal post as well as everything else. It is very endearing to find you so unmoved.

The whole of my present attitude is based on the assumption that you are the south side of the gap...

Jack was somewhere in Normandy, in line south of Rouen and Dieppe, not sure exactly where, but south of Dunkirk and the German army at that moment.

...and it is really rather heartless to be even temporarily relieved when one thinks of the people in the north. But now it has really begun I find that all my emotions are used up for myself and I have nothing left to spare for other people.

The BEF was back in England. Jack was still in Normandy, after Dunkirk. Returning in the train from London:

30 May, 1940

I met 3 BEF *(British Expeditionary Force)* officers last night including Gordon Lennox. They were simply heavenly. So pleased with themselves and their men. But they said it was the damnedest lie to say the Germans were not good soldiers. They were very funny about the Belgians who they said were never anything but an intolerable nuisance and very fast bicyclists in the wrong direction. They said they met Belgian officers driving out of Belgium as they went in.

The English are sweet today. All the BEF who are back smile broadly at everyone they see and in this carriage are 4 other people, and we are all offering each other cigarettes.

We are all barricaded up on the roads and I have been stopped 7 times for my identity card.

Fears of Invasion: Everyone at this point feared the invasion of England. Jack wrote sending plans for trying to find each other should England be completely overrun.

29 May, 1940

I'm afraid they're certain to try to invade England. If they do, you've just got to stay put. Should just stay on the farm, either Mary's or ours, and look as natural to the neighbourhood as possible. It sounds absurd to think they'd ever get anywhere near you, but everybody felt perfectly safe in Amiens and they were wrong.

German Invasion plan for September 1940, Operation Sea Lion

The first thing is not to be on the roads, and the second is to have food. In the event of complete chaos and our getting separated and unable to meet, I'd go to Lloyds Bank, St James's St. to get your address. Failing that I'd try all friends. Failing that I would go to the entrance of Gypsy Hall on the first of every month, from 12 till 2pm. Failing that to the pub at Shipbourne on the 10th of every month, same hours. Failing that, St Martin's in the Fields, steps Trafalgar Square 6-7am, 12-1pm and 9-10pm. If Norfolk were a clear area, I'd go to Runton *(their holiday house)*... If only the north were clear, I'd aim for Witherslack *(home of Maureen and Oliver Stanley)*... I hope all this is the most idiotic fantasy but intellectually I think it is a very real possibility. Remember that death will re-unite us.

 4 June, 1940

First of all I agree and acknowledge all your plans in the event of invasion and chaos. But have you kept a note of them because they are quite long and you will not remember for long.

Secondly I agree with all you say about England. I think I have already written it to you. Thirdly I agree that for both of us, if it should happen that we were asked to take a risk, England and the war must come first.

I cracked a bit on the night of the 21st when we heard Amiens has gone but that was on your account and also because Mary insisted on getting me drunk which is the last thing one ought to be when things are really bad. But except for that I have been OK though I had an awful week until I heard from you. The morale here was not too hot for a day or two either but never really bad. Then we have all been so tremendously revived by the behaviour of the BEF, RAF and Navy. It is the first time for 10 years the English have attempted the difficult (almost the impossible) and brought it off. I now feel.... how wonderful it is to be English.

Your letter was also sweet about us. I think we shall get through and I am glad in the end I have kept the farm for us and all the difficulties and risks have made me love every blade of it. And you have no idea what a warm little feeling one can have for cattle which one has paid for.

As for the rest, if things do go wrong I have loved you and you have loved me as much as people can love each other and that in itself makes everything worth it and to me is a reason for all human nature. I have not your complete faith in an after-life but I am prepared to accept your belief in it.

11 June, 1940
You say you have heard nothing from me. I didn't write for about 3 days ...it was such an awful time ... I hope you will forgive.

12 June, 1940
Of course during that week or two one did get the impression here that was apparently worse than the actual happenings. There was for instance an article in the NS & S *(New Statesman)* which said that the whole of Northern France was in ashes, that whole villages were razed to the ground under which lay unnumbered and unknown dead and that the worst of H.G. Wells' prophecies had understated the present situation.

I have since seen people who have returned and who say there never was any foundation for this sort of account. But you can imagine the sort of effect it had on me. And I had a vague and superstitious feeling that to write to you was to assume too much and to court disaster. I am so superstitious that I am terrified of putting even this much on paper now.

I remember clearly at one point when writing a letter to Jack that I wrote, "Dear Daddy, I hope you are not dead..." It must have been later in the war, when I had learned to write. Frankie said to me, quite mildly, "I don't think you should send that, as the awful thing is that it might be true by the time he gets it."

Every person we know is now back in England – except you. All very happy and pleased with themselves. .... of course taking a serious view of what happened. You tell me in your letters to be certain to complete the farm whatever happens, so it has all turned out very well. It is ours now and I mean to hang on to it.

One of their friends, Haschi, later Professor Wasserman at UCL, an Austrian Jew who had come to England to escape the Nazis, was interned. His wife, Anni Noll, was a close friend often mentioned in the letters.

30 June, 1940
Haschi has been interned, & Anni is madly upset. There is nothing in the world one can do about it & that makes it impossible to feel much about it.

3: 1940

The farm & difficulties with men

Jack returned to England some time after Dunkirk. There are no details in the letters as to how or when but the part of the army situated south and west of Dunkirk was not involved in the evacuation and returned later. He was located in Darlington in Yorkshire for about 4 months before posting in November 1940.

On the farm the chief difficulty Frankie faced was working with the men. Even today there is endless discussion about the problems women bosses face managing men. Frankie was trying to manage in an occupation which had been traditionally male-dominated. She was learning fast about farming but did not know enough to be able to manage 400 acres of difficult land, so she had to have a bailiff. A bailiff usually lives in the farmhouse itself and he makes all the decisions about the farm. Frankie was staying with the children in a guest house about 3 miles away.

The bailiff at this time was a man called Jones. Frankie was female, aged 32, small and pretty. Jones rode over her roughshod. He also cheated her and stole 23 sheep. Here is the story:

3 July, 1940

Jones is a complete tough and I don't pretend to be a manager of toughs. I meant to buy the milking herd at once and start milking in about 6 weeks. But I want to have full control of it when it comes and I'm sure I shan't get it with Jones around. As against this, everyone points out that I am taking a great chance if I upset him before the harvest is in.

7 July, 1940

I am having a harassing and really rather frightening time. I found out that Jones has been sending our sheep unfit to the market all summer, and we have lost about £100 this way. There are problems with the beef cattle and it becomes clear that 50% of the trouble is the result of mismanagement of a deliberate or negligent kind. I checked the books and found there were 23 sheep unaccounted for. I brought the matter up with him. He was immediately pretty bloody rude. I asked him if any had died. He said he didn't know ... some had but he didn't know how many. When pushed a little further he shouted at me and asked why he should know anymore than me? I made the obvious retort that I paid him to know and left the matter at that.

I went to see Mr Stewart to see if there was any possibility of getting a man to do the threshing if I told Jones to stop working for me. He said none at all and that I must hold off all rows for 10 days or so till the threshing is done. After that I must have a complete inventory of stock and threaten prosecution if any are missing etc etc.

Yesterday Carling came over and pointed out that our hay stacks were not thatched and we should lose the whole of the tops of the stacks if it rained. Of course it poured last night.

I was frightened that if I crossed Jones he would be rude enough to force me to get rid of him at an inconvenient time and I am frightened about the threshing. I estimate we may have lost something like £400 by robbery. I ought to have booted him out in May or June and chanced it.

10 July, 1940

All the fun here is spoilt by this Jones business. The only real reason for being here is the farm and I am fundamentally incapable of taking anything less than a full part in it. I find I have no sustaining interest unless I can really get on with the job.

11 July, 1940

I got rather a sweet letter from you which cheered me up a good deal. On the strength of being cheered up I decided that I was perhaps lying down a bit too much over the Jones situation & it would really be better to try a bit harder to make him do what I want. There is only one way to do this & that is to live in Wilmcote, closer to the farm. I am convinced that I shall do no good with the farm unless I do. Either with Jones or anyone else.

29 July, 1940

We cut the oats today. I wish you were here. It is really such fun. It was a good crop & I cut my arms to ribbons sticking it up into stooks. It is awful because there is always a thistle or something in every bundle as well as the oats.

It is more satisfactory & gives you a greater pride in possession than anything else in the world. You would really love it. A wonderful old boy of 70 who was a friend of the late owner's turned up (at my invitation) to shoot rabbits and foxes (don't say this to any hunting friends you may have because unless they have heard there is a war on it will put you outside the pale) which live in the middle. As you cut round the edges they go nearer to the middle & then at the end they have to make a dash for it. He was simply heavenly & the sort of old man who surreptitiously produces bottles of beer from all over his person.

He shot Thomas *(aged 4)*. He did really. At least a bullet richoted off a stone on to Thomas' leg & bruised & cut it. Thomas roared like a bull & I tore across the field. One of

24

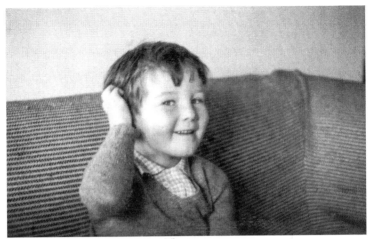

Thomas

the men called Newlands must have torn across behind me though I didn't see him.

There was a terrific sensation with everyone apologising & assuring each other it was quite all right. I suddenly noticed that T. had stopped crying & had disappeared. The man Newlands had quite quietly taken him by the hand & led him off to see the dead fox. Thomas was mad with excitement & saying "You see Mummy. Wasn't it a good think. Now he'll never be able to eat our chickens!" It was one of the kindliest & most instinctively clever things I have ever seen done & Newlands stays for life.

Altogether it was great fun & I ended the day by picking out with Jones six fat bullocks which will go to market tomorrow & bring us something near £200. I am pleased with life again & convinced that farming is **the** thing.

P.S. Still no news from the buggering War Committee.

The War Agricultural Committee was trying to make her plough up grassland which she needed for cattle.

25

14 August, 1940

We had quite a reasonable air raid last night. I heard some aeroplanes bang overhead. I was just thinking to myself "I'll bet any money those are Germans" because they sounded absolutely different from anything I had heard and with that a couple of guns went off. They couldn't have been many miles away and they sounded about half a mile away. I have had some wooden panels made for the upstairs windows because there is no other way of protecting the children from glass. I got up and tried to fit them up but it was absolutely impossible in the dark.

I got the children up and took them down to the hall which is the only place which has no glass. We were there for about one and a half hours and during this time three more lots went bang over us and each time a few minutes later one could hear the guns and bombs but the near one never went off again. After this I shall have to put the wooden panels up every night so that we can stay in our beds.

Later: The raid has increased in dimensions hourly and we are all agog. Apparently what I described in this morning's letter as an anti aircraft gun which was very near wasn't a gun at all but eleven bombs. Casualties here consisted of 7 cattle and one sheepdog at Gypsy Hall Farm, Wilmcote. She jumped over the half door of the stable and hung herself. Apparently she was always terrified of thunder. Mrs Jones says the farmhouse shook to its foundations.

Birmingham really got it I think. The telephone exchange man told me it was pretty bad and the story that has percolated to us is that they got the Nuffield factory and killed eleven men and injured fifty. Anyway we none of us can talk of anything else. I wasn't a bit frightened then but if I had known the noise was bombs I think I might have been and I rather hope they aren't going to give us a nightly visit.

The children were both thrilled by the raid. I always imagined one would spend the time in an air raid distracting their attention and making up all sorts of reasons for the noise etc. Instead of which I just said we were going downstairs because the Germans had come over to bomb us and it wasn't safe upstairs until we had got the wooden shutters up.

We spent an hour and a half giving our views on how many German bombers had been brought down now. Thomas always thinks they have all been brought down. Tonight he inspected the wooden things going up and insisted on seeing them up in my room as well as in his so that we should all be safe.

The farm is more satisfactory & gives you a greater pride in possession than anything else in the world. You would really love it.

P.S. Jones has wrecked the silage. He does this with everything he does not want to do.

On a happier note she wrote:

Darling Major D., Things are a teensy bit better temporarily. Jones, having been damned rude and tiresome for two days has I think thought better of it for the moment and is being a good deal less truculent. Long may it last – at any rate long enough to get through the next week or two until the time arrives for me to disturb his equilibrium again.

I long to hear more from you and all about being a Major and I long to see you.

Her troubles managing men were not over, but she found a much nicer bailiff, easier to get on with, although he still tried to keep her out of nearly everything to do with the farm, and would not help her acquire the more difficult skills. She managed without him in the end, but not for another year.

14 August, 1940

I have just finished listening to Anthony Eden who I thought for his class was not bad. But it is a lowish class. Outside Churchill they seem to be tiny little men. Maybe they're just bad speakers.

Management of Information in WWII. Frankie quite often wrote about the management of the war, and in particular the public relations aspect and the Ministry of Information.

18 August, 1940

Did you hear Duff Cooper's speech? I <u>hated</u> it. Quite apart from the vulgarity of all that boasting it is like flying in the face of Providence. Everyone hates it I think. The ordinary people are very brave and quite unmoved by the raids – in fact rather excited by them I think – and very pleased with the Air Force, but they like to take it all quietly and grimly only being pleased about what has happened and not counting unhatched chickens. When someone talks like Duff Cooper it is as though he brought bad luck on all of us. Winston's boasting is all right because he seems only to say "All right do your damnedest – we can take it" which is quite different. If only all the lesser men wouldn't try to copy him.

Frankie was in a bind because she did not yet know enough about farming to manage without a bailiff and any bailiff tended to be a man not happy to share the responsibility with a young and inexperienced woman, or be managed by her. He also realised that once she knew how to do things, he would be dispensable. So she had to deal with a man's natural misogyny and also his fear of being replaceable. Jones had these feelings in double strength, and even Carling, a nice man who came to replace Jones, refused to allow her to learn the skills or do very much on the farm, leaving her frustrated and unable to learn.

1 October, 1940

Day of troubles. First of all Oakley the deaf and dumb has run a fork through his thumb and is laid off. Then both Wyatts gave notice to leave this Friday. I said nonsense they must give week's notice like anyone else. So they said they did give it last Friday to Jones.

This leaves 2 able bodied men only, besides Carling. However, I am not got down – for 2 reasons. One is treatment of this sort which is just spite makes me feel tough and anyway I shall be damn glad not to have the Wyatts on the farm as they are bad mannered surly louts and I would never really feel a good atmosphere on the farm as long as they were there. So though it puts me temporarily completely on the spot, in the long run I am delighted to think I shan't have to see their dirty little faces every day. I believe with any luck I can weather it.

Jones is now refusing (not directly but in fact) to thresh the beans which are needed for this year's seed. However, I'm not really depressed. I can take anything now there is only a day or two more of Jones. I could never describe to you how much I hate that man or how glad I shall be to see the back of him.

4 October, 1940

Great goings on here. Margetts made the inventory. There were 22 sheep short which Jones accounted for by a series of remarkable deaths. I said to Highman, "Have a lot of sheep died on this farm this summer?" and he replied, "Well I did hear they lost one dipping". I went to a solicitor who told me it was a case for the police. He rang up the police and without mentioning any names gave them the facts and asked them whether they would investigate and take matters up if given the names etc or not. They said yes they would.

Now at this point stop and decide a) what you would have done b) what you think I did – bearing in mind he has done every oddish trick he could think of such as getting

Wyatts to leave without notice, insulting me etc etc etc and also bearing in mind that if police prove case then we can get money back i.e. about £60. Don't cheat - decide before turning.

New Page

Well, I think left to myself I just might have done it. But the Stapledons urged me not to – on the grounds that the waste of nervous energy it would involve sooner or later simply wasn't worth it and that if by chance the police gaoled him the feeling in the village might go either way and I might have difficulty with men etc etc. Anyway Stapes hated the idea and was very keen I shouldn't. So I have done absolutely nothing. I tamely paid their wages tonight and tomorrow I shall pay Jones £24 I owe him and £4 for this week's wages – knowing that he owes us double that. But if by any chance he doesn't get out of the house tomorrow, which he is supposed to be going to, then I may change my mind.

Well, I am not asking whether you approve because I am nearly 100% certain you will and it is just what you would have done. Personally I think it is pretty flabby but it may be worth it to see the end of all of them.

Carling has arrived and I think is going to be v. nice. We are on the spot for milkers and God only knows what we shall do but there it is. But anyway all the really sickening worries are over and if Jones goes tomorrow it will really start to be fun. If I ever had another month like the last I should sell the farm and that's that.

6 October, 1940

JONES HAS GONE. That is the chief news.

Some of the farm men, muck-carting. Mr Carling, standing. Mr
Highman driving International caterpillar tractor, Cyril Wheeldon
behind.

27 November, 1940
Lady Stapledon came to lunch and we talked about the war.
One gets so bored with these static periods and the fact that
we never do anything. What's the good of bombing Bari
one night and Durazzo the next? Why don't we bomb them
all, all day and all night? If it's still because we can't then I
think it's about time we executed the whole cabinet and
began all over again.

I'm glad to see that American journalists are at last
beginning to protest against the idiotic British censorship.
On the same day that the Germans say they have bombed
Birmingham our communique's still refer to a Midland
Town! The M of Information sends people round to see
what morale is like and, thank God, I hear that the reports
they get all say that morale is only bad where damaged by
their own bloody silliness.

I could tell the Ministry of Information that morale
would be a good deal better if any Government office was

31

capable of answering a letter under 6 weeks. Quite apart from no answer from the War Office, my especial grievance, I need 100 poles for fencing. Before I can get them I have to get permission from 3 different authorities, the first being the M of Agriculture and Fisheries. I wrote to the bastards about 3 weeks ago and no answer of any sort. What the M of Information needs to know is that the people of Britain want to get on and win this bloody war — and not in 1943.

28 November, 1940
After my rant of last night I got a letter from the War Office enclosing two forms on which I can cable at internal rates. The conditions are that I must fill in all your details including in what <u>country</u> you are serving. Now since not only do I not know but the <u>whole</u> idea is that I shouldn't know, this seems almost too good even for the War Office.

Frankie's conflict with men like Jones, and later to some extent with Carling, his replacement, was mainly with the higher managerial level of farm workers. Her struggles to assert herself and take control of the farm were also connected with the need to learn and achieve a level of competence herself. She was small, young and female and not their idea of a successful farmer. The main problem was their obstruction of her attempts to gain sufficient experience to be able to take over – though Jones was worse than that as he cheated her.

They were, of course, correct in their anxiety about their jobs and as soon as she found Pat, who became her adviser, she got rid of bailiffs and made a foreman out of Highman, who had no complexes or prejudices.

Although the battles with men could be described from a feminist point of view as prejudice, she also benefitted from the inequality of the sexes by becoming the favourite of various professional men in the Warwickshire farming world. Mr Stewart at Moulton Agricultural Institute, Sir George

Stapledon – a well known expert on farming and landscape - always, Clyde Higgs who helped her and bumped her into taking action, Mr Pattison, Pat, who became her prop and stay – a trusted adviser and later colleague, and Mr Dowler who sold her red poll cattle when he refused to sell to anyone else.

They appear throughout these pages, and without them she would not have triumphed as she did.

Pat, with Y-top stick and sheep-dog

Clockwise from the top:Clyde Higgs, Mr Stewart, Sir George
Stapledon

4: 1940

Bombing Coventry

22 November, 1940

Tomorrow I am going to Coventry to help in a canteen as apparently they are still very much needed for the homeless people. I am very much interested to see it as I imagine it is the greatest war sight which has ever been seen anywhere.

Devastation by bombs in Coventry 1940 (Topfoto)

14 November 1940 and following days, saw the Coventry blitz. This was one of the worst moments of the war and occurred fairly near to where Frankie lived with the children.

24 November, 1940

I went to Coventry. It is rather difficult to describe it because it both is and isn't what one had expected. The papers said the whole of the middle of the town was flat. Well, it is and it isn't. Whole areas are completely flat, but round them you can drive in quite ordinary streets with rather damaged buildings all round.

The Cathedral is demolished except that a lot of the outside walls and the spire stand. There is no water or gas at all, some electric light but no power. Everything was chaos on the organization side.

I spent the whole day buttering slices of bread. Some of the women seemed to have been doing it for 24 hours on end. I had no conversation with the people being fed but some of the bread-cutters were just ordinary Coventry women. I must say they were extraordinary. They were quite cheerful and full of dull jokes which I imagine only the English make, but which are very good in this sort of time. For instance when one of the women said she was going home for half an hour one of the others said, "Now don't you go having a hot bath and good lie down". In order to appreciate this one has to realize that we couldn't even get a glass of water to drink and that this woman hadn't had an ordinary night's sleep for ten days.

We asked them about the morale of the people. They all said it was wonderful. They said the only thing which got any of them down was when the papers said it had not stopped production, because they said, that, apart from the general chaos and lack of power, several of the factories didn't exist at all anymore. I do think it's silly. It just makes people distrust all official reports.

Coventry Cathedral after air raids in November 1940. (Topfoto)

On the way home the most odd thing happened. A soldier and his wife stopped me for a lift. I said something about having come from Coventry and the man said, "O, we're Coventry people but my wife left because of the bombing". Then she said from the back in a perfectly ordinary voice "We lost two of our children. The third was buried, but they got her out alright". They both spoke in such ordinary voices that I thought they could not be talking about something which had happened recently so I said, "This was some time ago you mean?", and they said, "O no, in the big raid last Friday". This was all they said about it and we might have been talking about the price of eggs. Is it the result of shock, or what? It seems to me to be absolutely terrifying.

25 November, 1940

I rode my pony to Aston Cantlow this morning to get it shod and in the blacksmith's I met a local farmer who told me I was potty to try to milk at Gypsy Hall as it wouldn't grow good enough pasture to get a good milk yield. I bet him in 3 years I would win the record milk yield for the County. He was a farmer of the old school who didn't believe in ploughing turf. This afternoon I had a go at milking myself and got on fairly well.

26 November, 1940

Children well — Thomas rather puzzled about prisons. "Will I go to prison because I <u>always</u> waste my food at breakfast?" — the man on the wireless having said people go to prison for wasting food.

Jack was posted abroad in mid-November of 1940. The address was censored but in fact Egypt – Ismailia and was at sea for 6 weeks on the journey out, thus contact was broken. For the next 4 years he went to most places that the British Army was sent to, organising transport and vital supplies behind the front line.

She went at this time to stay with friends (Leonora and Peter Cazalet) in Kent near the house that she and Jack had commissioned from Walter Gropius when they were married.

2 December, 1940

I motored down to Kent to see Leonora and look at the Wood House, and arrived about 3 o'clock. They were all taking a gloomy line about food here. They seem to think that, with the present rate of sinkings etc we should, in the not too distant future, get shortage of a type which England has never known. It does seem to me that the children must be alright as long as we can get eggs, butter, milk and vegetables from the farm — also rabbits and we could always kill an occasional hen. In that way we may turn out to have been rather far-sighted. They were all rather gloomy about the war, talking of a five years' war — and people with husbands in the Middle East can't take that sort of thing.

The Wood House built for Jack and Frankie by Walter Gropius, 1936

Going thro' London was rather remarkable. It has completely changed since we were there. All the rubble has been carted away into Hyde Park, all the broken windows mended or bricked up and everything tidied up. No-one seeing it for the first time would believe in the Blitz at all. The first sign of British efficiency I have ever seen.

4 December, 1940
I have begun to dig the garden at The Wood House where you left off. It is quite light land and I can do it quite easily. I have had some very rich pig manure brought down from the farm. This access of energy is as a result of the gloomy food talks at Fairlawne. We get regular and rather noisy air-raids now.

39

9 December, 1940

Last night I literally exhausted myself with grief and misery. I got up late and to the farm at about 11.30. The men were threshing and Carling said Harry was away ill and would I see if I could do his job on the stack. It consisted of pitching the outside sheaves to the man in the middle who pitches them on to the box. I did it until 1 o'clock which nearly killed me but I was determined to go on as I thought if I did it all right Carling would get the habit of counting me in on this sort of job. Then I went back and stayed on the stack until about 4 o'clock. Now this isn't happiness but it is something. The work is much too hard for one to be able to think at all. I am convinced it is the one and only solution for me. So there you are. I am sure I shall stay here and I am sure I shall not be too bad.

Some time ago Bob Laycock was ordered east so he sent Angie and the children to America. When halfway there he was recalled and made Colonel of the Commandos. And there was Angie, stuck in America. I now hear she has somehow managed to get back on the Clipper. Just as well, as Bob is not the sort of person to leave loose in England. They say he is a wonderful colonel, with a tough lot, Phil *(Phil Dunne, her friend Peggy's husband)*, Harry Stavordale, Toby Milbanke, Evelyn Waugh, but they all appear to adore him.

10 December, 1940

This morning I went early to the farm and bagged up 15 bags of chaff. Then I did muck-spreading from 2 till 4. I worked only about half as fast as a man but I think I would get quicker as partly it is a question of fitness and also a little of knack. After this I fed the hens and collected the eggs and I was by then so exhausted that I came home for tea, and did not wait for the milking. As a result of all this I have been quite o.k. and was delighted when Peggy (with whom I had arranged to go to London) put me off, because

I would much rather stay here and go on muck-spreading. This is all really rather good and if I can only keep it up I shall get much fitter and be able to do much more and then I think I shall be able to control the gloom completely.

Rose at Chadshunt, home of my godmother Peggy who called me The Orangutang

Gosh, I'm stiff to-night. I can hardly move and blisters all over both hands. I always think how much you would love it. However it is keeping me going even without you and for that one must be unendingly grateful.

12 December, 1940

The capture of Sidi Barrani, 3 generals and 6,000 prisoners seems almost too good to be true. It's wonderful to have legitimate feelings of optimism for a change.

The Battle of Sidi Barrani (10–11 December 1940) was the opening battle of Operation Compass, the first big British attack of the Western Desert Campaign.

Also a somewhat horrific note, different from his usual cheerful tone:

16 December, 1940
I'm sitting on a Court of Enquiry tomorrow to find out why certain drugs are missing from the medical stores.

19 December, 1940
Yesterday the Court of Enquiry was brought to a satisfactory end by a fairly senior officer confessing he had stolen the drugs. Poor devil he was an awful wreck. God preserve us from ever becoming drug-addicts.

20 December, 1940
The wretched drug-addict dies today — poor chap.

21 December, 1940
The children have just retired to bed having been excruciatingly funny all the evening. Rose was in one of her bad moods. She was very naughty at tea so she didn't get a sweetie. When I came in I said if they both did their exercises properly they could have one each. They started off but Rose immediately began to play the fool so I ignored her and went on telling Thomas what to do. So she went away and fetched both cats and dumped them down in the middle of the room just as Thomas was coming ponderously up doing "long steps". Of course he fell over flat and both cats rushed out of the room. Rose turned on him like a vixen and said, "What you frighten my cats for?" I said, "Oh, shut up Rose; that's too much". So she rushed out after the cats saying "Come here my darlings; don't take any notice of Mummy and Thomas". We continued to take no notice of her so presently she came and stood with her legs wide apart in the middle of the room bang in the road

of Thomas. He saw her in time and stepped round but she side-stepped so quickly they both went down with a crash.

I pushed her out and told her she was very naughty, and she rushed to the sofa and took up what has always been her favourite angry position. Head down and bottom stuck in the air. Thomas was by now tiptoeing past and he suddenly caught sight of the bottom. He turned round to me and giggled and said, "Shall I?" so I nodded and he caught her the hardest crack he possibly could after taking very slow and deliberate aim. This reduced her to such paroxysms of anger that she had to be carried kicking off to bed. After she had gone Thomas remarked in a very pompous voice "I've told Nora to tell Mrs Higley to tell Santa Claus to bring Rose nothink". I said, "Why?" So he said, "because she's so naughty. She won't drink her milk, she sucks her thumb and she hits me". I gave him a short lecture on telling tales and sent him off too. It made me laugh so much that the tears streamed down my cheeks. I think Rose's fat bottom was the funniest.

Thomas and Rose aged approx 4 and 3 years old

At this point in time Frankie had no idea where Jack had been posted as the information was censored and letters could not be sent during the 6 week journey. Ismailia is on the Suez Canal, roughly half way between the Mediterranean and the Red Sea.

The news from Egypt is by far the most exciting thing that has happened. It puts an entirely new complexion on things. I am beginning to wonder how the whole thing will affect you. You see you got your orders a month before the Greek thing started and things have changed so immensely since then, what with suggestions that Italy is cracking and so on.

I have a spent a fairly happy day and did some more muck-spreading. It is immensely hard work and I ache with fatigue. I rather like the idea that I shall get so fit because I always feel, with a war on, you never know when you may have some awful endurance test thrust on you like walking 20 miles with Thomas on your back and Rose under one arm.

We are getting about 20 eggs a day now which means we supply ourselves and one dozen to the Carlings and sell nearly 8 dozen a week as well. I am taking a dozen a week to Aunt Isy and when we have more than 2 dozen the Guest House get 4 doz, Mrs Higley 1 ½ and Highman 1 or 2. It is really awful fun because eggs are absolutely and entirely unprocurable for the ordinary person now and everyone is so pleased when we take them some.

Aunt Isy (as Frankie spelled it, but pronounced Izzie) was Lady Isabel Margesson, née Hobart-Hampden, and sister of Jack's mother, who had died in 1935. She was an eccentric lady, but much loved.

A good many things are short now. No fruit at all except the remains of the English apples; oranges, which are supposed to be still there have not been seen in this district for 2 or 3 weeks; great difficulty in getting toilet paper and soap. No wire, timber or concrete except by special licence which takes weeks and weeks; no silk stockings and very little make-up.

No one minds — it makes us feel we are getting on a bit. It also makes everything we produce i.e. eggs, milk, wheat inordinately satisfying. Our wheat looks good but we are worried about the beans. There is a very hard frost at the moment. I do love it. I don't notice scenery or lovely views very much and I am not one of those people who get pure joy out of the countryside. But I do adore the feeling of the country particularly when I am taking hard physical exercise. I expect you'd like a nice frosty day occasionally too — or perhaps by the time you get this you will really be in Iceland or the Grecian mountains and longing for a little warmth.

21 December, 1940

Much of the British Army stayed in England after Dunkirk, June 1940 until D Day, June 1944, preparing for a possible invasion or a second onslaught on the continent. Peter Cazalet was one of them.

Peter was very gloomy. He has got a battery made up partly of men from Chester, partly of men from other batteries and partly of new recruits. He says they are the dregs of the earth. Many of them can't read or write properly, a good many have v.d., they desert in hundreds, not permanently but for 2 or 3 days at a time, which means an appalling lot of trouble hauling them back and confining them to barracks. And they all cry all the time. He swears there is nothing unusual about this battery. He says all the later ones are like this.

 3 January, 1941
Well, my love, here I am in the second best hotel permanently attached to MC GHQ.

15 January, 1941 New address: Canal Base Area Middle East
I spent the last 2 ½ days driving round and looking at this area. I'm sent down here as DADTN Canal Area (for a month) and it presents some quite amusing railway problems, and quite difficult ones too.

I have not been able to find out what DADTN stands for. Possibly Deputy Assistant Director Transport. But N?

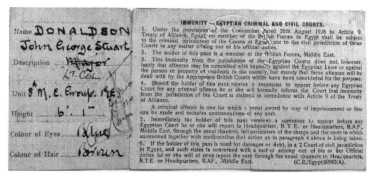

Jack's Identity card for Egypt and the Middle East

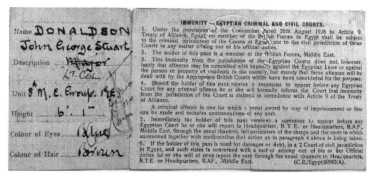

19 January, 1941

Do you remember I told you I had met a girl through Lady Stapledon who, I thought, would be an excellent governess for the children? Yesterday I engaged her full-time at £100 a year on the understanding that she would not be too conscientious about her work as I did <u>not</u> want the children looked after all the time but preferred them to play in the village a good deal.

22 January, 1941

The big news today is the fall of Tobruk, which is very exciting.

22 January, 1941 – Tobruk in North Africa falls to the British and Australians.

I keep wondering about you & whether it is exciting for you. I know you are not near there but it must be rather fun being with that army.

27 January, 1941

The belief in invasion grows and grows. George (*Martelli*) says it is partly British propaganda, to make people believe it is what the Germans want to do and if they don't we can say "Yah! You couldn't do it". He says British propaganda is terrific now and all news must be read in the light of it.

In the last week 2 people have said to me "So Jack is really part of the great army of the Nile". And I have said Yes with great pride and satisfaction, temporarily forgetting what it costs. I long to hear all about it.

Frankie, who may not have thought about politics much before she met Jack, was immediately sympathetic to his socialist ideas. She always said that he probably would have gone to Spain if they had not got married when they did. One large section of their friends came from the left wing. They had to exercise discretion during the war as many left wingers, especially members of the communist party, were sidelined because of their politics.

16 January, 1941

Phil (*Dunne*) came in & had a long talk with me about how he & Bob were more anti-communist than anti-fascist & if there was any question of winning the war by social revolution in Europe they would rather lose it, & were getting ready to fight any social revolution in this country after the war. I kept my temper well but said if they wanted to avoid social revolution they were setting the wrong way about it, as I for one was not particularly out for a revolution, but if there was any question of rule by a military faction led by him & Bob or Hinch & his lot or any other little lot with the same ideas I would fight to the last drop & so would everyone else who was not a member of Bucks Club or the 400.

Bucks Club was said to be the model for the Drones Club of P.G. Wodehouse

In this connexion I am sending you *The Times* pamphlet. I think it is staggering. I must repeat that it is not what it says which is astonishing but that *The Times* should say it. Ignoring with most superb complacency its record at Munich etc. & all the interests it has always stood for and adopting its usual all-seeing & all-knowing tone it proceeds in a series of extremely lofty articles to explain to the world in general that our present circumstances are due entirely to the lack of willingness we have shown to accept the principles of what, by any other leader writer, must be called socialism; & our only chance in the future is to accept them now. How about the following examples for a couple of peaches?

'The first step towards the creation of a new European order will be to feed the hungry, to clothe the naked & to house the homeless. No frontiers, no national rivalries can be allowed to impede this essential task. The old motto "to each according to his needs" is the only criterion which can be applied.' Can one assume that the eminent leader writer of *The Times* knows where this dear old motto came from?'

A biblical slogan used by Karl Marx.

Then how about this one?

'In 1940 the manufacturer forgoes his profits, the worker forgoes trade union restrictions on conditions of employment, the consumer forgoes luxuries & lends to the Government to finance expenditure from which no material gain is asked or expected. In 1930 a small fraction of these sacrifices would have sufficed to avert the unemployment crisis of the ensuing years &, at the same time, to bring to countries involved in war better housing, more ample nutrition, better education, & more amenities for the leisure of the masses.'

Really? Do you really think so? Then what can it have been that we were arguing about? I think it is their complete ignoring of the fact that they so willingly & eagerly represented the class which made 1930 possible, which seems so barefaced. What should one think of this now? Do they mean it? Or do they think it is good propaganda in America & elsewhere?

Two years later, In March 1942, she wrote that the Times had a new editor; had become an excellent paper producing the most staggering leaders and articles and had become her bible.

5: 1941

The Farm: Improving Standards

Frankie was always a perfectionist. Nearly everything she took on she did well at, be it golf, tennis, hunting, dog-training, now farming and, later, writing. It really irked her to see the poor standards maintained on the farm and this was an important part of her battle with the men who were in charge because she could not yet manage it by herself. She was determined to learn.

30 January, 1941
Rather a curious thing happened to-night. You know I don't always and entirely get on with Carling *(the new bailiff)*. I hate having to take an opposing line with him because I am never sure we shall get thro' it without badly annoying each other.

Well, the milking is not properly done. Quite apart from the fact that the cows are not stripped after the machine which they have got to be and I had already told him they had got to be once we got a decent head man, the whole performance is the most incredibly slapdash and slovenly business.

I went in today for the first time for a week or two and found Thomas *(the assistant cowman)* still doing it alone altho' the new and highly paid cowman has now been here nearly a month. He made no attempt at all to wash the cows, which is one worse than his usual flick over; if the machine fell off he shoved it back without cleaning it, and he whisked up and down at a speed which suggested he was in for a race, rather than attempting to do a decent job of work.

It is all quite serious because at this rate we shall lose our accredited licence which means 5/- today and will mean correspondingly more as our production goes up. So I had to send for Carling and have it out.

Frankie supervising the milking with landgirl Marjorie. She later took it over herself

I decided while doing it to force the issue over the stripping which has been a slight argument between us for some time. Net result I literally and actually sweated for one hour while waiting for him to come down and see me. I put it as nicely as I could but quite firmly and elicited the following from him: Carling not only agrees with all my criticisms but endorses them heartily and is equally worried about it.

I don't know what we shall do. It looks like trouble all round and more advertisements for men. The whole thing amuses me as it fits in with my latest theory, originally formed after reading your comments about lack of confidence among your brother officers. Almost nobody has your sort of confidence and it is the lack of it which causes almost all the trouble in the world.

In the case of Carling and me I fear that he will a) take advantage of my lack of knowledge and b) of my being a woman and consequently try to swing things over on me. While he fears that I will take advantage of my ultimate power as boss to give an order to swing things over on him. If we could both get rid of our fears all would be well because neither of us will do what the other fears unless the other does what he fears.

1 February, 1941

There is nothing to recommend today except that it is the 1st of February. No more January 1941. The winter is very old and stale and gloom-sodden. There is none of that grim and gayness which Mr Churchill was so eloquent about but only a sort of grim and greyness.

Last night Colonel Knox *(a US army official)* said that from American sources of information it is reasonable to believe that there will be an invasion soon and that gas will be used on a large scale. In case this is true I have had all gas masks equipped with the new attachment and I have decided that when Miss Hands *(governess)* comes in a fortnight, one of her duties will be to do regular gas mask drill with the children. If the invasion is in full swing when you get this letter it may be a comfort to you to hear it.

Thomas can now play Beggar my Neighbour, Old Maid and Snap with ordinary cards like a professional. The other night he went upstairs to have his hair washed and I played cards with Rose, who can't really play and is far too obstinate and proud to try to learn and therefore just fiddles. Presently she said to me "We play cards, don't we, Mummy?" Now this is just what Thomas used to say, but the differences in saying it were absolute. His face and voice held only eagerness and excitement and, one might almost say, joy in living. Hers held a whole world of feminine malignity. The remark really meant "You and I play cards while Thomas is upstairs and doesn't even know, so I am one up on him for once". But she has a sort of screwed up humorousness in her face which makes the whole thing less wickedly malicious than it may sound on paper.

4 February, 1941

Today, tho' it froze hard the snow was only thin on the ground so I took a walk round the farm in time to witness my first personal success. Wilkes uses a method of cultivation which is comparatively new and not much tried but he swears by it. It is to disc old pasture 3 or 4 times or 5 or 6 before you plough it. I wanted to try it and Carling and Highman, while pointing out the possible difficulties, fell in with my wishes.

Today when I went out Highman was ploughing the field and Carling was mending a fence in it. I said to Carling "This is a complete surprise to me. I had no idea you could plough with so much frost in the ground". He said, "Well, I don't believe you could any field except this. But with the discing it is alright and is ploughing perfectly". So that was rather fun and worked out well.

6 February, 1941

Clyde Higgs and Johnny Green of the BBC came over this morning. Green said they were going to revive the 5 minutes to 1 series and would I do one? At the beginning of the war it was a series at which cabinet ministers exhorted farmers to get on with it. Now it is to be farmers reporting how they have got on with it. I am to represent those farmers who have started farming since the war. I said I would do it, but as far as I can see it boils down to telling the same old story all over again but in even fewer words. Clyde Higgs said he'd help me.

10 February, 1941

Darling, I am playing with the idea of trying to write a book on my experiences and adventures as a farmer. It is a curious thing to say at the end of a letter as ill-written as this is, but I have a faint feeling I might be able to do it.

I am writing another page to tell you that an aeroplane came down in the field behind the row of houses yesterday. All the village of course went to see but this morning the wonder was over and so there was no-one there except Thomas who went over the fields by himself. He was very sweet about it. He stayed in the hedge and watched the RAF men repairing it but he had a good fright when the propeller started up. However, when he was asked by Nora what he was going to do when he was an airman he said airily, "O you don't notice it in the air. It's only on the ground it makes such a noise".

15 February, 1941

Last night and to-night I have begun to write my "book".

The farm is going very well. Carling is very efficient. All the beans have failed which means sowing spring ones but all the wheat looks good and Mr Stewart was stunned by the beauty of the ploughing which has been done.

2 March, 1941

Carling wanted to see me yesterday and it was to tell me that Bibby the cowman who is a shit but a bloody good cowman had announced that unless he got an extra 5/- a week he would leave next Friday. He already gets £3.5/-. I told Carling that a) it was blackmail but b) it was, at any rate, temporarily, successful blackmail. We can't do without him for the moment. I am perfectly certain we shall have one long struggle with cowmen until the war is over and we can build some cottages and get a good married man.

4 March, 1941

This morning there were 2 records on the wireless by Popeye the Sailor. It was really rather fun because it is the first time I have seen the children really entertained by an entertainment. They both pealed with laughter. It began with his making one of those queer noises. Thomas asked what the noise was. So I said, "It is a man trying to be funny". Thomas laughed uncontrollably and said, "Well, he is being funny as well". Rose laughed so much I thought she would be sick. It was the most enjoyable beginning to a day. The children are obviously going to have your sense of humour. It was a lovely, lovely day today.

During this period of the war, although Frankie struggled to control and run a few men, the bigger part of the labour became land girls. Photographs show how many there were at times working on hard physical jobs around the farm.

17 March, 1941

Apparently when I first began to dig the garden here the consensus of opinion in the village was that I had bitten off more than I could chew. If Molly had not turned up to help this opinion might have been justified but as it is we have now finished the digging here and are turning our attention to the garden at the farm. Mrs Higley said to Nora "Well, I must give those two girls best. They've certainly made a good job of that garden".

Land girls clearing mud, with Thomas helping

22 March, 1941

This afternoon Molly and I planted 24 black currant and gooseberry bushes.

I may soon have to give up smoking. I should have had to some time go but for Mrs Wheeldon keeping me a special supply and today for the first time I hear she has absolutely none in her shop. There are no luxuries now. Hardly any sweets or cigarettes, no fruit at all at the moment, no cheese, only 8 oz of jam a month (luckily we have a good supply), no gum boots (mine have started to let the water in) and so on with almost everything you want. Tho' we can't complain — we do pretty well with the farm.

It's extraordinary how much work I do now. Immediately after breakfast I went up to the farm to have an argument with Carling about the order in which he is sowing the seeds. Then I came back and wrote 38 letters and bills before and immediately after lunch. Then I took these to post. Then I went to see a man about fetching some coke. Then I went to the farm and wheeled down a barrow load of coal to the house as the men are too busy to bring it. Then I took the barrow back and brought down eggs which I took to the Guest House. After tea I washed the children's hair and cut their nails etc. Now I am writing to you and when I have done that I shall read the papers for ½ an hour and then write my book until bedtime. This way of living has one great advantage. The time flies.

27 March, 1941
Terrific news on the wireless. First of all the capture of Keren and Harrar in one day which must surely go somewhere near bringing all that to an end. Then the announcement of the coup d'etat in Jugoslavia and the reversal of policy. This last seems wonderful. I hope to God we shall back them up properly.

31 March, 1941: Moulton
I am at Moulton for a few days and nights to learn something about pig-keeping. I have an unfailingly good eye for pigs and have so far never failed to pick the best one out of every bunch I have been shown. It means when we are breeding our own I shall have a reasonable chance of picking the right ones for breeding or fattening.

This morning I mucked out, then put rings into some pigs' noses — fairly difficult as you can imagine. I successfully managed to do 2 of them. Then we exercised the boars which means going for a walk with one at a time, with a fat stick in your hand and whacking them. Then we mixed a week's ration and fed all the pigs.

This afternoon we fed again, this time me feeding more or less on my own; then I brushed the 4 boars and came in. I rather enjoy it. Whether I should for long is another matter. Here everything is to hand and everything you want exists. At home all is a makeshift with hardly any room.

Frankie feeding pigs

5 April, 1941
Our wheat is again a landmark and Mr Lindsay, who came over with me this morning said it was the best he had seen this year.

Frankie's father was a successful playwright but had always repressed any thought his daughters might have had of following him. She finds that writing the book comes quite easily to her, but cannot be sure it will be accepted. She naturally went to her brother-in-law, Dick de la Mare, who was a director of Faber and Faber and later its chairman. She wrote it in a very short time and it was quickly published, under the title "Approach to Farming". Dick was married to Katta, Jack's sister.

I finished my book today — or at least the structure. The last chapter is some very hot stuff on socialism and I am really pleased with it. Even if no-one else likes it I shall keep it to show you.

I am fed up about Benghazi. Oddly enough, the letters I just got from you are full of pleasure about its capture. I am also fed up with the propaganda. Why is it a stronghold with admirable port facilities when we take it and indefensible and with no value as a port when the Germans do? Gosh I'm sick of it all.

However, it now seems to have begun again. Yesterday German declared war on Jugoslavia and Greece. One fears the German army and I should like to be sure it is going to be alright.

February 6: Benghazi was captured from the Italians on 6 February 1941.

April 4: It was recaptured by Axis powers, led by Rommel

December 24: Taken again by the British, only to change hands again on 29 January 1942.

November 20: Benghazi was captured by the British Eighth Army after the Battle of El Alamein.

10 April, 1941

We had more bombs on the farm again last night. They made enormous craters and mucked an acre. I don't know how I am going to get all the holes filled up again. I went across that field this morning on my way to the farm. The first thing I saw was a thing exactly like a well but only about half the size in diameter. I went up to it and started peering down it and only then realised suddenly what it was. So it was lucky it didn't explode there and then. I think it is almost certainly a dud because it was just slung overboard with the other 2 by an aeroplane in a hurry and they both went off at once so I suppose this one was meant to. Coventry have had it very bad 2 nights running.

They say the casualties are as bad as last time and they got the Daimler works. The news is lousy. I wonder if we shall do any good against the Germans. Apparently the chief bomb officer came while Carling and I were both away and said that if the bomb didn't go off by 2 o'clock (which it didn't) it probably wouldn't go off at all. But if it didn't no-one must go into the field or work it until the bomb had been removed and they were too busy to remove it for 6 weeks. Well, this field is 18 acres and has been manured all over and prepared for roots. In 6 weeks it will be too late. Hell and Damnation!

Another remark the bomb officer made was that he thought it was not an accident but that they were aiming at the buildings which he says would shine in the moonlight and should be camouflaged. I haven't any money to have them camouflaged. I don't suppose it could be done under £150, but on the other hand I suppose one has some responsibility to the whole village. O Damn!

14 April, 1941
I went to Dick and Katta for the weekend, at Much Hadham. While there I met Mrs Mark Norman who had had a letter from her husband saying you had given him dinner in Cairo and you were one of the vital links in the chain to victory!

I forgot to tell you about the bomb. It exploded after all at 10 pm last night so the field is ours again, even if spoiled by 3 enormous craters. They are big ones apparently. Everyone who knows about craters says so.

The news about Libya and Egypt is terrible. Only people hardened by having heard of the fall of Amiens and Arras on the same day could stand up to it. It does seem to me there must have been some pretty bad miscalculations on our part for this to happen.

I am in a vile temper today because I have cut out cigarettes altogether. On top of this, gloomy news and no cable from you and Jan, who is staying here, must of course have the bath which means I won't get one. I don't really like having guests here. I would far rather have the bath. If only you were here I should burst my rage on your innocent head and in 10 minutes it would be over. As it is I have to bottle it up and I get crosser and crosser.

Frankie always smoked Craven A

14 April, 1941
The news is very worrying. We seem to have under-rated the Germans again and this seems to me unforgivable.

I was so pleased to get your cable. When anything horrid is going on send plenty and don't forget that because you know you are not in danger doesn't mean I know it too.

17 April, 1941
The news is very worrying. We seem to have under-rated the Germans again and this seems to me unforgivable.

The feeling here is absolutely general that appalling blunders must have been made and people are feeling angry both at the turn of events and at the way in which the news is presented. We are not children and we are all tired of being treated like children by people who are capable of making such a tremendous balls-up of everything.

There are many things which are on our side but, my God, the Greek thing makes one realize that there is much that is not.

28 April, 1941

I walked round the farm this morning and I must say I'm very proud of this part of our war effort. We have nearly 50 more acres of plough than when you were here last summer and, on the whole of this, crops are either going strong or, having been planted during last month, just beginning to show their heads.

I have just heard that the troops have begun to embark from Greece. Oh Dear! I do hate it. Not so much the defeat as all the deaths and all the sad women who will be left.

29 April, 1941

I have been wanting for some time to tell you about Rose. She is, for 3 ½, really extraordinary, I think. Today she spilled some food off her plate. Molly said, "That's what piggies do, spill food from their trough". Rose said, "This isn't a trough — see!" If she had said, "I am not a piggy", we should have said, "Yes you are" or something like that. But "this is not a trough" left us all speechless with surprise as it is not the answer we expected. There is nothing much to it but it is absolutely typical and goes on all day and every day.

P.S. Have just been up to say goodnight to the children, who are what Nora calls "wound up" i.e. very giggly. The joke was to call everyone by a wrong name — thus Nora Donaldson, Frankie Higley.

I said, "Thomas Pigley" and provoked those very refreshing peals of laughter which is the sweetest thing about all children. Then Rose said, "Let me tell you both something. Frankie Glasses and Nora Teeth". This is her idea of real humour and it seems to me at 3 it might be so....

Thomas and Rose with Nora in 1943

1 May, 1941

The news today is that at least 48 out of 60 thousand of the BEF in Greece have been got away and this seems to me the best news for ages.

3 May, 1941

In your letter you say you bet I will not finish digging the lawn as I have started farm work. You are quite wrong because we have dug not only the whole lawn but half the garden at the farm as well.

The news is rather frightening. They seem to be holding out well at Tobruk, but the news from Iraq is rather serious — or isn't it?

Jack wrote from Palestine where he was taking some leave. It was impossible for him to make the journey back to England, so leave did not bring them together.

5 May, 1941

Palestine sounds heavenly and I do wish I could have been there too. It is amusing that you should be in a place where

63

oranges rot on the ground while I spend most of the winter scrabbling to get 1 or 2 a week for the children. Now I don't even scrabble as there aren't any in the length and breadth of England.

To-night I am feeling really rather distressed because I had a set-to with Carling. I began it wrong by being made angry enough to tackle him in front of the men which he hates and is really wrong. But in return he was sufficiently rude to me in front of them that I shall have to see him tomorrow and tell him I won't take it, for the sake of future relations. I know by experience that for a woman dealing with a man and a fairly forceful one at that, it is no use burying the hatchet without having first ticked them off because they know it is a weakness and not a niceness on your part, and having got away with the situation they invariably presume upon that. Sometimes I hate having the farm just because of this sort of thing.

8 May, 1941

I am now waiting for Carling to come down and see me and, as you will imagine, I am in a slightly nervous condition. Last night we shot down 23 bombers over England.

Voila Carling!

Charming interview and everything o.k. Began with my saying I didn't take that sort of thing and his saying no, he knew and was sorry afterwards. Ended with a discussion of inferiority complexes of men trying to deal with women and vice versa. The interview has convinced me that at bottom Carling is a really good and nice man, so I shall find it easier not to be touchy.

News to-night of bombing of Suez Canal. I suppose it is as silly for me to worry about that as for you to worry about bombing the Midlands.

10 May, 1941

On Monday I am going to Birmingham; it will be May 12, six months ago bar 2 days since I saw you there for the last time. It has been in every possible way bloody, but I must say it doesn't seem like 6 months. That is the only good thing. I wonder how many more 6 months we have got to get through? I am afraid about 3.

(It was actually 6 x 6 months till she saw him – April 1944 - and 8 till he came home for good – at the end of July 1945)

11 May, 1941

Just heard the news which tells of bombing the House of Commons. I must say in spite of everything I find it difficult to believe in this kind of thing.

13 May, 1941

HOW ABOUT HESS? It seems to me to be the most staggering thing that has ever happened. Of course there is always the chance that the Germans are right for once and that he is potty. Then there are a host of too-good-to-be-true suggestions such as that things are going badly enough for him to be the advance guard of the rats. But I'm afraid this is too much to hope for. What I would give to be in the know over it!

On May 10th, Hess took a Messerschmidt 110 and flew it solo to Scotland where he crash-landed the plane.

I was in Birmingham yesterday to meet mummy *(Leslie Lonsdale)*. A great deal of damage has been done since we were there. Everywhere you go you see burnt and demolished buildings.

I shopped for the children and bought 2 summer dresses for myself. Our summer clothes for all 3 cost well under £10. Good, eh? I must tell you about the lunch we had because it will give you an idea of food now. We could have had fish or meat or rabbit (this was at the Queen's which as you know is the most expensive best hotel). I chose the rabbit because it was done with mushrooms and I thought sounded nice. Of course, I ought to have known better at the time of year and you couldn't even cut it much less eat it. Mummy had the lamb, which was alright. She wanted a dark sherry but could only get a light. They produced a tray of sweets to choose from. There was stewed Rhubarb, an open flan and a tart. We said, "What is the flan?" "Rhubarb." "What is the tart?" "Rhubarb." "What is the mixed fruit salad?" "Rhubarb and tinned plums."

I asked for cigarettes, not because I thought I'd get any, but just to see. The waiter said they hadn't seen a packet for 5 days. The position re cigarettes is that you can get them from your own shop (for me, Mrs Wheeldon) if you are lucky or have a pull, but otherwise you haven't a chance of buying them anywhere. Also they have begun to favour men. I am told that in factories and in shops in towns they keep them for men and won't sell any to women. Don't you think that's monstrous? I have cut my smoking to less than 10 a day — but because of the budget not because I can't get them from Mrs W.

Mummy said to Rose this morning, "Don't say moost, say must". Rose replied, "Must, must Mussolini, Moosolini", with a triumphant inflection on the last word. How's that for 3 ½?

6: 1941

Writing a book about it

15 May, 1941

As I hope you will have heard both by cable and pc I had a letter from Dick this morning saying they would publish the book. Apparently it was Geoffrey Faber's enthusiasm that had carried the day. It is much better like that as Dick is the in-law.

I enclose Dick's letter.

'My dear Frankie,

First of all I must tell you how very very much I enjoyed reading your book myself. It has got a delightful freshness about it which whets one's appetite afresh from page to page – my only criticism was one of disappointment that it wasn't a little longer. It has now been read by two others here, one of them being Geoffrey Faber, who was enthusiastic, so the next thing for me to say is that we should very much like to publish it for you in the autumn.'

Rose is at this moment yelling upstairs in her bath like a thousand bulls and I could easily murder her. Rose has been like a maniac for the last 10 days and in this small house one goes nuts with it. However she is also very sweet. She has a mania for picking wild flowers, particularly cowslips. She picks them very carefully with long stalks — at this point I was interrupted by Nora who came for my help as she can do nothing at all with Rose. Rose had bitten her and thrown water all over her and she could not get her nightdress on. I went up and smacked Rose's bottom as hard as I could. In spite of all the psychologists I can think of nothing else to do. All gentler methods have been tried for the last 10 days with no effect at all.

The new black dog Bunty is so sweet. I like her in a way I have liked no dog since I had the children. She sleeps on my bed and in all the best chairs. The kittens are also sweet, George, Georgina and Ginger.

Life on the farm continued. Frankie still lived in a house in the village. Her inability to take control of the farm was somewhat compensated for by the writing activities – the book was going well and had been accepted. But her frustration and irritation were only just below the surface. She would rather be fully involved, without time for expeditions into social life although these were a pleasure and at times a relief from the hard work.

19 May, 1941

I am just beginning to get warmed up to the idea of doing some more to the book and I really have the urge to get at it. But it's very difficult here. Children and maids and governesses and farm people pop in and out all the time and have no respect for a budding authoress.

I must tell you in detail how I feel about it because it is really rather sweet. I am so thrilled about it that I don't go to sleep when I go to bed and I wake up thinking about it. I am also completely incredulous and also rather nervous.

26 May, 1941

I am in a stew about the book — a) whether I can finish it, b) whether I should, c) whether it will shame me forever if it is, d) whether you will like it, e) whether Leonora will, f) whether Dick really does, g) whether anyone will when I have fiddled it about. I now understand for the first time why Daddy always goes on like a maniac about his plays. God blast it all.

1 June, 1941
Crete, I take it, is finished.

June 1, 1941, Crete, the last Allied stronghold in Greece, is captured by German forces at high cost to both sides.

I never did see how it could be more than a delaying action but then I never can see how anything ever will be. I suppose Egypt will be the next and then I shall have some horrible months.

I had a letter from Mr Stewart in which he said that he has seen no farm in either of the two counties which looked as good as ours. Rather extraordinary, isn't it? I am a bad letter-writer at the moment, but the book will be finished in a day or two and then I will go back to my normal habits.

Freddy Lonsdale

2 June, 1941

Got your cable re book and one for Thomas. He was frightfully pleased. Rose has a new dress on today. When she took it off she said, "There's a hole in my dress". We all looked appropriately shocked and surprised and she pointed to the arm-hole. I think she thought it up herself.

6 June, 1941

I wish I could give you a picture of the children's lives. Playing on the road outside the house there will be anything up to 30 children and 2 of these will be ours.

Rose rides the trike with a sort of matron-like determination. She has a blue and white striped summer dress with red braid on it and for some reason she looks very French in it. But like a Madame not a Mademoiselle. I think they are splendid children. Molly finds them quite unusual. She shows feminine traits already and has chums. These are chiefly the two worst behaved and most devilish girls in the village both of whom are about 8. They rejoice in the names of Sylvie and Ginette.

Thomas's chief friend is still John Highman but he is also occasionally patronised by much older boys who give him pennies and teach him to ride his bike. They both talk fluently and colloquially the same as the village. There are a good many rows and head-hittings but they solve all by themselves.

I have definitely finished the book. I can't do another stroke.

8 June, 1941

Yesterday I spent with Peggy. She was very depressed about the war. We discussed it and came to the conclusion that even to discuss it was all vanity of vanities. We have now got to the position where we have just got to go on. No talk of how we are doing or whether our leaders are any good serves any purpose. We can't alter anything but on the other hand there is no possibility of our morale being affected by bad news because the thing is too big for that. We have just got to hope that our leaders are better than they sometimes appear to be and keep on doing whatever we happen to be doing. One thing I am certain of is that the presentation of the news is bad. Everyone here is getting so utterly bored with being told that there are no airfields in Crete and the next that the Germans have got control of the airfields in Crete.

10 June, 1941

The bike is an uproarious success. He can not only ride it but do almost anything he likes with it. He is never off it now and thinks of nothing else. This afternoon he rode down to the post office with me also on a bike.

Thomas with his first bike, aged 5

We passed all the children coming back from school and T. kept up a running commentary. "Get out of the way, can't stop. Hello Baden — that's Baden, Mummy, the one with the gun. Hello Jim. Out of my way. Hello Michael — that boy's called Michael, Mummy," and so on all the way there. He's not a baby anymore — he's a little boy.

12 June, 1941

I've taken to bathing naked in the Suez Canal. It's very nice — one swims across and sunbathes in Sinai. But today it cost me my gold watch and £3 stolen from my clothes.

Jack used to tell us as children about this event.

16 June, 1941

On Thursday I was weeding the garden when I heard Rose say to a friend of about her own age "You see that girl over there with the red jersey and the black dungarees — well, that's my Mum". Our garden is a triumph and presently when it has all grown up higher I am going to take a photograph and send it to you.

I gave Carling £25 this morning. I don't suppose we have made a profit but Mr Stewart told Miss Strang that this farm looked better than anyone else's he had seen, and Dick said I ought to give him something. He was immensely sweet. He said he didn't really want anything this year and he wished I would take it and buy something nice for myself instead. We all enjoyed ourselves a lot and I'm sure it was a good move.

17 June, 1941:

This time last year you had just arrived in England. I feel sad. Tho' I shouldn't because if we could have been sure that we would both survive this year we should have thought that was something.

Rose did something to annoy one of the village women today who said jokingly, "I'll give you something when I catch you". R replied, "If you come near me I'll give you chicken pox next time I get it". You can see why we say she always has an answer.

Rose aged 4

18 June, 1941
I got a lovely letter from Dick today congratulating me on
my additions and alterations and saying he liked the book
better the second even than the first time, and saying he
thought it had an excellent chance. Also a draft contract
between F.D. of The Wood House hereinafter called the
AUTHOR. I never thought I would hereinafter be called the
author.

 23 June, 1941
Well, since I last wrote Russia and Germany are at war and I
have got a cable from you saying "Cheers for Uncle Joe etc"
which was great fun and I loved it.

Under the Codename Operation "Barbarossa", Germany invaded the Soviet Union on June 22, 1941.

No-one here is taking such a lovely straightforward whooping point of view but I shall now. No-one I have talked to gives the Russians credit for standing up to the Germans for more than about 2 weeks and they therefore feel that Hitler will get the wheat and oil without much trouble and then be able to sit back and stay out a long war.

When Churchill said last night that Hitler had turned from us to a weaker opponent he was voicing the opinion of everyone I have met. By the time you get this it won't matter as events will have proved one thing or the other. What will be fun is to see how we behave in relation to Russia. I bet we use every sort of evasion rather than call her an ally.

I have been sowing and singling mangolds *(a root vegetable fed to animals in winter)*. I managed 6 hours at it today which is good going for me. My back is nearly broken, but otherwise I am o.k.

24 June, 1941

More hoeing in extreme heat and so I'm tired again. I'm going to Birmingham tomorrow to fetch the new car so I will send you a cable from there. Our garden is a great sight and we already eat our own lettuces and mustard and cress and tomorrow our own spinach.

The London papers are quite objectively rather disparaging about Russian equipment. According to them their air force, tho' large is entirely of either obsolete or bad machines, they haven't much of a navy and their army is probably insufficiently armed. It is a bit depressing but I am cheered up by your cable and taking a bullish view.

June 25, 1941

Today Uncle Mag and Aunt Isy and a lot of vicars and people came over to picnic on the farm. I am quite a popular pet and my clothes cause much merriment. Aunt Isy said, "My dear I must tell you that I have never seen anything quite so awful as your overalls except your shoes". Vere is going to Abyssinia and Egypt and I should think he might pass right thro' Ismailia. I do so wish you could see Thomas on his bike. He is like a boy of 12 or so; full of agility and stunts and really awfully good.

 Jack wrote about Russia: 23 June, 1941
Cheers for Uncle Joe. How it will madden Victor and others. See you sooner. I missed writing yesterday as everyone was so excited about Russia. I think it's a tremendous thing. They may or may not put up a good show, but I was so frightened they'd do a Munich and let him have everything he wanted without fighting. You can't possibly beat Russia + America + England.

The United States had not yet entered the war but were expected to soon. Pearl Harbour effected the change, on December 7, 1941.

29 June, 1941
Russia has now been at war for one week. So far she seems to be holding them. If she does succeed in keeping them out of Russia it will be the most sensational slap in the face for all and sundry. And will answer a lot of questions. For instance, does socialism work? Well, in one respect, yes. With no more pre-war display of aggression than that of the democracies it would have succeeded in building up a war machine that was ready when the war came.

7 July, 1941
War time food is so dull. Here it is July, and so far we haven't seen a new potato, a pea or a strawberry. It just shows what a lot we used to import. Of course we are far

better off than anyone who has not got a farm. How the ordinary person lives I don't know.

Do you realise that the meat ration lasts only 2 days? There are no eggs, fish has been plentiful at 5/- a lb but now it is controlled I suppose it will disappear, no fruit, practically no cheese or jam, no cakes, rationed bacon, practically no chicken. The only thing which has remained plentiful up to date is green vegetables. Before they were controlled there were plenty of tomatoes at anything from 4/- to 16/- a lb (pre-war maximum price about 10p), but now they have also disappeared. Most pubs close 3 days a week for lack of beer and cigarettes are like gold. We do quite well for sweets from Mrs Wheeldon but in general they don't exist. I'm told that yours is a land of plenty, so think on all these things and bless the farm — that if our food is dull it is at least there — so far.

In July 1941, PG Wodehouse gave five talks on Nazi radio, from Berlin. No one in England heard the broadcasts, but making assumptions, some journalists criticised him. His most virulent attacker was William Connor, 'Cassandra' of the Daily Mirror. Many years later the Cussen Report, written in 1944, was published and cleared his name.

PG Wodehouse was also a very shy man and lived in a world of his own, limited by his study, his writing, Ethel and the dogs. Frankie was at school with his daughter Leonora and one day she said, "There's an extraordinary man down at the end of the drive". Leonora replied, "That's my father. He hides in the bushes and I meet him down there. He's frightened of the head-mistress".

I am going to enclose a cutting about Plummy's broadcast to America. The man obviously knows Plummy and just what he is like. He says "I guess he doesn't know. Perhaps he didn't think". The first is right. He doesn't know, and he never will. The sweet simple little man with his type-writer.

That's really all he is to life, as distinct from his books. I can hear him saying, as he did to me before the war... "I can't see what difference it makes — if the Germans want to rule the world why not let them?"

Plummy

7 July, 1941

I wrote an awfully stupid letter to Leonora about Plummy. I wrote 6 different letters and tore them all up, and all the time I was writing I had a picture of old Mrs Cazalet being patronisingly nice to Leonora about it; and I got more and more furious with her (Mrs C). I tried jokes, but it is obviously not a joking matter. By this time I was in despair and also in tears about poor Leonora and also about poor Plummy. After all, the real thing is it should never happen to him to get into such a position. Everyone who knows him knows he is not fitted to deal with it.

Anyway I finally ended by writing a far too melodramatic and far too protestingly affectionate and loyal letter and I know Leonora will think I have gone dotty. So now I am miserable about that. I find something to be miserable about every day.

11 July, 1941

Here is a good example of the sort of thing I invent to be miserable about, when I am alone. This morning I got a letter from Leonora beginning "Thank you for the sweetest letter I ever had in my life". I <u>was</u> pleased.

It is all this being alone. No-one to talk to and nothing good to think about. And I think, from a psychoanalyst's point of view, I behave too well. I am so practical and vigorous and forceful (apparently) and I go off and buy farms and bring the children up really quite well and write books and goodness knows what and I don't grumble much and I'm not particularly a bore to be with. But all the time I'm wondering how long it's going to be and how on earth I'm going to go on sticking it. And so I just take it out by inventing idiocies to be miserable about. The book has become more or less a torture to me. I wriggle when people talk about it, and am terrified that someone will find something shaming in it.

The Russians seem to be doing far better than anyone could have imagined and the papers say the German people are aghast at the trains of wounded which keep on rolling in.

12 July, 1941

There is a possibility that I did something to my inside threshing in the spring. Anni thinks I'd better see a gynaecologist, I don't think it will be more than a bore, two days in a nursing home and having my inside twisted round. It may account for my appalling and perpetual tiredness and depression.

One thing, one never gets away from the children and tho' they are sweet they are also odious. They yell and bawl and ask questions and always want to help when you don't

79

want them to and trip over everything and put their blasted little sticky fingers all over my papers and take my face cream, nowadays unprocurable, and squeeze it all over my dressing-table and fret and irritate me till I could cheerfully murder them.

Sometimes I really have to leave Rose because if I didn't I should beat her up. This house is really awful in hot weather. There isn't any shade anywhere and the house itself is like a cook-house. Whenever I want to write to you or do the books there are always 14 wirelesses playing in every direction. I don't really mind all that, but it gets me down from time to time and I feel better for a good grumble.

17 July, 1941: Lovelands
The woman doctor was unable to find out anything but wants to see me again in 2 or 3 days. I was tired and depressed, and Anni, who, as you know, lives here with Twinks, persuaded me to spend the 2 or 3 days here instead of going home and coming up again. So here I am, spending the whole morning in bed and writing to you. I feel much better already. I don't want you to get the impression that there is anything seriously wrong with me — there isn't.

London was pretty awful. All the girls have gone dotty. They are determined to get men to take them out if they bust but as there are so few men left this is a bit difficult. Bob *(Laycock)* had just arrived back bringing word that all the rest of the Commando would be coming too. This was the occasion for a sort of orgy of idiocy. Without much sour grapes it was obviously impossible for me to join in this, so that wasn't much fun.

25 July, 1941
I am writing under difficulties as I only sit down with difficulty having been tossed in the air by one of my pigs

and landed on my bottom. The old bitch did it exactly like a bull and from behind when I wasn't looking. Molly and I were moving some young pigs, always difficult because they are so nippy. We took out a bucket of food and let out one of the old pigs because we knew that she would follow the bucket and they would follow her. It worked all right. I had the bucket in one hand and a stick in the other and every time she tried to get at the bucket I hit her with the stick. Then I had to rush ahead to head off 2 little pigs and I forgot her. With that, she lifted me neatly about 2 feet in the air and I came down with an appalling crash, bucket and all and she got the food. Her name is Gypsy and she is that pig I picked out at Moulton and I love her so I forgave her, but I have an enormous bruise and sitting is not at all pleasant.

On our way home we found 2 cows right bang in the middle of the oats eating their heads off (the oats and their own). That took hours too and by then I could have cut them in half with pleasure. Animals are so inconceivably stupid and while doing all the things you don't want them to always look at you in a sort of luminously speculative way or else with a sort of eager but flat expectancy. They arouse all my most sadistic instincts. I think that is why I like farm animals. It is one's duty to hit them and one can work off quite a lot of stream. "That for Thomas and that for Rose", and so on.

Now I must go to bed. My bum is really very sore.

31 July, 1941
Another pouring wet day, and what was left of our crops is now flat. It is terribly disappointing and will mean a very difficult harvest and a good deal of loss of money. Still, that's farming.

3 August, 1941
I went over to the Stapledons where Buck is staying. He said that Uncle Joe was in a complete and piddling funk of an

appeaser of the highest order, who would have given in to the German demands only they were too stiff. I asked what they were, and he said, "Every gun, every plane etc etc". He said he didn't think that Uncle Joe would have got away with appeasement because the Red Army commanders wouldn't have stood for it. I asked for his evidence — he said it was generally held in London. Swiftly and with utmost relish I made the retort which this opening invited — too obvious to repeat.

Buck said he hoped it would not lead to too much optimism in England and everyone thinking the war was over. This gave me another opportunity I have been waiting for, for some weeks. I said I thought it was a pity that all the leaders of opinion in England were so anxious to squash optimism of which in my opinion there is not nearly enough.

I said, "What is overlooked is this. Because this is a people's war and anyone may get bombed any day, it doesn't alter the fact that no cabinet minister and no newspaper editor is living in one room, in the house of someone they hate and who hates them, because they have been bombed out of their own. Nor are the wives of cabinet ministers or newspapers editors having any direct experience of living while their husbands are in the Middle East. So they think it is a good idea to keep on telling all these people, who, in this war as in every other, are the ones who are really taking the hell, that they've got to go on taking it for at least another 2 years. Whereas the best chance is to let them have a glimmer of hope that it might be for only another 6 months or so".

This was very enjoyable because it really made a great impression and shook Buck up a bit. I hope he will repeat it to some of the other wiseacres who see that no day passes without the newspapers and the BBC re-iterating that there isn't any hope at all for at least 2 years, which they repeat in a schoolmastery way to keep the children good and not because they profoundly believe it themselves. We were drinking burgundy which had been slightly mulled owing to being heated by an electric stove so I was in really good form by then and maybe not making quite the impression I thought I was. But still, I thought I was, which is really all that matters in this dull life.

6 August, 1941

Carling and I walked round part of the farm together which is always a good thing to do. We shall be harvesting next week and once that starts there will be no time to discuss anything until November when all the autumn drilling is finished. Our great excitement is that windfall apples have started. We have been entirely without fruit for 4 months and it is with the greatest pleasure that we go prowling round to pick them up. Life is cheap on a farm and also plentiful compared with other people's lives. I don't suppose there will be apples in the shops for 2 or 3 weeks and then they will be an enormous price and very rare. We shall try to store enough to see us through most of the winter.

When you were a child did you have 2 circular pieces of cardboard with a circular hole in the middle round which you wound wool and which after being cut made a woolly ball? This is the children's latest craze. They wake at 7 in the morning and start winding at once.

7 August, 1941

I had an aircard today in which you said you understood about feeling incredulous (about the book) and you felt like that when you got your firsts at Cambridge. The feeling didn't last long with me but it ought to have and your card gives me a slight return of the feeling. Of course having a book published is not really on a par with a double first. But I know what you mean about it being something you have done yourself and no-one can take away.

11 August, 1941

We had a very good afternoon cutting thistles. They were in the pig place which is up behind the cottage. We cut about an acre. Sometimes they were waist high and thick like a jungle and we went 4 in line swinging our billhooks like golf clubs. We finished it and came home pleased and tired.

I don't think I told you that a few days ago Thomas helped me drive 2 full grown pigs from the buildings down to the cottage. He really helped, beating them on the way they should go. A year ago he would have been terrified. It's a pity that you have to miss it all. You would love it.

14 August, 1941

I have just finished reading rather a good book of memoirs by a woman called Stella Bowen who was once married to Ford Maddox Ford. At the end she says something about Munich — then "We are fighting for our lives, that is understood. But it might have been for so much more". That was well put, I think and I am not sure it is answered by Winston's and Roosevelt's 8 points announced by Attlee this afternoon. Have they given us anything more to fight for than our lives? One still thinks of "Free to all like the Ritz Hotel". Roosevelt is all right — he has always done his best. And Winston is all right too because without him we probably wouldn't even have our lives left to fight for. But is a peace created by him and the Beaver *(Lord Beaverbrook)* really going to be any good? I don't know. I wish I did.

The Atlantic Charter was a pivotal policy statement issued on 14 August 1941, that, early in World War II, defined the Allied goals for the post-war world.

22 August, 1941

It still pours with rain every day and the position for us as for every other farmer is really very serious. The corn is sprouting (germinating) in the stooks which means it is useless. Not all of it but some. Soon it will be all if this goes on.

A large proportion of the English members of the British Army spent the period from Dunkirk (approximately June 1940) to D-Day (June 1944) in England. As well as tactical training they were used to help around the country with important labour intensive jobs such as farming and bomb damage. Frankie has trouble with some of them, as well as with her own employees.

Yesterday 10 soldiers came to fill in the bomb craters. The position is that I pay the army and we are paid by the war insurance, but nobody pays anything till after the war. One of the 10 was corporal. When we had settled the 9 men to work he came back to the farmhouse because he said there were some forms to be filled in. These turned out to be forms which should have been signed in the evening when they left agreeing the number of hours they had worked. Then he messed about the farmhouse talking to Mrs Carling. Molly and I went down the fields and on our way we met one of the soldiers coming up.

He asked us if we had seen the corporal. We said we thought he was at the farmhouse. He said, "Well, if you see him tell him I've gone to the village to get some fags". This should have left 8 men working there but when we got there there were only 7. I suppose the eighth had had a sudden desire for some sweets. All 7 were leaning on their spades talking. In the afternoon we went down again and there were 8 men there. 3 were working and the other 4 leaning on spades.

On our way back later in the afternoon we met the corporal and one man coming down. I went up to him and said, "I want to see that." I asked him for the paper I signed this morning. He said, "Why?" I said, "Because I'll sign for 7 men this morning and 8 this afternoon, but if you've got 10 down for either I'll cancel my signature". He said,

"Why?" So I told him in well chosen but quite moderate language why. So he said, "Well, you see, I'm sort of here to supervise. I'm not supposed to work".

So I said, "Well, that's ok by me but I don't pay for supervision specially not for supervision done at the other end of the farm while the men lean on their spades". So he said, "Well, I had to go and look at the other bomb holes". I said, "Why?" This completely flummoxed him.. So I said, "Well, you look at bomb holes to your heart's content because I won't".

This did a bit of good and after that a little, a very little work was done. It doesn't matter very much because in the end it's the War Insurance that pays. But it makes one feel a trifle nervous that this is how the British Army behaved in France and are behaving in all sorts of places. Perhaps not. Perhaps they behave better in other countries. But at the risk of being a colonel Blimp, there doesn't seem to be much discipline about the British Army.

All the farmers who are having them for harvesting report the same kind of behaviour and what's the use of a man with 2 stripes, who I imagine is equivalent to at least a foreman, if one of the men can say, "If you see him tell him I've gone to get some fags" in the middle of a morning's work.

It has rained solidly for 42 days (that is raining even after the St Swithin's period is up). Carling estimated this morning that we had probably not lost more than £300 to date (I think a gross under-statement) and anyway it hasn't finished yet. Every farmer in England is in the same boat and the seriousness of our position is slightly swamped by the seriousness of the position from a national point of view. Nobody is in despair because when there isn't one God-Damned thing you can do about it's not worth even being despairing. But there are farmers offering fields of wheat or oats to anyone who likes to come and cut them.

Everyone is cross with Rob Hudson *(Min of Ag)* because a week before any field of corn was cut he announced publicly that it was the best harvest in history. If he had used the word "crops" it would not have mattered but we all think him an ignorant swine who brought misfortune upon our heads by counting our chickens before they were hatched. The better the crop the worse is the hit.

1 September, 1941
I am in a furious temper today. Molly and I always want to work on the farm but except for the very dreary jobs like hoeing and thistle-cutting it somehow happens that we never do. Whenever we say to Carling "Can we help?" there is always some reason why it would be much better if we didn't. Every day now there are appeals on the wireless for more women to join things and do munitions and both Molly and I are beginning to feel that, unless we work all day on the farm there is no justification for our arrangements as they stand. She at least ought to join something and I at least ought to let her go.

I have never been able to pin on Carling the fact that he is deliberately trying to stop us joining in but he is certainly incredibly stupid about using us. This morning I said to him that Molly and I were going to work today, and we would either stook or go on the cart, whichever he preferred. He said they weren't going to stook and he wasn't quite sure what he was going to do until he saw whether the soldiers came. (We sometimes use 1 or 2 for harvesting.) He had got on a poker face and he said he would let me know later in the day. As I went down on my bike I saw the cart and 3 men go down to the field. So I fetched Molly and we just went down there and I got on the cart and she pitched on to it.

We got on very well and every time Carling, who was driving the tractor, came down with the empty cart to take away the loaded, there was our cart loaded up and ready, so nobody could say we were holding them up. However the third time he came he brought 2 soldiers with him which meant that there was nothing left for us to do, as they had enough without us. So, as I am very brave, I walked straight up to him and asked him why he had brought them. He said he'd got a lighter job he wanted us to do. So I said, "We don't want a lighter job.

5 women + a female dog helping to load hay and straw

We don't find this heavy, we enjoy it, and as the cart's always ready I assume we are doing it all right". So he said, Well, he wanted us to restook some oats which had fallen down and were getting wet. "If you don't do it the men will have to".

So I thought it was undignified to go on having an obvious barney in front of the men so I said all right we would do it. But I was furious. The oats did need doing but I was convinced that he would never have asked us to do it if we hadn't been doing this because he never asks us to do anything, and I am convinced he thought of it to get rid of us. Anyway, he won the first round and I am not sure what the next move is going to be. But it's going to be something. And I refuse to pay soldiers to do work I can perfectly do myself. And Molly will have to leave if this goes on. Anyway, I'm not going to be beaten by the bastard.

2 September, 1941

We worked fearfully hard today. I am determined that, if there is to be show-down with Carling over our working it shall be on the right terms of reference. So, since he said the oats needed stooking, we bloody well stooked all day. I am not going to leave him an opening to say we are choosey or won't do what needs doing most. I did about 7 hours work today. That is a good deal when you actually do it and I am very tired.

We are going to London tomorrow with the children to buy their winter clothes.

3 September, 1941

When the train was waiting in the station at Paddington Thomas suddenly said in a very loud voice to a crowded carriage, "A soldier just passed with a thing on his front like Daddy's" I said, "What has Daddy got on his front?" Terrific gestures to his chest — "You know, that red thing". Slightly embarrassed I said, "Oh, you mean the ribbon". He said, "Well you know, the thing the King sewed on". I explained amongst a good deal of laughter that the king hadn't actually sewn it on and he said, "Well, anyway, it was because he was brave". We had lunch at Gunter's with Anni and Jan and Dave.

9 September, 1941

Today I have done the hardest day's work of my life, 9 – 5.30 with the men all day. I either go on the cart and load the sheaves that are pitched up or else as a change I pitch. But our wheat is so heavy I can only just pitch it. The potential argument with Carling as to whether we should work or not has dissolved into thin air as we are so short-handed he cannot afford to ignore us. In fact he is reduced to asking us rather shamefacedly if we think we can stick it all day as they can't do without us. It is really great fun and real sweat of the brow and all the old ones like leading the horses in or riding on top of the cart you have just loaded. It's so funny that you've never done it. We do it all day and every day and it is a part of our lives but it is much more your sort of thing than mine. You would be very jealous of my hands if you could see them— they are really horny now. Well, I think I must go and have a bath. I'm getting cold and stiff.

 19 August, 1941

As you know, the colonel went to Suez, and now has asked for me to go too. I probably shall, in about a month, when we've worked the new colonel in here.... *and 2 months later:* ...It's satisfactory to get one's teeth into a job which needs doing. Ismailia was too well buttoned up to be fun.

 10 September, 1941

I have been meaning to tell you about the food situation and how well the farm has worked out. I think the things people miss most are eggs, fruit, jam or things instead of jam, and soon it will be milk as apparently there is going to be a shortage.

Milk is rationed to ½ a pint and some will get dried or condensed instead. Neither milk nor eggs affect us at all. We have just got 40 lbs of our own honey. We have plenty of jam as we had saved some sugar and had our own fruit and tho' we can't have fruit all the year we get an awful lot from the windfall time onwards and we have bottled quantities of plums and are about to bottle quantities of damsons. So I think you can feel very pleased about the farm from that point of view and the children look frightfully well and have so far not suffered from the lack of anything vital.

14 September, 1941

I haven't written for 2 days because I worked late the last 2 nights. I shall now write a long letter to make up for the two days. Today is Sunday and by rights we should still be working as the Minister broadcast an appeal to farmers to do so. But the men are tired and one horse lame and the tractors haven't been looked over or been oiled or greased for a fortnight and it is no use flogging the willing horse so we decided to knock off.

We have only about 4 acres of wheat left to get in, we have finished the oats, and we have two fields of beans, one of barley and one rather large field of mixed corn still to get. If rain will hold off we shall finish next week. The whole position is a lot better than it looked at one time. We lost a lot of oats but we got the wheat in in "fairly good nick" and the crops are very heavy. I am really tired. My hands, wrists and arms are stiff and sore. I can hardly knit my fingers are so stiff. But I think I'm fitter than I have ever been in my life.

I posted the book proofs air-mail and I think they should get thro' the censor because it is obvious what they are.

Evening

I have spent a real worker's Sunday. I was so tired I just wrote letters and read and slept all day and never went out at all except to feed the pigs. I'm reading an excellent book by David Garnett called *"War in the Air"*. He is in intelligence at the Air Ministry.

He says, "The Chamberlain government had always been in that tragic dilemma which is so frequently revealed after the financial crash of a great company. They could not tell the country how near the brink of disaster it was for fear of precipitating that disaster …. but they never faced the results of those mistakes or admitted them, and had clung to power hoping to remedy them, much as a financier hopes to restore the reserves which have been wasted". I think this is completely true, but it should not be overlooked that financiers go to prison for this sort of thing and are treated as a menace, whereas politicians as a rule get completely away and continue to menace society not only by their errors of judgment but by their ability to keep secret their errors of judgment.

Then there is Moore-Brabazon. *(Minister of Aircraft Production 1941-2)*. He is charged with saying roughly that we are glad to see Russia and Germany weaken each other — Russia being our ally. Churchill gets up and says, whatever M-B said he (Churchill) knows he didn't mean it as it was interpreted …. and it does harm both to Russia and England to publicise such a thing. Neither of them attempts to explain what he did mean if he didn't mean what he appears to have meant. And he doesn't resign or even get ticked off and that's all there is to it.

15 September, 1941

We have done another good day's work, turning beans. They were not stooked so they all had to be turned over and 3 rows turned into 1, so the carts can go through to pick them up. It is hard work but not so heavy and is a change from team work as you can go your own speed. We worked all morning and all afternoon till tea-time and the interesting thing is I'm not at all tired. Also about the garden. We have now been eating nothing but our own veg for about 4 or 5 weeks and look like going on for months.

16 September, 1941

Today's hot news is my biceps. You know I have always had flabby arms with no muscle at all. Well, I happened to feel them this morning, and what should I find but two cricket-balls. We got complimented on yesterday's work. Carling said he was immensely pleased to find the beans all done when he got there and he said Highman, who was ploughing in the next field, had remarked to him how extraordinarily well we had worked. This is high praise from

Carling, who always puts us on the dullest jobs and then regards us with a fishy eye.

Anyway we women have managed to make ourselves felt, as we are now no longer given time to do urgent jobs in the garden and one morning we were not even allowed to feed the pigs who went hungry till 11 o'clock. I am not sure that is good farming but we never disobey orders. The policy is to show we are useful before throwing our weight about. But we are never allowed decent tools to do the job with. The men take all the best pitchforks and leave us with the heavy ones and when I remark on it no-one so much as blinks. I have circumvented this by picking out the two best and hiding them. Farm men are rather sweet. Peter *(Cazalet)* once said, "you'll never own anything. It's always 'my pigs, my cows etc' ". But what he didn't know, it's "my pitchforks" too. Carling often says to me about some tool or other "I shouldn't borrow that one. It's Joe's". Borrow!

17 September, 1941

This afternoon I was sent off to horse-rake the oats. It was a great test because the rake was in the field and I merely went off ½ a mile from the farm armed with the horse. The question which filled me with sweating apprehension was, could I get him single-handed into the shafts? It was really a question of weight. Could I lift them? If I could, useful citizen worth her salt. If I couldn't, B.F. and dilettante useful for a couple of hours gang work but otherwise useless. I did it all right and raked for 3 hours. It wasn't really nearly as difficult as I had apprehended but my stock was up when I got back and I had obviously been doubted.

19 September, 1941

The news seems bad. I think Kiev must either have fallen or else so nearly have done so for it to be only a matter of time. And this must be very serious ….

19 September, 1941: Nazis take Kiev. 29 September, 1941: Nazis murder 33,771 Jews at Kiev.

Large cart-horse, led out to the field and backed into the shafts of hay rake. Frankie was 5ft 2

What is the good of listening to the news or doing anything else except pitch fork? Pitchforking is good. I did it all day yesterday until 7.30 at night. To me it seems a miracle that I can, that's why I keep on telling you about it. When we first started the harvest I couldn't get the sheaves on top of the cart at all when it was loaded high. Now I do it all the bloody day and at the end I'm not even more than reasonably tired.

7: 1941

Much Hadham and Walter de la Mare

Jack's sister, Katta, was married to Richard de la Mare (Dick), son of Walter. They lived in a beautiful house with a huge garden and a swimming pool, a luxury for us, in the village of Much Hadham in Hertfordshire. We went there often in our childhood, usually unaccompanied except by Old Nan, to stay in the school holidays.

Old Nan in 1936 with Thomas at his christening

*Old Nan had been Katta's nanny as well as Jack's. He was, of course, her perfect boy. She always used to tell us how much better the de la Mares and the Shawcrosses (our other cousins) were than us. We were humbled by this and it was not for many years that we found out that she gave them the same treatment about us, praising us in comparison to them. Although always rather disapproving of Frankie she came to accept and love her. She even stooped to using garlic on the salad bowl and other such newfangled ideas. She always said to us, "No one but your father would be able to put up with your mother". She may have been right, as though wonderful and stimulating Frankie was a difficult personality, given to depression and euphoria in an unpredictable way. Once, when she was dying, I asked Jack how she had been that day. He replied with satisfaction, "**Much** better. She's giving a **lot** of trouble."*

 25 September, 1941

We are going away next week to Katta's. The children are madly excited. I am being very grand over the food question, which is always a thing nowadays when you stay away. I'm sending one chicken, an enormous cut off our pig, 1 pot of honey, 1 doz eggs (I can't pack any more) ordinary tea and sugar ration, lashings of butter and all the sweets Mrs Wheeldon has been able to collect in a week. I hope this will properly impress Katta. When I go on Monday I shall take some rabbits.

26 September, 1941

The children went off this morning. They woke up at cockcrow and began to prepare. When they were ready and we were finishing the packing, they ran outside and one could hear their voices up and down the path "Good bye, so & so. Good bye So and So. You won't see us for one week and one week-end". On the platform Thomas was very self-contained but Rose ran round in circles making rather pretty gestures with her hands. The house is like a grave without them. I never knew before how much they mean to me for themselves. I always hold the theory that I care for them chiefly for your sake but I don't think it's true. I have missed them all day, and all day I have thought "now they are in the train. By now they will be in London" and so on. They had two new blue coats (the ones I dreamed about) and they really did look sweet. I do wish you could see them.

27 September, 1941

Still no letters. I got three broadsheets from the Planners on food distribution and production.

The plan takes no account at all of soil suitability, the personal preferences of the farmers, the fact that high-yielding dairy herds are bred not bought, nor of the fact that the only way to avoid abortion is to rear your own stock; you can't just buy every year from supply farms. It never touches the real problems of agriculture, such as rural housing, water supplies, roads, wages, prices. I have written out what I consider to be a very good and devastating criticism of it.

I shan't in fact deliver this. If I do go to the conference I shall tell them privately what I think of it, but I shan't speak publicly at all. I think it is really horrifying. Apart from the fact that they are a lot of able-bodied people with at least sufficient intelligence to do a routine war job, think of the paper they waste. Lay people always go on so about composting, and sewerage, and blood from carcases. They seem to think a few enlightened intellectuals could put the whole thing right in two minutes.

I wish they would come and try. I wish they would come here now and tell me a) whether to thatch my ricks, b) or to cut my silage or c) to go on ploughing and cultivating for next year's sowing. All three are important and all should be done at once and someone has got to decide which to do first or to do a bit of each and not finish any. When they had decided this they could tell me where when and how to make the compost heap and rub their noses in it. And then they could mend my gates and do my fencing, and paint our doors and saw the wood for the winter and then we should all be neat and tidy and fit for the approval of any intellectual. And I should be jolly pleased because I can't get it done in any other way.

Yesterday, for the first time for about a year, the thought flashed across my mind that we might not be going to win the war after all. Everyone here is a bit downcast by the failure of American production. It is a bit discouraging to think that all the war has done so far is to give the Americans more purchasing power to buy automobiles which ought to have been tanks. If the Germans got to the Caucasus the Russians would fail and then where should we be? I don't know. Maybe somebody does. I am sick and tired of politics, politicians, leader-writers and all controllers of propaganda. I never believe a word they say anymore.

It is horrible here without the children and I long for Monday.

30 September, 1941: Much Hadham.

The really exciting thing is that my book is going to come out on October the 9th *(Jack's birthday)*. I shall send you a cable to tell you this, so the news when you get it in this letter won't be as exciting for you as it is for me at the moment. It is quite accidental as Dick had no idea it was your birthday.

It is really lovely here. Katta and Dick are awfully good hosts and it is so nice to sit up drinking tea and talking — so much what I need. I can see that I must really go away more. I get so depressed at home but cheer up at once when I get the stimulus of company.

The children are having a lovely time. They get on extremely well with Katta's and are not a bit shy. Old Nan is here. I am afraid she is really getting rather old now. I notice she is a trifle piano compared with her usual self. Of course she is over 70 now. I wish you would write to her occasionally.

1 October, 1941
I am really rather enjoying myself here. The house is littered with books that I more or less want to read, so immediately I have fulfilled the minimum politeness of a guest, I bury myself in an armchair and read for the rest of the day.

Yesterday I was taken by Katta to pick blackberries for the Women's Institute. Three other leading lights of Much Hadham came with us. One of the three women has a husband in Egypt. He is an R.E. and is on some job too secret for her to know what it is. She is very unhappy and she spoke to me as a kindred spirit, with complete intimacy. She said she couldn't really imagine how she had got as far as she had. She had always thought she would be dotty by now as it made one so lonely. And she said she was getting old and bitter and when other people's husbands came home on leave she could hardly pretend anymore to be pleased. She said at one point "But I am used to going about alone now". And I knew that, for her, that was almost the saddest thing, like an insult, a humiliation.

I know how she feels, because just at the beginning I felt like that. I think that all over England women are suffering like this and I think seriously that it is devastating. But nobody cares or even remembers them and the war will go on for years yet. So what? Dod says the first and greatest casualty of the war is the family.

Meeting Walter de la Mare: Dick's father, Walter de la Mare, was renowned as one of the great English poets of this time. He is famous for the poem 'The Listeners' *and the novel* Memoirs of a Midget *among many other writings.*

Walter de la Mare has been here for the night. I got on very well with him. I know this by all the ordinary tests and also with certainty because when he left he said good-bye to me twice; the first time he said, "I hope we shall meet again soon. I should like to see your farm". And the second time he said, "I must say good-bye again. It was lovely to have a talk". He also asked Dick to send him a copy of my book.

I must break off here to tell you another odd and, to me, pleasing coincidence. yesterday I went to London and I went to Dick's office to travel down with him in the evening. I was shown into the waiting room where his father was also waiting. So we went into Dick's room together. Dick came forward with a book in each hand and said, "I've got a book for both of you". they were the first advance copy of my book and the first advance copy of a new one of his. I liked that.

He suddenly said to me after dinner when we were discussing the two books, "Are you able to talk about your book alright?" I said, without taking thought, "I had a period when I squirmed if anyone mentioned it. Now I've got that in control. Is that what you mean?" Believe it or not, it was what he meant. So what I had always regarded as an unpleasant and neurotic idiocy suddenly became in some way a qualification of some sort of integrity and anyway a guarantee of some sort of sensibility and a password to his friendship. He said he always had it with every book and never got over it.

Later he asked the company generally whether they ever felt depressed in the mornings. He asked it shyly and rather shamefacedly. I replied, "Always". I could see that he was relieved at sharing in some way something he was vaguely ashamed of. However, this was not quite so romantic as we eventually boiled it down to cigarette smoking.

100

He was doing an anthology on love and he is interested in time and dreams. I think I could have told him things that might have interested him. You know how he cross-examines you. But I couldn't with Dick and Katta there. I think he knew that too. He is a very charming person, isn't he?

7 November, 1941
The children are amusing. Their characters are so different. We were pulling mangolds today. T. works hard but never stops talking. Then Rose arrives and with a portly gesture of

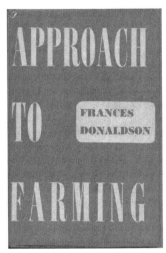

Walter de la Mare, poet and writer and, right, the cover of the book

defiance and provocation, pulls two mangolds out of a row we were not working on, throws them at my head and walks off. But they are both sweet and charming with each other. Thomas looked out of the door this afternoon and shouted, "John, tell my baby sister to come to tea!" I do wish you could see them.

Frankie liked tough people and I was always tough – to the point of being impossible. She says at one point, "Rose is a vile child. I could eat her". Thomas was a more delicate flower, sensitive and often brought to tears. She had more trouble with this and although she loved him the pressure and worry of the farm and the war made her more impatient. Their relationship deteriorated a little over the years. In this photograph I am looking challengingly and with confidence, while Thomas has a slightly tentative expression.

Thomas and Rose standing by the car

13 November, 1941

It is a year today since I saw you. I do think it is wonderful that I should have got thro' a whole year.

18 November, 1941

I have just got a cable and an airgraph. You are sweet to be proud of me. The Airgraph I had this morning says you have been in Suez a week and are busy and happy but gives no details. YOU MUST GIVE DETAILS, you blockhead. I must say in some ways you are the most unsatisfactory husband one can have. I must quickly add you make up for it in other ways. Nanny went this morning. I really love her, but I'm glad she's gone in spite of having to get my own supper and fill my hot water bottle because she gives me no peace in the evenings.

20 November, 1941

Today we heard the news of the attack on Libya. I wonder how it will go. I am almost sure that the Marshall Arthur Coningham must be a man known to his friends as Mary Coningham. If so I knew him very well and he was the first man I was ever seriously in love with, at the age of 12. No-one over 12 would be seriously in love with him as he quite mad and odd in a way. See if you can find out if he is a New Zealander and wears his hair en brosse. If you ever get near such grand people introduce yourself, as I couldn't know him better. Tho' the war is odd. I would never suggest your introducing yourself if he wasn't in his present position. But he is awfully nice and frightfully brave. He brought down God knows how many aeroplanes in the last war.

Your description of hearing my broadcast was thrilling. I am glad you heard it because one of the things which influenced me to do it was the thought that it would be such fun for you if you could hear it. The Carlings come back tomorrow thank Goodness.

21 November, 1941

This morning at about 7 o'clock I was woken up by Nora who said that Gypsy Hall was on fire and the flames were shooting into the sky. I knew that the telephone on the farm was out of order so I had to decide whether to go up to the farm or down to the village to telephone the Fire Brigade. I went to the back of the Eighteen Cottages. All I could see was a very small light which flickered occasionally, so I went up to the farm. Highman was in charge (Carling is still away) and with the aid of a stirrup pump he had got the fire out — thank God I bought the stirrup pump. We employ a mental defective as cowman — quite nice and efficient, but slow and defective. He had gone to fill the tank of the engine with a 2 gallon can of petrol in one hand and a lamp in the other. As he poured the petrol the fumes ignited from the lamp. He was so frightened that he dropped the 2 gallons of petrol and ran, thereby adding a good deal of fuel to the flames.

The whole engine is burnt out and the cows will have to be milked by hand until I can get it all renewed which will be God knows when. What had happened was this. The whole of the cowshed is wired for electric light, including the engine room, but as the boys used to leave the light on Mr Clever Carling removed the bulb. I hold Carling entirely responsible. How can he be so stupid as to go off on holiday leaving a mental defective wandering around with a bicycle lamp? I have the unpleasant job of ticking him off when I see him tomorrow fresh from his holiday.

24 November, 1941

I HATE the children's hour in the winter. I LOATHE playing Snap with everybody yelling and I DETEST reading gloomy children's books.

Nobody sympathises with you more than I do for missing the children's youth, but you are lucky to miss all this. I shall have to do it every day for at least four months now. It's enough to drive anyone away from home. Thomas has developed this new trick of indulging in angry tears about everything. Today at tea he said, "whenever Mrs Butts went to Stratford, Manning asked her to bring him something". I said that was like other people I knew. T. immediately burst into tears and yelled at me, "Yes, but you never bring anything". I bundled him out of the room.

I'm sure one should treat these psychological difficulties quite differently, with great patience, and wait for him to grow out of them. But I'm not bloody well going to. I've seen Daddy indulged all his life and I've seen Harry Sackville, whose tempers were very much indulged as a child, grow into a spoilt young ass and anyway I like to enjoy my meals in peace and I'm not going to have them spoilt by having to indulge Thomas all the time. What do you think?

28 November, 1941

I am rather shocked at times by my generally rather suicidal mentality. I use the word figuratively. But, for instance, when Nora came to tell me about the fire at Gypsy Hall. I had no spontaneous reaction but rather the feeling "O well, let it burn. Nothing could be bloodier than life is now anyway". That is an exaggeration but in a way describes my whole attitude to life. There is one factor in relation to G.H. and the fire that is that I am always thwarted of responsibility there.

My attitude is, I suppose, "O, Well, the men will look after it". I am more than ever determined to have a small farm after the war. I want the children to have fresh food and I want them to grow up in an atmosphere which demands effort and initiative from them and in which they constantly see everyone at work and since a farm gives all these things I want always to have a farm.

28 November, 1941

I dined with Wogan Phillips last night in Stratford. He is quite exceptionally nice and you would like him. Apparently he went to Spain, not in the International Brigade as he is C3, (*Conscientious Objector*), but as an ambulance driver. He was turned out of his local Home Guard unit because he had been in Spain — they called him a fifth columnist. What an odd commentary on the general knowledge and understanding of the English. Of course, this was before Russia was in the war.

30 November, 1941

The tendency here is to be slightly worried about the Libyan campaign. At best it seems our casualties must be huge. At times like these I begin to think I have much to be thankful for. But the Russians turning the Germans out of Rostov is good.

November 20, 1941: Germans take Rostov. December 5, 1941: German attack on Moscow abandoned.

I should say it's the first time the Germans have been turned out of anywhere big enough to count. It looks as tho' they bit off more than they could chew with Russia.

5 December, 1941

I went to a farmers' meeting which was very enjoyable. It was the first meeting of a new discussion club run by Clyde Higgs and the War Committee and the new agricultural adviser who is called Pattison. It was a very good meeting addressed by a man called Mansfield, who is a considerable pundit. My dear, it really is fun, being a person of some importance. After the meeting was over I went to join and pay my subscription. Clyde Higgs came up and said, "Hullo, authoress" in a loud voice and asked me how the book was going. Then Wilkes came up with Mansfield and said, "Do you know Mrs D?" and Mansfield said, "Unless I'm very much mistaken, Mrs D must be the author of a very charming book I have just read". Mrs D covered in blushes and enjoying herself like mad.

I talked to him for a long time and then went to pay my subscription. There were two rates, one for farmers and one for farm labourers. The man said, "Farm labourer?" and I said, "Farmer". He looked a bit surprised and said, "Well, Miss Mrs ...?" "Mrs Donaldson". "Oh ho, Gypsy Hall". Then we went all through it. Then Pattison was brought and introduced. He said he hadn't read the book because he had asked for it at the Library, and the girl said he would have to go on a very long waiting list. All very enjoyable. I do wish you were here to see it.

9 December, 1941

I am getting like the German people were always supposed to be, too used to sensation and crisis to be aroused by anything. I am very much less interested in the new Japanese war than I was, for instance, in the Italian attack on Greece. I no longer believe that any one thing can bring in its train a quick end to the war. They are all to me simply phases which have to be got through. The end of each month is a far bigger event in my life than anything the Axis can do. I am only interested in time.

10 December, 1941

I have just heard the news of the sinking of the P.o.W. and the Repulse, which has chastened me a good deal.

10 December 1941 HMS Prince of Wales and HMS Repulse were sunk near Kuantan on the east coast of Malaya, by Japanese torpedoes and bombs, there being no worthwhile defensive air cover. About 1200 men were lost.

When we sank the Bismarck Eden said it was more important than the loss of Crete, and tho' I suppose, as we have more ships, it is not as serious, it must be in the order of a major defeat. The Japs seem to be having some luck and a considerable initial success. I wonder if the Americans are any good?

11 December, 1941

I am very depressed about the news. It seems so odd that the Japs should have succeeded in sinking one American and two British capital ships in three days considering the Germans haven't been able to do it in two wars.

P.S. What a good gesture on the part of China to declare war on Germany and Italy! It may not mean anything at all as I suppose she can't do more than continue the war against Japan, but after all these years of lonely fighting it is a very pretty example to the rest of the world.

December 5, 1941: German attack on Moscow is abandoned.

December 9, 1941: Chinese Government declares war on Japan

December 7, 1941: Japanese bomb Pearl Harbor;

December 8, 1941: US & Britain declare war on Japan.

December 11, 1941: Hitler declares war on the United States.

P.S. again. There is rather a scandal going on because Basil has been taken out of the army by Brendan and appointed to a cushy job in Ministry of Information.

Basil Ava, Marquis of Dufferin and Ava. Brendan Bracken, Minister of Information 1941-45, Churchill's "faithful chela" and founder of The Financial Times

Questions have been asked in the H. of C. Apparently people are particularly annoyed because it is common knowledge that Basil has done quite excessively badly in the army and has anyhow now drunk himself into a coma.

P.S. Since America is now at war with the Germans I must write another line. It is rather a big occasion and I feel now that the Germans can never win. But there is one rather amusing thing. In spite of our bad record at Munich etc we do share the distinction with France — who has now lost all claim to distinction — of having declared war on Germany. Every single other country waited to be actually attacked.

12 December, 1941

Apparently the Japs have no secret weapon. They were just very efficient and we were rather inefficient.

I have just had the only cheerful thought I have ever had about the war. Hitler has been forced to play his last ace with Japan. If we have trumped his ace with America (which, unless Japan continues her quick and spectacular victories, we surely must have) it is now at last really a question of time. The length of time it takes Britain,

America, Russia and China to defeat Japan, Germany and Italy. But there can be no more large set-backs, no new navies thrown in to alter the balance etc. So that now at last the war seems to have got going in earnest and any victory we achieve will be a real one and a step forward. All the preliminaries are over and the war really begun. At the same time I think we shall have to do a bit better. Neither in Libya nor in the Pacific can we be said to have been very brilliant. And slow but sure is not good enough if our casualties are as great as they have been lately in both places.

14 December, 1941
I am rather optimistic about the war. You cannot get away from the fact that the Russians have got the Germans on the run in Russia while we have at any rate got them walking in Libya.

This is typical not only of Frankie's somewhat volatile temperament but also of the swings and changes of wartime news. On 11 December, 1941, 3 days before, she had written, "I am very depressed about the news..."

Bob Laycock is missing. I wonder what that means. Poor Angie! I wish I was you — always surrounded with people. It is the loneliness and the hours of contemplation which get me down.

17 December, 1941
T has just made a divine remark and a perfect commentary on Molly's teaching. I told him you had written him a pc written in big letters so that he could read it. He said, "Does it say anything about cats?" I said, "No, why?" And he said, "If it did, I could read that".

19 December, 1941
The Farmer and Stockbreeder people are coming tomorrow, so I hope I shall have some photographs of the farm to

send you; also an article about it which you can boastfully show to your friends.

22 December, 1941

The F & S *(Farmer and Stockbreeder magazine)* people came and took lots of photographs of the farm and me feeding the pigs and not feeding the pigs and so on, and it will be great fun if they are all good because I will be able to send them to you. The Farmers' Weekly, having already given A to F a kind word have now reviewed it again amongst a list of books for Christmas. These are the high spots. *(the 'she' referred to is Frankie)* "One of the interesting things about her account of it all is that no-one could say, grudgingly, that she was lucky. Luck had nothing to do with it. She has had a great deal of invaluable help, but simply because she cared so wholeheartedly about this experiment and was so clear-headed and intelligent in the way she tackled it, that she found out where to go for advice, and the people she asked were glad to give it to her. Her own personality comes spontaneously thro' her narrative. The rest of your interest will be divided between the interest of her progress and the integrity and acuteness of her own observation."

I have now had a letter from H.J. Massingham, a writer of some small distinction on country life. He says, "I write to tell you how much I enjoyed and admired your book, so well written and full of such admirable good sense and good judgment, and with vision too, which most books on farming so sadly lack". Now I think that The Farmers Weekly review and this letter, added to the TLS *(Times Literary Supplement)* review, express the whole of the success of the book. I am surprised at its sort of "prestige" success. I am surprised at being backed so heartily by the farming papers and at getting good reviews from literary papers and most of all at getting approval from so many farming intellectuals, all of whom give me credit for "vision", or "a sense of values" or something of that sort.

8: 1942

Tobruk and Jaundice

Jack was selected especially to organize Tobruk logistics and supplies. He immediately fell ill with jaundice (hepatitis) and was moved out to hospital. When he recovered the job he had gone to fill had been passed to someone else, so he was sent to Baghdad and then Tehran. When Tobruk finally fell we were told that this had saved his life as so many people were killed then.

27 September, 1941
I am to be moved immediately to Tobruk. *(Followed by delays.)*

6 January, 1942
9th General Hospital *(Code for 8ᵗʰ Army hospital).* Now at last I can write to you all about my week's series of accidents. I wrote last from Cairo, which I hope Randolph took back to you, bringing you up to date so far. I went round to HQ to see various people and felt distinctly shivery, and thought I was starting a cold. I had to start by air, leaving the Hotel at 5.30 am.

I knew I was ill, but there had been such flap trying to get me a seat on the aeroplane and it as all so urgent and all that, that I thought it better to take aspirin and carry on. The aeroplane was four hours late — I felt like hell all the way — and went straight to bed as soon as I'd met my new colonel, who seemed alright and at least had the sense to see

111

I was ill. That afternoon we drove over to Tobruk, where I went straight to bed again.

Next morning a doctor, who suspected jaundice. Next hospital, and next evacuation by hospital ship. Two days on board, one day (yesterday) on the train, and here we are. The Tobruk hospital was incredible. I'm sure they find it very difficult to get supplies and everything is sunk and all that, but nothing but deliberate sadism could excuse its squalor. It's in an old but not badly bombed Italian hospital, with all doors and windows blown in. This has completely beaten them. They got as far as nailing a blanket over a door, but to nail two and put weights on their bottom was too much for them.

The day I arrived I was put into ward 9, a long room with about four doors and windows on each side, and everywhere blankets blowing horizontally into the room, and gaunt cowering figures trying to bore thro' their pillowless beds to escape the pitiless draught. The medical inspection was pretty funny. Two doors were in a straight line either side of the room, (horizontal blankets of course). You wouldn't credit it, but they placed the examination bed between the two and on it sat waiting patients. The food was minimal, not that I minded, the rain poured onto the bed next to mine, and it took actual physical threats to produce a cup of hot water to shave in.

All thro' sheer hopeless incompetence, — no ill will at all. In fairness, their job is not to treat, but to diagnose and evacuate. But all the same it was a bit over the odds. Evacuation was held up by an air-raid, and it wasn't till 10 pm that we finally dressed and went down in an open ambulance to the docks. Here it was pouring with rain and blowing hard, and we had to get into open boats and be towed out to the hospital ship. By this time I was past caring, but when we finally got aboard we were treated to everything in the world. The ship was a real paradise, exquisitely run with charming people running her. Now I have a comfortable room to myself and am quite content to be apathetic and get well in my own time. I don't feel well but not ill either.

Jack recovered and went to Baghdad. He stayed there some time, not particularly enjoying the work or the people, but finally struck gold when he was transferred to Tehran for special liaison with the Russians. Although the Russians were our allies, most English and Americans feared them as much, if not more, than the Germans.

Jack was a declared socialist, and had very nearly joined the Communist Party and fought in Spain. He had strong positive feelings for the Russians and got on well with them, which made him successful in this new job. My ex-husband, Nicholas Deakin, was lunching recently with a well-known historian who specialises in this period and subject. At one point in the conversation, the historian remarked reflectively that relations with the Russians in the war had been bad everywhere except in one place – Tehran – and nobody knew why things were so much better there.

14 January, 1942
I got a cable from you today saying you are in hospital with jaundice. How horrible for you. I expect you are very fed up just as you are starting your new job. It is disappointing. And jaundice is a very depressing disease. Have you any books? If not I am afraid you will be very melancholy.

January 21, 1942
The first number of "The Dairy Farmer" has arrived, and contains a review of A to F. It says "Its author has manifestly learnt more about farming in one year than many people do in a lifetime". I like good reviews from farming papers.

The news has just begun. How inconceivably badly we are doing in the Far East. The Japs seem to be able to do exactly what they like.

24 January, 1942

We seem to be literally throwing the war away in the Far East.

Quentin Reynolds, broadcasting from America last night, threw in the remark that 1945 would be the peak year for U.S.A. naval production. If this is the beginning of accustoming the public mind to an acceptance of 1945 in place of the long promised 1943 I am going to throw up the sponge and stop trying at all. The muddle and inefficiency is becoming so obvious that it can no longer be completely hidden by constant exhortation to all the people who are doing their best to do it harder. I for one am beginning to be extremely bitter and angry. I look forward to months without letters and years without seeing you …..

I wrote you a letter some weeks ago explaining that the milk position on the farm was very far from satisfactory, and that this was due partly to the fact that many of the cows weren't quite good enough and partly to the fact that the labour in the cowshed was inadequate. Nothing was done quite well enough and it was no good buying better cows until the management was better. It seemed a good moment to have a TT test done in the hope that some of the reactors would be cows we were going to sell anyway. This worked out quite well. We had five, two good and three bad, which would have been sold anyway. We shall probably get the licence which would mean an appreciation of £250 in the herd's value.

If I could once get the management right it would be quite easy to improve the cows.

I wish I knew where you were and I wish you'd have a spell at Wilmcote and me in Tobruk. I personally think mine is by far the harder part — but then I think of the flies and

114

the heat and the lack of water and I begin to wonder. This morning's airgraph told about Shellaker. I guessed it was that. What a nice reward to get invalided home. You might try a jag. Phil said there was only one way for ordinary people to get home and that was to disgrace themselves.

30 January, 1942

It turns out they will need chaps for the two places I told you Reggie Fellowes is going to, ending in N & Q, and some of these would be railways jobs, so Thicknesse thinks I might go to one of them.

Iraq and Iran. He went to Iraq first and later to Iran. There is no other mention of Thicknesse, presumabluy an officer.

3 February, 1942

I got two airgraphs today. I hadn't realised you were ill directly you got to Tobruk. I have never had the cable from there. I thought you had worked there for at least two or three weeks. Your descriptions of the hospital there remind me of the Crimea and make me feel perhaps I should chuck everything here and force my way to the front as the 1942 Florence Nightingale. It makes me so angry. It couldn't happen nearer England, the fuss would be too great, but when this lousy country has sent people to the ends of the earth in its defence it's safe to treat them anyhow.

Our new cowman arrives today. I do hope he will be a success. It will make the whole difference to our future fortunes.

I have decided to take the Tribune again and the Labour Monthly. Would it be alright to send them on to you? Or are they too noticeable a colour to be discreet? Not that you seem to care much about discretion — you write some staggering things on airgraphs. You ask if your letters are censored. They show no sign of it.

The news is bad. We have obviously lost Singapore, tho' there is no announcement yet. Criticism of Winston seems to be growing not so much because people are dissatisfied but because he is so dictatorial, and makes so many statements like "The responsibility is mine", as tho' that were relevant to the situation. But the whole community really loves him.

13 February, 1942
I got three photographs this morning and one of them is really like you. Jan, who is staying here, was trying to find out the other day if the children really remembered you at all. I showed this photograph to T. and said, "Who are these two men?" He said at once, "That one's Daddy but I don't know who the other is". Rose was there so it was impossible to know whether she would have known or not but my impression is that she didn't know you from Adam. She hardly could know you. She wasn't two when you went away nearly 2 ½ years ago.

Clyde Higgs was an eminent local farmer from Leamington Spa. He supplied milk to all the area around Stratford upon Avon. He was an energetic man with an original mind. His milk bottles were famous, and carried slogans such as 'Higgs milk, Higgs heggs / Keep the workers on their legs'; 'No milk for seven days makes one weak'; 'Your cat miaows at milk from our cows'; 'The milk's thine, / The bottle's mine' .

I went to a weekly boarding school in Stratford when I was about 6 and we used to sing, 'Clyde Higgs, Milk for the pigs'. I did not realise that we were taking him off, and just thought we were being deliciously naughty.

116

9: 1942

Some Important Advice

14 February, 1942

Today the most extraordinary thing happened. I went over to see Clyde Higgs to ask his advice about the cows etc. When I had been there about three hours, he suddenly said, "Of course you'll never do any good until you get rid of that bailiff of yours". I sat up as tho' shot and said, "What do you mean?" He said, "Well, what are you doing messing about? You're not making money and you're not doing anything except sit in that house in the village leaving about £12,000 worth of capital in the hands of a man you pay £4.10/- a week to. I thought perhaps you were writing but you don't appear to be. You're not the girl I thought you were".

He meant I should run the farm without a bailiff. I made all the obvious objections and he just pooh-poohed the lot. He said I'd never get anywhere this way, that I couldn't make much of a mess the other way, and that in any case if I found after six months that I was making a mess of it, good bailiffs were two a penny anyway (I believe this is true) and I could easily get another one. He repeated, "if you haven't got the guts to do it you aren't the girl I thought you were and you'll never get anywhere".

This only happened an hour ago so obviously I oughtn't to make any comment on it. But I'm going to. I'm going to do it. I know I oughtn't to until I have consulted you and waited for an answer but I also know that you don't mind risks really and that if you were here and understood all the complex difficulties you'd agree and let me do it.

The very thought of it makes me feel good in a way I haven't felt good for over a year. I know I can't get anywhere this way and I know I'm not doing a job that's worth doing. I'm dying of inanition (re-read some of yesterday's letter). I can't do any of the things I want to, I'm thwarted at every turn, I've got nothing like a full-time occupation, I crawl round the farm unable to say boo to a goose, when I get good advice I can't take it because I can't make Carling, I can't get my pastures grazed the way I want them grazed, I can't take on the C.O. *(Conscientious Objector)* because Carling thinks he ought to be in the army and so on and so on. ... It's reduced me to the point where I can't bring myself to get up in the morning. If we were making a pot of money it would be worth it, but we're definitely not. If I make a bad enough balls we can sell out. We are bound to take out as much as we put in. Anyway I know in my bones I must do it.

O boy, am I excited! I've been wanting someone to say this to me for weeks and weeks — months and years — and nobody would. I hadn't the guts to do it off my own bat but now I damn well will. If you knew the humiliation of my position — writing articles, meeting farmers, always being cracked up as a success story when really I'm nothing but a miserable, thwarted and neurotic creature entirely in the hands of a bailiff.

You've got to forgive me and back me 100%, and you've got to grin and take it when I've lost all your money. I absolutely know it is right. I know I don't know anything but I know damn well I can learn anything I want to if I want to. In about two years from now I shall write a book called "The adventure really begins" and that will earn us all the money I've lost in the meantime. Hurray, Hurray, life's going to be fun again!

½ an hour later:

I'm so excited I have to write some more. I see all my insoluble problems melting away. I know there will be others and in some ways worse ones to take their place but there will be a bit of life about it. I shall be able to employ who I like — something quite new. I shall live in the farmhouse, but I shall keep this house on in case I want to import outsiders. When someone says to me "Will you or can you do this?" I shall be able to say Yes or No, not "I'll think about it", which, being interpreted means I'll sound Carling. When someone who knows what he is talking about says "You ought to do this" I shall be able to do it instead of having to go home biting my nails with frustration and temper.

16 February, 1942

I'm so madly excited these days that I sweat slightly most of the time and can't keep my mind on a book or a conversation or anything. Mr Stewart was not nearly so disapproving as I expected him to be. He thought that, having Highman, it would be perfectly possible for me to manage the outside work, but I must have a cowman who was just as good.

I used a very telling argument with him. I said that when we had a good cowman yield was good, and when we had a bad one it was bad, and that Carling's presence didn't alter this fact. Mr S agreed that providing there was some intelligence at the top, the ploughman and the cowman were the key men and not the bailiff at all. I maintain that, if I'm to keep a grip on it, I <u>must</u> live at the farm where anyone can see me at any time of day or night. The difficulty is to find somewhere for a married cowman, as the present one, who is single is sure to leave with Carling as he is his friend.

Mr Stewart says there is one week in five when most of the land girls have gone and I could go to the Institute for a week. I was rather pleased really because it shortens the time before I can tell Carling, and get on with it. I simply

119

can't wait. You don't know what all this means to me. It gives me back my self-respect. I'm so tired of writing articles etc about what I have achieved when I know I haven't achieved anything except a home farm without a home. Also it opens up such a vista for the future. Everybody regards me as news and a possibility but I can't ever get further than "I bought a farm" because quite frankly I haven't got any further. In about two years from now I shall be able to write dozens of books and articles and broadcast practically every day.

I've had so much to say I haven't mentioned the news which is so ferociously bad that I don't, sometimes, think it's important what I do. We could easily lose the war this year. I suppose you've gone back to Tobruk just when Rommel is on the move again. Oh dear.

I'm still so excited about all my new plans I can't sleep at night.

17 February, 1942

I'm delighted that you're joining Reggie Fellowes (*In Iraq*). It takes a great load off my mind, and you like him and it is new so I'm sure you'll be happy for a bit.

I have been threshing all day. It is killing. Even the men admit to extreme tiredness at the end of the day.

I don't want to start saying horrible things about Carling immediately I have decided to get rid of him. He seems so nice in many ways, but he often does odd things. Today we were threshing wheat which is always the worst and it was our heaviest crop and it was really beyond anything. Carling came on to the rick in Joe's place. Joe is usually with us and he is always very sweet and does the worst job and skips about doing extra bits to relieve us. Carling took the easiest job and during periods when he was ahead of his job he just leant on his fork and watched us. In the end I said to Molly "Stop trying – just lean on your fork and then he'll have to work or the drum will stop". It is rather odd isn't it? Molly thinks he's just a shit but I really don't know what it's all about. Directly he goes Joe will start to tell me what the men really think about him. Everyone appears to like him except Molly and me. I am bewildered by him and unable to like him.

I am so awfully tired, but bless you for February 20th (wedding anniversary).

13 March, 1942

Rather an exciting post — a letter from Jesper from Suez. It is an absolutely charming letter written as if he knew me and really sweet about you and saying you were going to Tobruk because Hewer said you were the only officer who could fill the bill and he knew Hewer was right because that was why he had got you to Suez, and telling me not to worry and saying all the arguments for thinking Suez was really much more dangerous .. Don't you think it was sweet? I was so pleased because it gave me a feeling of your being with real people who love you and appreciate you as our friends do and not just vaguely "with the Army" which to me never represents anything except a string of names. So I feel much cosier about you.

We seem from the news, now going on, to have got very much the worst in the naval battle with the Japs off Java

The Battle of the Java Sea was a decisive naval battle of the Pacific campaign of World War II. Allied navies suffered a disastrous defeat at the hand of the Imperial Japanese Navy.

18 March, 1942

Your new job sounds quite fun and hard work and you will be happy for a bit.

I hear on all sides our shipping position is formidable and we lose such a lot as a result of their having to travel in rough seas to avoid the enemy in calm. People say we can't start a second front because we haven't got enough ships to get the soldiers there, much less supply them. But who knows?

Today's news is a blood row with Carling. When I had my long talk with him I told him I wanted to learn to drive the tractor etc and I did say I'd let him know when the children were better and I was ready to start milking. This morning it was a lovely warm day and as I came up from feeding the pigs I saw Highman starting to sow nitro-chalk on the 8 acre field which was the first one we put down to grass. So I thought Good Idea — I'll have a go, and I walked over to him and said, "Highman, I'll come with you and you can teach me to drive it". He said OK but it would take him about a quarter of an hour to fix the drill. So I said I'd go up to the house and see Carling and come back.

Now I knew Carling would be furious. I can't tell you why and no-one believes me because it is so unreasonable but he definitely doesn't want me to do things and also he hates me having anything to do with the men. Sure enough, he looked as black as hell when I told him and put up a couple of reasons why I had better not. I took very little notice and said his reasons weren't very important, and then had a talk with Mrs Carling.

As I left the house he followed me. He said, "About this tractoring — are you really going now?" I said, "Yes". He said absolutely definitely, "You can't do that" (on my oath, because he later denied it). I said, "Just what do you mean?" He said, "Well, you said you'd let me know when you wanted to go. I was going to start you on drag-harrowing". I said, "Well, what difference does it make?" He said, "Well, you've got two drills on the back and it would be a mess-up if you were to turn them over". I said, "There are two answers to that. One is, I won't. The other is, they are my drills". And walked off and left him.

Then I went on the tractor and discovered what several people have told me, that there isn't anything to learn. If you can drive a car you can drive a tractor, the only difference being that a tractor is far easier, as you don't change the gears and it has a wonderful lock. This made me absolutely boiling over with Carling.

If there had really been any difficulty or danger one could have found some reason for believing it wasn't just ordinary spite but as it was as easy as falling off a log and no-one but a half-wit could possibly come to harm - mind you with Highman on it as well - there was no excuse at all.

Frankie driving the tractor

I boiled and boiled and boiled all morning. My temper was added to by thinking of all the impertinences and humiliations I have swallowed from him in the last eighteen months, and also that this episode proved conclusively that he had been deliberate every time.

So after lunch I went down to the farm and I drew a long breath and then made no attempt to keep or recover my temper for ten minutes. I told him just exactly where he got off in about six different ways. (I enjoyed it like mad because after the first sentence I realised he was going to take it — I quite see how Hitler has got the way he has) and then I asked him to tell me one good reason why I should ask permission before driving my own tractor with my own drills behind it on my own farm. He took the line a) that he hadn't said it and b) that he hadn't meant it. So I ended up by saying "All right, we'll leave it at that but you be a bloody sight more careful how you talk to me in the future".

We then spent an amicable half hour looking at the cows.

The really wonderful part of the story is this. I then, in order to show my independence, went off and had another go at the tractor, and, thro sheer carelessness, I _did_ put the drills in the hedge. Luckily Highman got them out without damage. I said to him as a joke "I'm glad you got them out because I wouldn't have liked to go and tell Carling what I'd done". Highman roared with laughter and said, "Well, you needn't worry. He always does it with the caterpillar. You can always tell where he's been by looking at the hedges". Rather a good end to an absolutely wonderful day.

The extraordinary thing is, one spends years trying to be nice to people and trying to consider their prejudices and so on (only partly out of niceness, partly out of fear) and they are absolutely bloody to you and do everything they can to spoil your fun. And then one really good crack of the whip and they rush to heel and behave like human beings for the first time. In future I'm going to be tough …. I never had any real happiness over the children till I got rid of the nanny (and from that day onwards I have never been difficult or uneasy or hysterical about them) and I shall never have any fun out of farming till I do it myself. And I'm sick and tired of being fretted and thwarted and humiliated by people I'm employing and I'm never going to be again. I wonder!!!…

24 February, 1942
On Saturday I got a message that Carling wanted to see me and found him looking rather white and wanting to know if

124

it was true I was going to manage the farm myself and was only waiting till the threshing was over to tell him. I said there was some truth in the first part, none in the second, and he and Mrs Carling had better come down and talk to me.

He blustered a bit at first, but I stood up to that and said if he wanted to conduct the conversation in that tone he could, but he would get a month's notice and nothing else. He came off it at once and she was a miracle of intelligence and tact throughout. The upshot of the interview appeared to be that they were so anxious not to go that they would do absolutely anything I wanted rather than have to. This left me undecided. If he would behave quite differently and really make an effort to teach me what I want to know etc and take orders better I should probably do better to keep him, as undoubtedly the other way would be an appalling worry tho' much more fun and also I might lose a lot of money if I made a mess of it. I told them I would think it over and let them know in about two weeks. I should think it would almost certainly end in my keeping for a bit longer.

Frankie was always surprised and delighted with the reaction she got from Jack whenever she struck out independently. In response to this and similar letters he wrote:

 (No date) How I loved the letter I received yesterday — your outburst on Carling and its immediate success. It's very hard on you, because these softnesses are all my fault, and, tho' I may in many ways have been a good influence on you, I've helped you to forget your native toughness a bit. However, now you're getting it back, which is all to the good.

I have absolute confidence in you, and anyway am fully prepared to crash as long as the preliminaries are fun. You know my views. I want <u>you</u> to do the farming, not a bailiff.

2 March, 1942

I had a fourteen-page airgraph yesterday (only one page missing). In it you give me a lecture about getting depressed and losing initiative and impress on me how important the farm is. This was really very timely, as I think I have begun to lose my sense of proportion. Mr Stewart was over today and I put to him all the pros and cons of the Carling case. He was quite decided I ought to keep C but insist on really learning and on getting my own way when I want to. He said directly you came back we could manage the farm ourselves, because you would be the man in the house and if you killed a cow with the wrong dose you would be the boss entitled to. I think this is very sound and I am going to do it.

6 March, 1942

I got back from London and the BBC last night. I think my broadcast was really good. Now to get it straight, I don't mean wonderful. It was short, only 600 words, and factual so there was no scope for being wonderful but I think it was good. On the preliminary run-through Green, the producer, said, "It's excellent". Then, after I'd finished, Vincent Alford, who produced me before and fancies me a tiny bit, and who later took me out to lunch, came in and said to Green "Well, if you knew the whole series was going to be like that you'd be a happy man". Then I got a wire from Diana De La Warr saying "Congratulations on excellent broadcast"; and then Mr S rang up and said everyone at Moulton had listened and thought it "quite uncommonly good". Add to that the fact that I also thought it quite good.

7 March, 1942

I simply do not know what to do about the children when Molly goes. I'll never get another girl because now they are all in war-work. If I send them both to the village school they won't learn a thing. I do feel that, as they ought both to be reasonably intelligent, they ought to learn to read and write early enough to get a good start. It is depressing. Let me know what you think about the village school.

We both went to the village school for a time, but I immediately contracted scarlet fever and Thomas impetigo, so Frankie was somewhat put off the idea. Eventually Thomas went to a 'prep' school in Henley-in-Arden, weekly boarding, later to Summerfields in Oxford as a boarder. The health of the poor in those days was much worse than now and so the risks of constant illness were real. I went to Swann's Close school, a delightfully progressive establishment, in Stratford as a weekly boarder when I was about 6 (ie in 1944).

About the Carlings. We fixed it up very nicely. I am going to learn to milk and to drive tractors and set ploughs etc. They were both really nice and of course the whole episode has proved very useful as a shake-up for them. I shall find it much easier to get my own way in the future.

Frankie decided that farming is not difficult to learn. She was a tremendous perfectionist and this side of her character contributed to her emotional swings. When facing a challenge or succeeding in meeting it she was always elated. Delays or failure to succeed cast her into the depths of despair. Jack understood her and had an extraordinary tolerance and acceptance of everything, so he was not upset by her letters. When there in person he could keep her steady, but this side of her character made separation especially difficult for both of them.

She says at one point that she loves him and needs him because he brings out the best in her whereas nearly everyone else brings out the worst. She found most aspects of farming easy to learn, including driving heavy machinery and managing the enormous cart horses, even judging when the crops were ready. She finally concluded that farmers, like many experts, try to shroud their work in mystique and impenetrable pessimism as a means of boosting their self-image. They need to give the impression that it is far too difficult for ordinary people to understand or succeed at. The reason that farming is difficult is down to external factors like the weather, also the seemingly irrational behaviour of animals or their illnesses, and sometimes sheer overload and volume of work rather than to any mastering of the theory or practice.

26 March, 1942

You ask about pig feeding. They should get potatoes and a certain amount of swill — so should our hens. But these need boiling every day. I can't do it because I don't live at the farm and therefore I should do it one day and not the next.

Frankie driving the Fordson tractor.   The International Caterpillar

Mrs C won't, she is too lazy. So both our pigs and our hens get a perfectly orthodox pre-war diet which is taken from the coupons which are issued for the cows as we produce enough home-grown for the cows. This is a very good example of the sort of thing that gets me down and completely spoils my fun.

27 March, 1942

This was my day. Started a bit late to feed the pigs at 8.45. Finished about 10 and went into Stratford to cash cheque and do week's shopping. Came back and went up to farm and mucked out one lot of pigs. Lunch. Went on International Tractor with Carling for 1 ½ hours. Turned out also to be easy. There is something to learn this time as it works on entirely different principles. Two joysticks and two brakes and you turn by judicious application of the brake and joystick on the side you want to go. Very simple, but I haven't the guts to tell Carling it's dead easy and any half-wit could do it so I let him instruct me.

Came back to farm and prepared food for pigs. Tea. Fed farm pigs then went to Broadlow where I was supposed to try and shut up a sow and litter who had to be brought up to the house tomorrow. Very very difficult without supreme luck as no-one can catch or drive six young pigs. Found mum and piglets all out together on the wheat. Chased them up and down for about ½ an hour trying to get them in. Then realised that everywhere mum went the pigs went too. So decided to take a chance and chase mum up to the farm there and then. Very anxious-making as if any one got lost on the way complete chaos would ensue. Got them as far as the farm gate when they all separated as mum gave up playing.

However, Carling, Hall and Marjorie all turned out and in about ¼ of an hour they were all safely in a box, which will save three men about an hour's work tomorrow. Came home and dug deep and manured four rows and dug over three rows which were dug deep in the autumn. Result, now pretty tired. To go back to tractors. Look here, whatever I do or don't do in the immediate future, I absolutely know I could run a farm without a bailiff provided I had proper cottages for a good ploughman and cowman. It is really rather exciting because it means that you could if you wanted to when you came home.

I wear your socks with gumboots. They are all wearing through. When any shrink so that you can't wear them please post them home to me.

31 March, 1942

Mr Stewart has fixed for me to go for a short time as a pupil to a man called Wilkins who is wonderful on implements. I shall only go for about a week now but if I get on well with him I shall go back in June or July when he is ploughing for summer fallow.

I never mention the war now. There are too many places involved. So I just don't bother and I get along better.

8 April, 1942

I took the car to London. When I got there I went shopping all day and Buck took me out.

I liked him very much but they gave me a lot to drink so that may have coloured my views a bit. Then I picked up Eddie S.W. *(Sackville-West)* and took him down to Fisher's *(the de la Warr house)*. I do like Eddie. He is so sweet and simple and not all difficult in all the little ways I would have expected him to be. I think he is rather remarkable because fundamentally he must be a neurotic, but, if he is, he has got complete control of himself and doesn't really show it at all. I expected him to be detached and bored by the discussion of his own subjects by people who are not his equals. But we talked nineteen to the dozen all the way down and all during the week-end he was ready to discuss Tolstoy or agriculture.

I started off about Hemingway and he said that he hated the book so frightfully that he had made an opportunity to drag it into an essay which was about something quite different. He thought he might be prejudiced but he was also quite sure he was right. But later on I found he admired Emlyn Williams who in my view can only be described by the jazz word "corn". So I came to the conclusion that intellectuals are not infallible in taste any more than anyone else, although they may make fewer mistakes. Anyway it cheered me up because if he can like Emlyn Williams I can certainly like Hemingway. It is the same with Edith Evans

130

(the actress). All you highbrows like her but I heard her the other night in a modern play and I know she is utterly bad.

I hate it here. That's about all there is to that. It's so squalid and unattractive and there is no warmth and the whole thing is a very dignified uphill struggle where I have no friends and no-one who regards me as an equal but just hundreds of people to whom I am just "the Missis", and who regard me with varying degrees of like and dislike but never as a person like themselves. But when I went to Fisher's this week-end it was like getting into a warm bath and not wanting to get out of it. I basked physically in the whole atmosphere. Not only because it is comfortable and they are all kind to me and surround me with affection but also because of having people like Eddie to talk to. And here there is no-one and it is like going back to school.

In a month or two when the petrol ration is stopped altogether it will be even worse because, altho' I shall have petrol for the farm, one will be liable to be stopped on the road and asked where one is going and what for; so one will never be able to use the car except for strictly farm business and I shall never be able to go to Peggy's or Hannah's even on a Sunday.

I wanted to be a farmer. I have no interest here in this farm. Well now, I could just take a little farm either as an extra to this, which means raising more money, or let this and take a bigger one. Or I could sell this. Now here is where ambition comes in and the need for your understanding and approval. Deep down I believe very strongly in myself. I don't really want a little farm, tho' I think I should be quite happy if I decided that way. But ultimately I want to be a big farmer and a great business woman. I believe I could be, too.

Of course I shall feel quite different some other day because I always twist and turn and play with a lot of different ideas before I actually make a decision.

This morning Thomas and John Highman *(younger son of Highman)* came in and said they could help by digging the garden. I remembered their little spades were at the farm and thought by the time they'd fetched them they would only dig for 10 minutes and then stop, so I said yes. They both looked so eager. My dear, they have dug literally and absolutely the whole garden and put a load of manure in. But they only dig about an inch deep so it is just a mess of soil and manure, so how in Heaven's name shall I get it right? They are so pleased with themselves and have dug like maniacs all day.

10 April, 1942

This morning I got an aircard from you in which you say you have just got an airgraph telling you I had decided to do without Carling and that you are very excited and anyway you'd rather I spoilt the farm myself than had someone else run it. I can't think why I ever thought you would disapprove because of course you are really far more courageous than me and like change and new excitements even more than I do. I am whooping with joy about your being on my side, but I sent you a cable today just to make sure you don't mind what I do.

12 April, 1942

I am going to Wilkins for a week (I told you about him earlier) to learn how to set and use agricultural implements. I don't think I shall stay very long, probably a week, and try to make a success with him and his family so that I can go back in June or July when he is ploughing for summer fallow. Sometimes I wonder how much of what I write makes sense to you. Do you, for instance, understand the term Summer Fallow? I suppose you do, and, anyway, your great mind can work it out.

I got £300 in for wheat yesterday and paid every other debt we have in the world. I have several expenses still in front of me but I also have enough to cover them coming in for the next few months. So, by the time you get this, you can, without going in for wild extravagance, let up a trifle on any economies which really spoil your fun.

13 April, 1942: The Manor Farm, Brize Norton

I am here to learn as much as I can about ploughing and cultivations etc. This is a most remarkable family. There are two sons, one of whom was once at Moulton. The father is a farmer, with about 650 acres. The sons live at home, but they run a contracting business and have a smaller farm of their own. They are super inventive mechanics. Normally a Fordson tractor is only used to pull a two furrow plough. These boys use — under good conditions — a four furrow with a Fordson, or under less good conditions a three furrow. As far as I can make out it has nothing to do with hotting up the tractor but merely with exquisitely fine adjustments of the setting of the plough. I think all that will remain beyond me, but they are intelligent boys and are going to teach me how to plough. I arrived here last night. I have learned three or four things already.

1. They fill the tractor wheels with water instead of air. This gives more grip.
2. In operations like rolling, harrowing etc, they go round the field instead of up and down. It is quicker because there is so much less turning and doing the same bit twice on the headland, and I can't think why everyone doesn't do it.
3. They grease the implements like maniacs all day, once every hour rather than once a day.

14 April, 1942

Yesterday I tractored all day until 8.30 pm. I was cultivating. I drew a compliment from Ted *(Wilkins)*. He said he had always thought tractoring was a man's job, but he thought he might have to change his mind. I said, "Do you really think I'm getting on all right?" He said, "Well, you're getting on far better than I ever expected you to."

21 April, 1942

I am back here for the second week of this horrible tractor course. I think agricultural people are the most tiresome and the most conceited in the world. They have an attitude of self-importance which no-one else in the world has. I think it is because they never go anywhere or do anything but their own job. If they got out bit they would find out about all the things they don't know.

Ted has exactly the same kind of conceit that Carling had — I recognise it a mile off now. However I've managed in the last two days to plough twice for about twenty minutes each time. I've made this discovery. IT'S EASY. But never make the mistake of telling people that I say any of these things are easy. If we want to be accepted as real farmers we shall have to go on pretending it's all very difficult only we're so brilliant we can do it.

The principle is easily understood, tho' it might take a long time to do it well. When I can explain to you in ten minutes something that it has taken me ten months of patience and control to learn it may make it all seem worthwhile. <u>Tomorrow I am going home.</u>

April 27, 1942

It is so odd to think of you having breakfast in bed sucking oranges while looking at the Mediterranean while I am here in this absurd little house. All your life you will say things like, "When I was in Iraq" and I know that in twenty years time I shall still feel slightly cross when you say it because I can't bear you to have any life without me.

I think we shall certainly make a profit on the second year, that is very good, isn't it?

2 May, 1942

Well, I have put the children to bed and how tiresome they were and how I cursed them. It seems curious to think of me putting the children to bed and getting bored with them while you haven't even seen them for eighteen months. I wonder how long your excitement at seeing them would prevent you getting bored with them. If I know anything of you, for about ten minutes.

3 May, 1942

Today is Sunday and I have been tractoring all day. Pattison came to look at the wireworm in the wheat, and he advised harrowing it again with heavy harrows, top dressing it, and then rolling it with the tractor wheels. I thought I'd have a go. It turned out to be perfectly practicable and not nearly as slow as one would imagine. I should think I did three acres — I certainly did all the worst patches on the field

I had also to mind the children. I disposed of this problem by taking them on the tractor with me.

Riding on the mudguards of the Fordson tractor, aged 4 and 5

135

I remember quite clearly, on more than one occasion, riding on the mudguards of the tractor during farming activities, usually puling a plough or harrows immediately behind. We enjoyed it enormously. I was 4 years old at this time and Thomas nearly 6. We had no sense of danger.

Molly, who kindly fetched them at tea, said they looked too sweet for words hanging one to each mudguard. Tractoring is very tiring. I am dead beat tonight.

4 May, 1942

I rose at 6.15, dressed in ten minutes, and was at the farm by 6.30.

Hall, our cowman, is a neat, youngish, rather vague-looking man with considerable personal charm and horn-rimmed spectacles. Apparently he has the devil of a temper.

 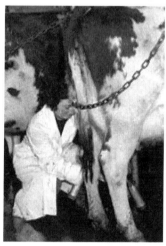

Marjorie in BBC internet page, and, right, at Gypsy Hall milking cows

Marjorie, the land girl, hates him and everyone keeps out of his way. This morning he was quiet and efficient with the cows and very good and charming at instructing me.

When I went up to the farm I met Mrs Carling, full of smiles, and said, "what's the joke?" "Well," she said, "we consider you've done a good job in the milking shed already.

Usually the swearing and cursing in the shed can be heard all over the farm, but this morning there wasn't a sound". Apparently Marjorie had gone round in high glee calling all the men to come and listen to the silence. Carling told me he asked Hall how he got on with me. "Quite all right" he said, "a bloody sight more sense than Raymond." As Raymond is a mental defective under the statutory Act, this was not quite the class of compliment it might sound.

Marjorie in bbc.co.uk/history/ww2peopleswar: "I was sent to Gypsy Hall Farm at Wilmcote to work for a Mr and Mrs Carling; the bailiff of the farm. Gypsy Hall was a much larger farm and had a pedigree herd of Ayrshire cattle. They had long horns and seemed to love jumping hedges. I can still remember the misty mornings that were a sure sign of another hot, summer's day. My time at Gypsy Hall was very happy as we all got on so well...... I never went back to the city...I always look back on my time at Gypsy Hall as one of the happiest of my life."

6 May, 1942

I've been in the cowshed twice a day and yesterday I went tractoring as well and I got tired. There is one thing I've noticed before about Carling. He'll fight to the last ditch to stop me doing things, but once I've forced my way in and can do something he'll always use me and be glad to. I am now looked on quite seriously as a spare tractor driver and always summoned when he is short. I think I'm getting on quite well with the cows.

I'm happier on the farm than I have ever been and I am getting on better with Carling that I ever have. For one thing he has taken to minding his p's and q's with me and for another, since I've been doing more work, I've got on better terms with the men. I used to feel completely separated from them and that made me feel uneasy. Raymond the half-wit is really the sweetest. He is not as stupid as all that and he is quite uninhibited and straight-forward. He has very good manners, but in the cowshed he orders me about as tho' he was head cowman and without any self-consciousness. I find it most endearing.

I wish you could see our leys (*grassland specially cultivated for best milk-production*). They are at long last a triumph. It is very fine but dry and there has been no rain for weeks and all the permanent pasture is like a billiard table but the leys are glossy and green and fit for a queen. I am glad, because last year they were so disappointing and they are my one real contribution to G.H.

Frankie later, in 1955, wrote a book called Milk Without Tears where she discussed ley farming in some detail in the chapter on Grassland Farming, Summer Milk.

9 May, 1942

I had a divine cable from you this morning. I really am glad that you are going to farm with me after the war. It makes so much to look forward to.

10 May, 1942

Have you heard or read that in thirty-three by-elections lately an Independent has been returned in spite of the fact that the Government candidate was backed by the Conservative, Labour and Communist parties? It is a symptom of the feeling which is affecting nearly everyone in England and me along with them. It's not that people necessarily want to out the present government. Almost everyone is still behind Churchill and no-one thinks that there is a better lot of men waiting round the corner. It is more a feeling of "Down with vested interests".

18 May, 1942

You appear to have been much amused by the row with Carling. I like your attitude about it being best to get on and manage G.H. very much. But the chief disadvantage is there are no cottages and, as I have often explained, it is absolutely fundamental to be certain of the two key men. I believe the War Committee might be persuaded to give me a permit to build. There are one or two new factors which weigh on your side. One is, I have made rather friends with Pattison, the agric. organiser and I think he is rather a good man — much better than I originally assumed. He is the son of a farmer and appears to have a genuine knowledge of stock and also of the routine running of a farm, which springs more from a farmer's mind than Mr Stewart's, which is slightly collegy. For instance, he gave me the hell of a ticking off for wanting to pick some pigs with him and without Carling. He said no decent farmer would ever pick out his stock without the man who looked after them. I'm sure he'd help all he knew how, if I was on my own, even tho' disapprovingly. There is only one crab to this, and that is, unless I'm dotty, he fancies me. But he is very shy and easily choked off and so far I've had no difficulty in managing him without the bucket of boiling oil I had to use with Mr Stewart.

Pat became an important part of our lives and a friend of my parents for life. I drove Jack, aged 89, to his funeral near Stratford, a year or two after Frankie died. He was a constant feature of our life in the war, coming regularly to advise. We often spent Christmas with him and his wife Eileen, whom he married after the war.

21 May, 1942

At last I have found someone who understands the beauty of my bookkeeping. Dave said Margetts wasn't really good enough and I ought to have a proper chartered accountant. So I wrote to Clyde Higgs and asked him who did his books. He wrote back that his man had definitely refused to take on any more clients but he said he would speak to him. The man, who is in Leamington, said he would see me, but if the books were the usual farmer's bloody muddle he wouldn't touch it.

I went in fear and trembling and he said they were lovely and he only knew two farmers who kept double entry and one was Clyde Higgs and the other was me. He's going to do them and he's going to set a proportion of labour and feeding stuffs against the various accounts and draw up proper costings and a balance sheet for me as well as seeing the books thro' the Income Tax.

I am awfully pleased because the books are a lot of work and I always do them very carefully and as I'm so bad at addition it is a great sweat and I've never had anything but kicks for my pains before. I'm sure you will be pleased because you like all that side, so you can carry on when you come home.

Some weeks ago when I was talking to Pattison he said how I ought to farm was to have foreman instead of a bailiff but pay some good farmer to come over regularly and advise me. I didn't take much notice as I thought I wasn't short of advice and the full details of the suggestion didn't strike me at the time. But I got your letters about really preferring the original Clyde Higgs idea to anything else.

Then yesterday I was talking to Clyde Higgs on the telephone. I asked him when he was coming over. He said it wasn't any use saying that because I hadn't got a telephone and so a busy man couldn't be bothered getting hold of me. And I said, "Well, I asked you to do something about getting me a telephone but you don't do it". And he said, "No, I'm not going to — the telephone is there — all you've got to do is to move in beside it".

Then he started to browbeat me in his usual way for about five minutes. All this started me on the track of how to do it and I lay awake for hours last night. And then, when I was thinking, I was suddenly struck by the full beauty of Pattison's suggestions. You see, if I could find someone good enough who would come over once a week for a couple of years, it would be so much less frightening. They would tell me when the corn was ready to cut etc. and I could discuss the cultivations of each field in detail before doing them and then if there was something wrong, they would spot it.

1 June, 1942

It is Thomas's birthday today — the third one without you. I wonder how many more. There isn't any cable but I'm sure you sent one. I gave him a bow and some arrows and a swimming belt like a life-saving outfit from you. You may think that dull, but I scoured London and he is very pleased. After the end of this month there will be no petrol so I suppose no bathing. — unless I buy a trap. The birthday parties are always the same. Nora always manages to produce a jelly and chocolate biscuits and a chocolate cake with candles on and I always make the same remarks to the effect that no-one would think there was a war on etc. We have four village children to tea. They couldn't be duller and no-one could say our children have a wonderful time on their birthdays, but since they don't know anything better they think it is o.k.

2 June, 1942

One or two people seem to have been able to get permission out of the War Committee to build cottages. I am seriously thinking of trying to get permission to build two. If I had two cottages, a girl in the house, and at the same time an arrangement with some farmer as Pattison suggested, I don't believe I could go far wrong. So I believe Clyde Higgs may win in the end.

I had an aircard and a cable saying you may be going further east. I'm so glad for you. I simply hate your present job, but I can't make out whether you mean Persia or still further. You have always talked of Persia as North before.

Jack was sent to Tehran for a job he loved – liaising with the Russians, our war allies whom most of the British establishment hated. Later he became a Lieutenant Colonel and received a medal - the order of the Patriotic War - from Russia.

26 May, 1942
Reggie is definitely putting me forward as AQMG Persia, which would be just what of all things I should have chosen. It will be exciting to live in Tehran and meet Russians and feel one is mixed up in that part of the job.

18 June, 1942
It'll take a little time to get going, but then it will be a really fascinating job. I shall be the main intermediary with Bill's friends *(the Russians)*, all of which will be most instructive. I believe they're absolute bastards to deal with. But it's going to be fun.

Frankie and Jack were afraid of reprisals, especially against Jack's war career, if their political orientation were noticed too clearly. So they devised a code for referring to the Russians – Bill's friends – based on the name of a communist friend and influencer (possibly Bill Carritt or maybe Bill Alexander) and for the Americans, Johnnie's friends, based on a strongly pro-American friend called Johnnie Miller. It is interesting that this kind of caution was felt necessary in war time Britain, even when speaking of our allies.

8 June, 1942
We had a party for the death of Heydrich and I stood drinks all round.

Reinhard Tristan Heydrich, "the Hangman," stood out as one of the most brutal mass murderers in Nazi Germany.

10: 1942

The war carries on

Frankie felt optimistic about the war at this time..

May 27, 1942 – SS Leader Heydrich attacked in Prague.

May 30, 1942 – First thousand-bomber British air raid (against Cologne)

4 June, 1942

The war news is really rather good — Russian offensive followed by two 1,000 bomber raids, followed by a definite stand in Libya. Very different from any other spring. The feeling here has undergone considerable change. Instead of thinking the war against Germany is going to take years, people now think there is a real good chance that it will be over by this time next year. But as against that, they think the war against Japan will take at least four years, unless Russia gives us the only possible jumping off ground, by declaring war against her, and everyone is convinced Russia will not do that.

Pattison came here last night. I am a little excited. I discussed with him my project for having an adviser and said I would rather have him than anyone else. I think he would be the ideal person. He knows his stuff and I get on with him.

I am a little sorry I didn't take the plunge when Clyde Higgs suggested it. I was so certain and full of faith then.

5 June, 1942

Pattison rang up this morning to say that I must write to the Ministry of Works and Buildings asking permission for the cottages; they would then check with the War Committee and (privately) the War Committee would back my application. I shall apply at once, without feeling it absolutely leads to any particular decision about Carling. I don't think it can be wrong on any count.

6 June, 1942

Today we have suffered a severe loss and a grave setback. Joe Newlands has given notice. He is the only man on the farm who understands stacking and thatching; he is the carter and the shepherd and he was my favourite man. Both Carling and I are very gravely shaken. Haymaking begins next week and harvest is not far off. We are completely hamstrung by having no cottage in which to put a man and a complete shortage of local labour. It is not worth trying to get the cottage Joe will vacate for two reasons. Two or three months ago his landlord gave him notice. This was pure bluff as he hadn't the slightest chance of getting him out. I explained this carefully to Joe at the time but I knew then that he didn't believe me and I recognised that I was up against all the pathetic insecurity and ignorance of the past. This proved to be true, and the little man has been looking for a job with a cottage ever since. He has done it very badly and given a week's notice at the beginning of haymaking but I can forgive him because I realise that he could not know that, if he had told me two months ago he was looking for a job I shouldn't have said, "Well, take a week's notice then".

It sends a wave of insecurity over the farm. People look at each other gravely and say they wouldn't be surprised if Highman wouldn't soon like a change and so on. The most serious thing for me is that it does away any chance of my being able to do without Carling until two cottages are actually built on the farm. I could never weather a crisis like this without Carling and without a cottage in which to put a new man. Supposing Highman left with Carling here — well. Carling can plough ....Only if I had cottages in which to put a new man could I face these supposings. I must go now, because Hall is away and Carling out, and I have to milk and then feed the pigs.

Evening

Pattison went into my figures the other day, and said immediately that the reason the farm didn't pay better was the cows. Not only are they not good enough (which I know), but too big an acreage is given to them. You see, until he pointed it out, I never realised that, if you add the arable acreage given up to food for them to the grassland, they are using about two thirds of the farm and they are not converting it into nearly enough cash. There are two things wrong. One is that too much oats and beans are grown. The other is there is still too much old pasture not pulling its weight. A third and probably the greatest reason is that Carling neither manages his grassland well nor is willing to make the colossal effort necessary to get the most out of it.

I am rather ashamed that it needed Pattison to point the facts out to me. But it is odd, because I have always shown my cropping programme to Mr Stewart and he has always taken the line that I was rather short of grass. But there is one thing. As from when Clyde Higgs gave me that piece of advice I have taken on a new lease of life and I am not only learning all the time but also getting a firmer grip on Carling. So if I do have to keep him for a long time I shall at least be getting somewhere which I wasn't before. I am now going to have a cold bath because there is no hot water. You see how tough I have become.

7 June, 1942

I am depressed a bit. I always knew that the idea of running G.H. without Carling was nearly too dangerous as it well could be and that, with a run of bad luck, it could turn into a terrifying situation. The incident with Joe has convinced me that it is as near as nothing damn well impossible. I shall go ahead with the building of the two cottages because I think it might be difficult to sell the farm without them. Even two is not enough, you really need one per 100 acres. That's four in this case. I'm sure it's right about the cottages. But for the rest I feel right back where I started from.

Landgirls hoeing potatoes

8 June, 1942

I did six hours hoeing today, which, coupled with the fact that I milked and fed the pigs before breakfast, makes a damn good 8 ½ hour day. I'm tired but there are two things I thought of today which I want to tell you. One is that, tho' I had a very bad period just before Clyde Higgs started me off on my present wild goose chase, since then I have been both busy and definitely after something. It gives me a great zest for life, which practically nothing else does. It is quite different from happiness, which is more basking. I can't describe it exactly, but I definitely want to go on and complete the pattern.

16 June, 1942

Something happened today which I took as an omen. We were making silage for which you need a lot of water. One of the men was fixing a pipe. There was an elbow joint between two pipes and he broke a bit so that there were no threads left to screw the joint on. Consternation! I thought to myself how, when I am the bailiff, I shall have to deal with this sort of problem and I simply don't understand them and black out in face of them. And I had that sinking of the tummy which I often have when I think about being without Carling. I went to watch — he tried one or two futile ideas and no-one had any idea of what to do. Then I said, "You know there's a rubber elbow joint exactly that shape on the milking machine". Terrific smiles and general relief all round, <u>and</u> it worked and I was privately fit to bust with pride! As an achievement, not very great, but as an omen, lovely.

There was a heavenly bit in your letter, where you said there was one thing you couldn't approve and that was the once mentioned suggestion that I should send the children away — in fact, you wouldn't allow it. Of course I should never dream of sending the children away. What would I do without them? I must have been at a very low ebb the day I suggested that.

23 June, 1942

I have painted the garden side of the house the blue of the cowshed and white. You have no idea how pretty it looks. I think it has put £100 on the value of the farm. And I am having some barn roofs mended and all the doors in the yard mended and painted. I don't know how I'm going to pay for it. I shall do the inside of the house as nicely as I can in wartime and it will all be great fun. And perhaps next year you'll come back and share it.

I have started to learn to hand-milk. The first morning Carling came to show me and he didn't believe I had never

147

done it before. So I was pleased. But this morning I had another and more difficult cow and I found out there was something to learn and that Carling was quite good at teaching. So I was pleased at that too, because I love learning.

The news is awful, isn't it? I can't stop thinking about that jaundice and how I should be feeling. *(Jack would still have been in Tobruk if he had not had jaundice.)* I should also very much like to know where you are. I hope it is Persia, but I have a faint feeling it may be further, as you spoke of flying, and I shouldn't have thought you would have to fly that distance. I do hope it isn't further.

Thomas's arithmetic is really brilliant and he is beginning to read a bit. I think you could now start a serious correspondence in block letters with him. Make the words short and simple and he will be able to read it and to answer himself.

This country is now absolutely lousy with American soldiers so I suppose there really is going to be a second front. Everyone says we haven't got the ships to get them there, much less supply them.

24 June, 1942

I work hard and I am tired but, in spite of the appalling war news, I'm happy. I'm excited about the farm. I'm awfully pleased with the painting and the house looks so absolutely sweet that I bicycle right round it to get to the buildings just to have a look at it. I dream of next winter when I shall chop down all those ghastly laurels and plant flowering shrubs. When I have made a garden in addition to all the concrete and paint, and when I've done the inside of the house, no-one will know the place.

I'm getting on slowly but fairly surely with the hand-milking in the morning and in the afternoon I am more or less permanently second cowman. I must say I find them all pretty stupid. I've only been milking a short time, but if I was head cowman I would reorganize the whole routine and system of milking and I absolutely know I'd get better yields.

The war news is unbelievably awful, isn't it? I believe they'll get Egypt. Anyway, thank God you're not there. *(June 21, 1942 – Rommel captures Tobruk.)*

30 June, 1942

The news is appalling *(June 30, 1942 – Rommel reaches El Alamein near Cairo, Egypt.)* — I don't believe we've got a dog's chance of holding Egypt and I think the papers have already started preparing the public mind for the fact that we may have to get out of the Mediterranean altogether. I wouldn't mind so much if it meant home for you. But I'm afraid it could only mean imprisonment by the Germans or India and the Japs, either of which would be so much worse than the present.

In the meantime I am becoming quite a good cowman, but this morning, I wielded a scythe and my hands, which I thought were so hard, are now covered in enormous water blisters and I shan't be able to hand-milk for a few days. I thought of you while scything.

 1 July, 1942 Iran

I've been terribly busy, and the heat down south here is so intense it leaves one hardly able to get thro' the day's work. The day before yesterday I cracked, and produced a temperature of 103, which may be sandfly fever. However, I'm in quite a comfortable hospital, and will have lost Terence the tape-worm by the time I go out. To give you some idea of the heat — at 5 am the bathwater is still too hot to get under — you can burn your hand by touching metal in the shade — nobody tries to sleep in the afternoons — you sweat too much — it's been 123/4 in the shade lately — there have been a number of deaths from heatstroke. The job is going to be a very good one and a very exciting one, and I think I can make a go of it. It will carry a Lt.Colonel later, which is all to the good.

2 July, 1942

The most interesting thing here is that Bill's friends are, so to speak, the chief customers. They seem to be very sticky and narrow-minded, but I feel confident, probably wrongly, that by a little bullying I can make them less so. It's nice to see an occasional red star in the streets. They seem a tough and simple lot. This for them is a sort of rest from the real war.

 ## 3 July, 1942

Two rather depressing things. Most farms were surveyed about eighteen months ago, but for some reason (incompetence) this one hasn't been done yet. Pattison came here a few nights ago and he asked me whether I thought anyone could possibly say the farm had gone down since I had it. I said no, quite definitely not. There were a lot of things I wasn't sure about, such as the cows, but I was absolutely sure of that. Then he asked if I was still absolutely determined on getting rid of Carling as he thought it might lead to trouble. So I said, "Come on, what is all this?" He said there had been a meeting of the local War Committee at which someone had said G.H. was going down and was not what it was when Plant had it.

Most of the professional men and farmers who knew Frankie both liked and respected her, but she was unusual in her time and not surprisingly, the target of malice for some. She was straying into what was largely a man's preserve and making waves which were bound to annoy. It is perhaps surprising that she did not have more opposition.

This last remark is like the Mad Hatter's Tea Party because Plant didn't farm it at all. He merely sold hay off it. It was Field and Jones who began the ploughing and slagged it and so on. P hadn't been at the meeting, but he was told about it afterwards and he was obviously a bit worried because he thought they would be out to survey it within the next fortnight and would I be sure to let him know when they had been so that he could make a point of attending the next meeting.

The whole thing is mysterious, because no single member of the Committee except Gordon Davis, who is the district officer and very nice and heavily on our side and always says he thinks the farm is wonderful, has seen it since I have been here. So that, whoever started this has done so without seeing the farm.

P came right round the farm that evening and examined every field. I asked him what he thought and he said it was obviously all rot but he still seemed a trifle worried. I said, "I've always taken it for granted it would be graded A. What do you think?" He said, "B plus." I said, "But why?" He said if he was doing it he would grade it A but he didn't believe they would because of four fields.

One is a really good ley which has kept the dairy cows for nearly the whole of the summer and on which they went up to twenty gallons. But it hasn't rained for months and it's dry and burnt up and nothing looks so awful to an uninformed eye as a burnt up ley. The next field is the root field. It is rather a mess. Then there is a wheat field, which was very badly eaten by wireworm in the spring. The fourth field is also wheat, and it is simply an only moderately good crop.

As against this we have two fields of beans which Clyde Higgs says are the best he's ever seen, three first class wheat crops, a good crop of winter oats, a very fair crop of spring oats, some S 23 for seed looking well and some first class sugar beet. Also some very good and extremely useful leys.

The thing that gets me down is not what was said at the War Committee because I know they are nothing but a lot of sour second rate gossips (they hate Clyde Higgs and one of the remarks that was made was that I was never off the telephone to him — I've spoken to him three times in my life on the telephone), but the fact that Pattison seemed to be taking the whole thing seriously. He seemed to think it was a reason for re-considering the Carling decision, and he seemed to think they could make my life a hell if they wanted to. I said they could go to hell until such time the farm was so badly farmed that they were able to dispossess me. But I feel there may be something more in it than he has told me and I feel they are all coming out to look for crabs — and there isn't a farm in England where you can't find crabs if you want to, and I feel that, for some reason I don't know, they have always had it in for me if they could get a chance.

I think I ought to explain that the War Committee have complete powers to do anything they like. But as we are not yet a completely fascist state they obviously have not power to abuse their power. If you are not doing very well, they have power to tell you what to do and to force you to do it, and if you are doing badly they can dispossess you. But unless and until you are doing badly they have no power that I know of to interfere with the running of the farm. And that's why I simply can't understand why P is worried or why he thinks it is any damn business of theirs whether I or anyone else sacks or keeps their bailiff until they prove that they can't manage without one.

Matthew Naylor wrote, in the Farmers Weekly: *Saturday 19 October 2013: "The war ag committees made several such interventions. These committees were run by progressive farmers with tough principles. They were empowered by the Ministry to take 'firm measures against the recalcitrant or hopelessly inefficient' and were permitted to take 'all necessary* *measures to secure that land [was] cultivated to the best advantage'. There was no third party to whom appeals could be taken.*

In the spring when I first thought of getting rid of Carling the news fairly whistled round Warwickshire and everyone discussed it and everyone except Clyde Higgs thought I was mad and would be broken and bust within a year.

We were told a long time after the war that Nora used to read Frankie's letters to Jack and pass any interesting news around the village. Frankie could never understand how all her secrets got out.

It may simply be that Pattison thinks if I do it now it will cause endless gossip again and may cause the War Committee to keep an eye on me. But, from my point of view, if he and William Davis will refrain from repeating all the more unpleasant bits to me, I shan't give a damn what they say and if I'm going to do badly the War Committee may as well find it out as anyone else. And as Pattison is to be my adviser in chief, it is up to him to see I don't do badly. But it depresses me and makes me feel persecuted.

6 July, 1942

I spent the week-end with the Hudsons, during which I bought three really good heifers at such fantastic prices I don't think I shall ever be able to tell you what I paid.

Anyway, I was thinking about it today, and I thought I never would have bought them if I'd thought they were going to be managed by Carling and Hall. They simply aren't conscientious enough, either of them. I'll never do any good till I get rid of them both, and I couldn't get rid of one without the other. All very satisfactory as I'm going to anyway

9 July, 1942

I wrote to you last week about the War Committee crabbing the farm. I think that has blown over. Two of them came over late one night when I was in bed and Carling took them round. They said the beans and the sugar beet were the best they had seen anywhere and the corn very nice and they went away saying they were pleased with the farm. Also, Clyde Higgs has issued a proclamation saying we have some wonderful crops. Then Pattison told Hughes, the chairman of the War Committee , that, if it had gone down since I had it, it must have been one of the show places of the Midlands before I had it.

Yesterday, after Mr Stewart had been right round I said, "Do you think the farm looks reasonably well?" He said, "Reasonably isn't the right word". I said, "How would you grade it?" He said, "Well, if there is such a thing as a grade A farm this must be one". So I think my enemies are scotched. I think they are enemies. It isn't apparently the main Committee who have got it in for me. It is the Stratford District Branch. They are all pooping little men and apparently it is A to F (*the book*) which has annoyed them. They think I think I know (so I do). Anyway they seem to have overstepped themselves this time because, if they wanted to say the farm was going down, they would have done better to take a passing look at it first.

The farm keeps me going and I feel that if you like your new job that will keep you going. I wish I knew where you are and if you are happy and whether you are a colonel. I think it is a most wonderful thing that you weren't in Tobruk and now you aren't in Egypt. I have really started to believe in our luck again, for the first time since you went to France …

Just got your letter from new job. (*?Tehran?*) Still a major! I've been too previous!

11 July, 1942

I went to my accountant and finished up the book. The profit is really £406, but this includes eggs milk and butter etc supplied to the house. On this Carling gets £20.6/-. I have decided to divide between the men the same again. I have written out a cheque for each of them. The largest is 6.10/- which goes to Highman and the smallest to Cyril Wheeldon who only works part time. In addition, I'm giving £5 to Mrs Carling because her poultry unit performed the phenomenal feat of making £299 gross and £185 net profit. I am awfully looking forward to giving the men their cheques which I shall do on Monday. It will be a surprise and I do hope they will be pleased.

12 July, 1942

Two things I've been trying to say; One, yes, I agree with you at feeling slightly sick at large scale bombing in Germany. And I found the slight jubilance in press and BBC about the homeless absolutely nauseating. Second, if you can send any more sweets. Please do, as they are going to be rationed now, so we should be awfully pleased. I don't know whether it is wrong to ask. If you ask for things from America your letters get stopped, but they seem to treat the Forces differently.

 **17 July, 1942**

A small thing happened which pleased me very much yesterday. Robbins and I were having a meeting with Bill's friends. *(See photograph shown at 13 November, 1942)* The Colonel (they are mostly colonels) said that the General, whom I had met with Reggie, had been favourably impressed by my business like attitude and hoped that my presence would make a real difference.

20 July, 1942

Please try and write as often as you can, because, quite apart from the fact that I wilt without letters, I am fascinated by your job. (And madly proud of you. I go around telling everybody you are entirely responsible for the whole of the transport in Persia and that, now the Russian army is split, Timoschenko relies almost entirely on you).

My mouth is stuffed full with some of the sweets you sent. I must say they are wonderful. But unfortunately nearly all gone. I do wish you could see Rose. I'm sure you would adore her. She has very fat stout legs all over mud and scratches, and her face is almost pretty and awfully attractive, and she is really a bitch. I absolutely dote on her.

There seemed to be no fear of the dangers of sugar in those days, and sweets were clearly an important part of daily life, often mentioned. Sweets from the Middle East were particularly delicious

21 July, 1942

There is a parcel on the chest of drawers in my room. Rose asked me what it was. I said, "Shoes". She turned to Thomas and, in a conversational voice, said, "Lucky beggar. She's always having new shoes".

Carling arrived to fetch me to go to see a War Committee farm which was open to the local farmers. It was most interesting. Derelict in 1940 it was mainly fallowed last summer and the cultivations done by the plough, four ploughings in May, June, and August, then drilled. No manures of any sort. Result, the best crops I have yet seen. Clyde Higgs was there. He is very pleased with me because I have twice taken his advice, Carling and having the cows abortion tested, (results not yet known). He was rather sweet. I think he must have known that the Stratford bums were trying to spread the rumour that G.H. was going down.

Anyway, I was talking to him and Hughes who is Chairman of the War Committee and several other Committee people, and I said I thought the crops were wonderful. Clyde Higgs said, "I've only seen one better lot". Someone said, "Where is that?" and he said, "At Gypsy Hall". The really sweet thing is that it isn't true. Ours aren't as good as theirs and since he isn't a fool he must know it. But it was sucks for anyone who happened to be standing around and had made dirty cracks in the past and it puts me quids in with the main committee, who are the people who count.

26 July, 1942

I'm going to describe the farm position which is now sorting itself out and becoming very interesting and exciting. First of all, Pattison will be free to be my paid adviser. I have agreed to pay him 20% of the profits with a minimum of £150. You may think this is an awful lot, but it is the wage of one labourer. I think he will be worth anything. You see I've had to deal in the last two years constantly with people who say nothing is possible and cut down and vitiate all my most progressive ideas. If I say to Carling "Let's do so and so" he finds 40,000 reasons why we can't. As a result I've got very dulled and cautious myself.

Now Pattison is the opposite. He gives me hell about the low production of the farm and is always telling me I must do this and that. I advance Carling's 40,000 reasons why we can't and he simply scoffs at them. In addition I would pay a good deal for the negative fact of having someone there to see that I don't do everything wrong and make a dead loss. So I hope you will agree. By the way, he will also get the use of the old car, as he will be 10 or 12 miles from here and he is very short of capital and won't keep one for himself. If he didn't have it the police would take the tyres off it to melt down for the rubber so I don't think it makes much difference.

Now as to organisation. I should really get a first-class cowman and put him in this house *(Didcot, our house in the village as she was not yet able to move into the farm)*. I don't really want to because the thing about first class cowmen is you can't interfere with them much, — they are in a minor way like bailiffs. If they are really first class this wouldn't matter but if they are anything less you are stymied again. Also I love the cows, they are my favourite thing and I want to fiddle about with them and work out the technique for a milking bail (which has a lot of snags) for myself.

Caterpillar tractor pulling a plough, not discs which were round and cut the surface.

William and three members of the Surrey War Committee arrived to look round the farm. There seemed to be quite a lot to show them. In the first field we were discing before ploughing which they had never seen before. William was delighted because they had been on a field of Clyde Higgs the night before and he had said he ought to be discing it and Clyde Higgs had said it was too hard.

We were making a lovely job of it so William was awfully pleased, and the others very interested. Then we have some winter oats of a new variety which everybody is interested in, and the S 23 seed production is new and our beans are the best anyone has seen and we have one rather unusual and very good variety of wheat and a lot of quite interesting leys and they all seemed interested and pleased and they all went away congratulating me. So I feel better because, to tell you the truth, I have been smarting under the dirty cracks of the War Committee even tho' they were made by people who hadn't seen the farm.

The children are just going to Sunday school. Last Sunday Rose went for the first time. Thomas has never been able to tell us what happens there except vaguely that it was all about a man called Christ (just like Father). But we asked Rose, and she told us the story of the widow's mite, only she thought it was mice.

Life is very dreary as the sweet rationing has begun and is 2oz a week. I haven't mentioned the war, which seems to be going extremely badly. The only thing is not to think about it at all. We never thought it would be as long as it has been did we?

Stooks in a field, cut and tied into sheaves, in the days before combine harvesters

29 July, 1942

Last year there was a certain field of oats that got wet and kept getting blown over in stook. Molly and I and any other women available stooked and re-stooked it innumerable times. Yesterday at lunch I said I was going stooking and Thomas said he would come and help. Rose said, "I shall come and push them over". I looked very shocked and said, "You wouldn't do that!" She then said, "Well, Manning and I did last year". (Manning is a little village boy). She then told how, when we had set up some stooks and turned our

159

backs, she and Manning pushed them over. She said with a great deal of relish that "Molly came along and said O my Goodness, 'ere's another one fallen over". She knew she was telling a monstrous story, and when she is conscious of guilt she looks fearfully shy but covers it with a sort of brave bitchiness. We asked her where it was she had done this? She looked rather disconcerted and then said, "You know, in the stooking field". There was something incredibly sweet about that. She was only 3 when she did it and is only 4 now. She is an endless source of wonder to me because I can't think where she gets it all from. She is not like me — she has more humour — and she's not really like you. I'm sure you were never slyly mischievous in the way she is when you were little, tho' her guts and her trust that everyone is going to like her probably comes from you.

Yesterday morning I was woken up by a German aeroplane letting off a machine gun outside my window — the first I have heard. No casualties as far as I know — it was really several miles away.

31 July, 1942

Samples of everyone's milk are tested by the Medical Officer of Health every so often. There are two tests, one is called the Methylene blue test and is for bacteria which may be present for a number of reasons and is difficult to trace. The other is for bacillus coli which can only be present in the milk if dung or urine has got in, i.e. thro' dirty production. It is not only rather a disgrace to have a dirty test but also you may lose your TT and Accredited licences if you have too many.

We have had three dirty tests and the last two have been Bacillus Coli. I have threatened and implored etc and done everything I could and now we have had the third I have just said I won't have Hall in the milking shed anymore but will do it myself. He is a slovenly slut and doesn't make any pretence of trying to produce clean milk, and I am fed up with it. I have said I will pay him the same money to work on the land for two months if he will stay, but otherwise he can get out with a week's notice ... Either way I'm not going to have him in the cowshed anymore. It will mean I shall have to get up before 6 (which, until the extra hour comes off, is before 4) because I shall have to get the cows in myself and this takes ½ an hour, but it will be a good opportunity to get a lot of experience while Carling is still here to advise me.

Dairy cows bags (udders) being washed by landgirls before milking

6 August, 1942

I am now head cowman and the alarm wakes me at 5.30 a.m. and I rush out to fetch the cows. Last night I went to bed at 8 o'clock. With the double summer time it really means that one is getting up at 3.0, which is practically the same as doing a night shift. I hope I shall adjust to it and finally not get too tired. It is all going very well. I am (very privately) convinced that I am a better cowman in every way (except stripping) than Hall. Not only is the shed spotless throughout the milking but the cows are up 5 gallons since I started. That can't be counted to me as they have been moved to a field with more keep but as Carling predicted they would go down it is at least satisfactory.

The only news is that, thro' a mistake or bloody mindedness, the Labour Exchange are threatening to call up Nora to a factory, in spite of representations made by me that I could not carry on the farm without her. I think it is a mistake, but if it isn't, by the time I have marshalled the War Committee, Buck and if necessary Mr Bevin himself, they won't be able to get away with it. But it worries me unceasingly just the same.

The war news is so utterly terrifying and awful I scarcely dare think of it or turn on the wireless. I have found myself asking myself whether it is conceivable we are not going to win this war.

8 August, 1942

I had a letter from you today written in the train and all about Bill's friends. You say you hope I'm interested. Now just so as you shall have no excuse I must tell you that I am ABSOLUTELY FASCINATED. I want to hear every detail and all they say and do and what they look like and whether you have any political discussions and whether they like you and if you like them. My picture is of everything on our side being madly standoffish in a thoroughly boring middle-class way and then you arrive with real geniality and charm and friendliness and also are very efficient, and we deliver twice as much as ever before. For the first time I really envy you your job and please do what you can to allay jealousy by telling all the details.

10 August, 1942

The war news seems so much worse than it has ever been. How do we think we're going to win if the Russians get beaten?

July 9, 1942 – Germans begin a drive toward Stalingrad in the USSR. **September 13, 1942 – *Battle of Stalingrad begins***

Personal news is quite good. Carling saw the War Committee and quite likes the sound of their job and has gone to Northampton today about another job, and will probably take one or the other.

Then, (this is a superstitious one) I lost my watch, the one you gave me. The strap broke and I only knew I had lost it somewhere between here and the canal bank. I was slightly depressed. It seemed so horrid losing that particular thing. This morning the children were up at the farm and Thomas (whose arrival it marked) found it in the orchard. Just as there was more rejoicing over one that was lost and found, I find this is a good omen.

12 August, 1942

You say you are well and busy and I can see you are thrilled and for the first time I feel you are getting the right sort of fun out of life. You also say Reggie asks for Colonel Donaldson. It is grand, isn't it? I wish they'd hurry up and put it through. For one thing, I'm told it makes a very real difference from the money point of view.

Rose in macintosh hat standing by the Hillman Minx

The other day Rose and some of her beastly friends were at the farm. It was raining and she had on a macintosh hat. She came back without it and said in an airy way which nobody questioned that it had blown off, and she had lost it. Today at lunch, Thomas (who is a fearful tell-tale) told us that she had put an egg in it and the egg had got broken, so in order not to admit to the broken egg she had chucked the whole lot, hat and egg away. She really is a vile child.

I remember this episode clearly. I thought about the fuss that would ensue over breaking eggs into the hat and decided that it would be considered a worse sin than losing it, so made up the lie. I judged the reaction incorrectly. Grownups, you know. They make such a fuss about everything.

I had a blistering row with Carling this morning, which probably was a mistake and I probably wouldn't have done it if I wasn't so frightfully tired. Have I told you that the other day we had an abortion? It really is a good one as the cows were tested only four weeks ago, and we had the most wonderful clear test. Then we get our first abortion in 2 ½ years.

There is of course a chance that it was simply an ordinary abortion and not contagious, but one must act the other way. Anyway, this is particularly difficult to deal with because the animal aborted in the night at not more than three or four months and I simply found the foetus when I went down for the cows the next morning. We have therefore been unable to trace the cow as they close up again immediately at that stage and so we can't do anything for a month as since they were only tested a month ago they wouldn't show any reaction in less than two months from then. But it is frightfully important to isolate the herd from everything else on the farm. We've got a lot of dry cows and heifers down the end of the farm and they have a nasty habit of getting out and coming home.

Yesterday they got out and I saw them in the field next the cows. It never occurred to me that Carling would leave them there and anyway it's simply a waste of time my giving him any orders about the movement of stock because he doesn't take the slightest notice. This morning when I went down for the cows three of the dry cows were in with them. It was only luck that all the others weren't in with them too — a risk of £500 to £1,000 worth of stock. So when I saw Carling I bawled him out — It didn't do the slightest good, in fact only harm.

You see he so sincerely thinks he is simply wonderful in every way and quite incapable of making a mistake that, when he is rebuked, he not only finds it tiresome but extremely unjust. So he becomes very rude indeed and very self righteously indignant. None of which improves my temper and we still have six weeks to go. He is going to take the job with the War Committee. Clyde Higgs is chairman of the Demonstration Committee. I hug to my heart the belief that one day Mr Higgs will tell him all the things about himself he ought to know.

19 August, 1942

I've bought a little pony for the children. It's arriving today. They don't know about it yet — they only know there is a surprise coming. We are all excited and it will be great fun taking them down to the station to get it. I paid £10 for it and £1 for the saddle and bridle and 30/- for the rail fare. I told them it was from you and me together.

21 August, 1942

Terrific excitements. Pattison (whom I now call Pat when I can remember) arrived yesterday to go thro' the cows and decide which we would cull. He was so horrible about nearly all of them that I was reduced to despair. Then we suddenly decided to have a farm sale to get rid of all of them except about 10 or so and buy new and better ones with the money.

I have decided already to get rid of the sheep for the moment, as we have ploughed up so much; and the hens will have to go as without Mrs Carling there is no-one to look after them, and I want to simplify all these small things to start with. So we will have a wonderful sale and we shan't stand to lose anything because Pattison will post six men round the ring to buy in anything which doesn't fetch enough. Isn't it exciting? I've been longing to get rid of all those beastly cows for ages.

Anni and Haschi came over on Sunday, and Anni started a tremendous campaign to make the house really comfortable even at the expense of a good deal of money. She takes the view that a) I have lived like a pig for two years and both

166

deserve and need a break and b) that when you come home we shall have to live in a reasonable way and things will become more and more difficult to get. Of course I very soon got hotted up.

We went and looked at the house. I thought that, if I put an Aga in the present dairy, that could be the kitchen and the other room would be really nice for the children and for meals. This is impossible without first laying and lighting the fire, as one can no longer get a Primus stove or anything like that. With an Aga all I would have to do would be to boil the kettle. Anyway, I think I shall probably get one if I can, so I hope you won't disapprove.

Aga cooker with 4 ovens

Then the next thing was that the bathroom is lovely but has an exceptionally mean and uncomfortable bath in it. Of course baths and bathrooms do mean rather a lot to me. I could always restore myself to happiness by going into a luxurious looking bathroom and lying for hours in the bath. And Anni painted a tremendous picture of you coming home and being quite unable to get your legs into this one at all. Then I am going to do the decoration fairly lavishly. I feel a bit guilty — I don't know quite from what standpoint. I think it is because you are away. If you were here I'm sure we should be most extravagant together.

I'm going to London in the afternoon and shall be away for two days. It breaks my heart to leave the cows even for that long because one of my new and expensive heifers has calved and I like to watch every move she makes in case something goes wrong. But I've simply got to order all the things for the house.

30 August, 1942

I had a very good time in London and succeeded in getting everything I wanted, and luckily remembered the two Peckham Agas and asked Dod and Pete if I could borrow one, which would save the pleasant sum of £77. I got lovely wallpapers and a bath and went in to Sybil Colefax and sat talking to John Fowler for hours.

Colefax and Fowler were smart interior decorators in Chelsea.

They are going to make me some lovely curtains for my sitting room out of dark green black-out material (which is coupon free) and dark and light green fringes, and some of our old linen sheets for drapery.

I am rather depressed. Everything is squalid and dirty at the farm and I can't get it right without better men and I have no men, good or bad, even in sight. However I am perfectly certain it will be alright and I will feel gay one day and when the farmhouse is empty I shall do a dance in it even if there isn't one man left on the farm and I have to do everything myself.

31 August, 1942

It is all pretty depressing. We haven't at the moment got so much as a smell of a man and you know our existing staff, with the one exception of Highman, consists entirely of half-wits and untrained girls. They are none of them capable of doing a job without supervision. Idiocies occur every day and are awfully apt to undo in five minutes one's cherished and carefully arranged work of a week. In addition it pours with rain every day and we are very much behind with the harvest. It is even becoming doubtful whether we shall have finished before Carling goes. So one can't help being a trifle gloomy. But I don't regret anything.

Frankie on Rose's pony

I had a very amusing letter from Daddy *(Freddy Lonsdale)*. He says about Chesher , *(his secretary)* , "Of course I know she's well meaning, but then she means well in such extraordinary hats which makes one doubt her sincerity". He says "tell me about Jack and give him my love and tell him I never cease to think of him. It would be nice to all have dinner together like we used to do".

Frederick Lonsdale, portrait by Simon Elwes. NPG

3 September, 1942
The depression is immense and it is now raining and raining. The trouble with me is I'm really tired and stale with

all this milking. I could only just about do it with comfort if I was a land girl and had nothing else to do or think about. I find it a bit too much. But don't think I am seriously grumbling. I wouldn't change anything if I had a chance to, only I wish it would work itself out a little better. I have very slight cold feet as the time draws nearer for Carling to go. As a foreman Highman is an unknown quantity, and I'm not sure whether I shall know what to tell the men to do in the morning or not.

4 September 1942

I really ought to have a tremendous lot to tell you but there is so much going on that I am in a maze, and can't sort it out. If you can imagine having all the small details of moving house, plus engaging and trying to settle in new staff, plus making arrangements for a sale, plus doing the milking, plus trying to get two cottages built, plus finishing the harvest, plus making sure the seeds will be here for the drilling, plus the thousand and one things there are to see to on a farm anyway, plus arranging to get the children off to Katta's and get their winter clothes, plus go to Moulton tomorrow and deliver a speech to twenty children who have won a six weeks course there as a prize in a Farmer's Weekly competition, you will have some idea what my life is like.

16 September, 1942

For absolutely no good reason I'm feeling rather gay. So I'm taking ½ an hour off to write to you and whilst doing so I'm having an orgy of Jack Teagarden.

Jack Teagarden, jazz trombone stylist of the pre-bebop era.

Tomorrow I take the children to London and hand them over to Nanny who will take them on to Katta's *(his sister)*. I shall have a long day because I've got to get their winter clothes and then get back here.

Old Nan with Rose and Thomas, helping Frankie in wartime

For the last two days I have relieved Highman ploughing for an hour at lunch,so if there are two long strips where the corn doesn't grow I for one shall know exactly why. At the same time it's great fun and makes me feel it's all going

to be most enjoyable, in spite of being short of every sort of labour.

Highman is frightfully nice. It is a pleasure to talk to him. He is so straightforward and sweet. He practically never says anything but yes, anyway, which is just what I like. Then the milking is going better. I've got Cyril Wheeldon and Margaret (Pattison's girl) in there now and they are both coming on a lot, especially Cyril. They are as quiet as mice with the cows and very clean, which is something quite new at G.H. and makes milking a pleasure.

Tho' I have to supervise a lot, we have practically got to the point where I can turn up late and leave early if I want to. Of course, all this optimism won't last and tomorrow I shall be telling you how awful everything is. Still, I'm sure, sooner or later, it's going to be such fun as has never been known. And, of course, if one has enough fun, one does not have to make such terrific profits because fun is better than money anyway and I'm sure you will agree.

11: 1942

Farmer Donaldson at last

21 September, 1942
Note the date — now I am a FARMER, tho' you wouldn't think it if you saw me, because I look like nothing so much as a housewife rather inefficiently moving house, into Gypsy Hall farmhouse. I haven't got cold feet at all and I think it's going to be fun and I have only one wish — that you were here.

Carling had finally left and Frankie had now moved into the farmhouse at Gypsy Hall. With Pat to advise her she was now in full charge of the farm.

I don't know where to begin. But I suppose the most important thing is the farm. I think it's going to be o.k. I thought before that the first week would be a nightmare trying to decide what everyone ought to do etc. It's quite easy with the tractor drivers and the stock people because they just do routine work but what, I wondered, did people like Oakley (the deaf and dumb) do before breakfast and on days when there was no obvious gang work like hoeing or harvesting? However, it doesn't arise. The difficulty is to find enough people to do all the thousands of little odd jobs that need doing. All that you just swing into without difficulty and don't really think about. It's all going well.
I must describe the staff. First of all Highman is super as a foreman — at least for me. He is a man without an inferiority complex and you know how rare that is. He's never touchy and never obstructive and he's quite obviously

174

out for the best. So that, if he disagrees with me or advances some reason why I shouldn't do something, I never suspect an ulterior motive. Then he turns out to be awfully good at a lot of things. When Carling used to earmark the pigs he did it with two men and fiddled about discussing which way the numbers should go for hours. Highman did it this week with one girl and a speed and precision which was a treat to watch. He's obviously keen to make a success of it and looks awfully eager and happy and is sweet to everyone.

His faults probably are that he doesn't think ahead, isn't used to organisation and may not be forceful enough with the men. But I think I can supply all that. Anyway I'm much more pleased with the first week than I ever thought I would be. By the way, I'm giving Highman £4 and paying his cottage.

Frances Donaldson with Mr Highman who became her foreman when she stopped having a bailiff to run the farm and took over herself

Then there's Cyril Wheeldon aged 18 rather lacking in force but quite a nice pleasant little cowman — would be perfectly good as second to a good man and very useful as a relief tractor driver. Both he and Highman have been ploughing by moonlight up to about 9 o'clock. Cyril was getting the under 21 standard rate of 45/-. I've raised him to £3 which is the over 21 rate as I don't think I could replace him for less. Then there's Oakley, the deaf and dumb. Then on Monday Sharp starts.

That's all the men, but, including me, there are five women, and Pattison calls it the Nunnery and Oakley has been heard to announce that he's sick of this bloody Women's Institute. There's Jessie who four months ago was a typist in Birmingham, came to us in July and is absolutely first class in every way. She does the horses, the pigs and the hens, which is too much and she will have to be relieved soon. Then there's Margaret, who's the girl Pattison got and who was not good to start with but who has come on 100% lately. She is supposed to be difficult and moody after the first three months and maybe she will be, but she's Scotch and touchy and seems to respond to being treated rather well, so maybe she won't. She's excellent with stock and a great help temporarily.

Then there's Peggy who is the tractor driver in the canal cottage. She's not 100% on a tractor as yet — she can't start them yet and sometimes stops them and so on, but she's not too bad and a useful relief driver and a very nice girl and quite fairly intelligent. Then there's Sheila Rees-Mogg who is Mummy's friend, awfully stupid in some ways but quite useful in others. That's the lot and it's not nearly enough but it's all fairly good and everyone is mad keen and working hard and I — much to my own surprise — am taking it without anxiety or neurotic worrying. I think it's because I'm so damn busy I haven't the time to turn round much less worry about anything. And I think it will go well, probably with occasional horrible lapses.

I think I'm going to like the farmhouse quite enormously. I am spending an unreasonable amount of money on it in an effort to make it easy to run as well as pretty and comfortable. It has a nice atmosphere now I've got rid of the dark brown paint and I think it's going to be really gay and jolly. Anyway I love it so perhaps we'll stay here for some time after all.

27 September, 1942

One effect of being so busy is that I never worry. You know how I normally stew over things. Well now one passes on to the next thing so quickly one simply hasn't time. It makes one's attitude to life much more like a man's.

29 September, 1942

About the cottages. I got the permission but it now turns out that it is next to impossible to get any materials or anybody to build them. Well, I've fallen in, by means which I needn't describe, with a building contractor called Shellabear. He is building aerodromes and is a small scale Billy Rootes of the building world. He has produced plans, will supply all the materials and will send his building foreman once a week to supervise Cox, the local builder. BUT his ideas of a really nice house are any road development house and that is what ours are going to be like.

2 October, 1942

The carpet layer starts in three days from now, and as he moves round the house so we shall move after him. The wallpaper on the landing and stairs and in the bathroom is lovely and the bathroom is going to be the best we have ever had, except for one thing which is that I could only get one piece of lino in London and that was the shiny oilcloth type with a hateful black marbly effect on white. I put a new bath in and when I got here I found the lavatory was an absolute bugger and took ½ an hour to fill which is really impossible with me and two children and two land girls. So I bought (£7.10/-) a new one with a modern low cistern and now it works a treat. The paint is white all over the house and it is wallpaper everywhere — white backgrounds with patterns on. I think I shall have spent about £300 on the house.

6 October, 1942

At this moment I am writing in a room with one man papering and another painting. They are both very cross as I am considerably in their way, but I have just said that if they paint me I am still going to stay here so they may as well get on with it.

I haven't heard the news or looked at a newspaper for days and haven't the slightest idea what is going on in the great big world. I get pretty tired but I don't mind it and I must say it is all rather fun and I love managing the farm and do it quite alright only I wish I had more men. Pattison gave me a farmer's stick with a top like V where your thumb goes and I walk with it doing a terrific pose and poking animals in a critical way with the end of it.

11 October, 1942

Yesterday was the sale. I don't know where to begin. It has been such hard work and everyone on the farm has been at it until after dark all this week. Firstly it was a success in every possible way. Financially I think I must have got much more that I gave in the first place.

Then the sheep. I paid 72/6 for 45. We sold 36 in 3 lots of 12. The first lot fetched 93/-, the second 79/- and the third 84/-. There were 3 left which weren't fit to go in and they will fetch something or other. The rest have died but the lambs of the lot had already brought in what I paid originally for the sheep. Then the heifers must have averaged nearly £30. I bred and reared them. The calves sold badly but were only thrown in to make up the sale. The gross total was £2,029, but Barnard's fees and advertising have to come off that. The nicest thing is that it was done absolutely slap up in every way.

Pattison was argumentative and irritating, cancelling every order I gave and taking all the men on his job and leaving me with about one girl for all I had to do but I must say he brought it off. We had a great bit of luck in that a super cowman whom I have engaged to come here in the spring when the cottages are built was on his holiday and he came and got the cows ready. He is a showman and knows all about it and he made them look wonderful. Pattison had spent about two days doing the same thing himself for the sheep and they looked wonderful. Then his organisation of the men and the sale ring was perfect and everything went without a hitch.

We had really swotted with the yard and roads round the house and everything was tidied up and dirty old bits of wire replaced by timber rails and cowsheds whitewashed and hedges brushed and so on. All that was done in the last two days before the sale as well as everything else. On top of all this the house was just ready in time. It is too pretty for words.

I had lashings of food and tea and beer and I even secured a bottle of gin and I did it slap up like a party and asked everyone in. Anni had been all last week and done the flowers beautifully and the whole house looked wonderful. It put Gypsy Hall on the map in quite a different way.

People kept saying to me they couldn't believe I had done all that in two years, and I had to refrain from saying two weeks, you mean. It was great fun in retrospect and I am awfully proud and pleased, but it was dreadfully hard and it nearly killed us all and it only came off by the skin of its teeth.

The sale was at 2. I had asked lots of people to come in early for drinks and food, but by a quarter to one I was still trailing round in a pair of dungarees with no buttons on one side showing my underclothes and a filthy face and in an absolute panic because there were still six cows which hadn't been tied up and no-one knew where the sheep were and the calves hadn't been separated. But it all just worked.

Jack was giving parties too for his Russian comrades:

7 October, 1942

Reggie is coming up with us on Saturday and we're going to give a party for our Transport Russians. Bos (Monck) is bringing the Minister and we shall get all the grands we can, and then get tight first and make it a party. We shall have lashings of caviar and vodka and a violin and accordion in the gallery. R & B and I will put up £10 each, and Gifford will give us £20 from his entertainment allowance at Kuibishev which he never spends. I hope it will be fun. Meanwhile Stalingrad stands, and I think it is now obvious that it will stand.

13 October, 1942

The party was very much OK. We got two bands in the end and a real lot of caviar and loads of drink and it swung very well. We had about 20 Russians, and every single one was blind *(drunk)*. Some 70 to 80 people in all. It started at 7 pm, and all the Russians arrived first, in a body, a bit sticky to begin with. However it all warmed up and by 9 o'clock we were having Russian songs and solo dances. The Minister was there and saw, probably for the first time, how to throw a party for the Russians.

12 October, 1942

There have been several good rows since the sale. One gentleman pinched deliberately another's much more expensive sheep. So this morning we just went over and took them back. He was out but he telephoned later. I put him on to Pattison who chewed him up so well that when he came to collect his real sheep he was meeker even than they were.

Tomorrow I am going to Reading to see if there are any Ayrshires to buy. Wilson came today about the cottages. We've got the plans passed now and he says we ought to start building next week and be finished by Christmas. He also said that they'll cost £750-£800 the pair. I don't believe any of it but if it is only about half true it would be wonderful.

Because Jack and Frankie had commissioned a house from Walter Gropius, assisted by Maxwell Fry (a leading British modernist architect), they had standards to live up to. In wartime Frankie could not either find or pay for an architect to design anything which they would have liked, and she needed accommodation as quickly as possible. These cottages were built first, to house the Highman family and the Price family, the cowman. Later they commissioned a second set of cottages from Maxwell Fry.

14 October, 1942

The cottages are going to be dreadful, but you mustn't mind, at least not more than I do, because they are going to make the efficient running of this farm a possibility. I must say I have been lucky in running into Shellabear and his talkative Mr Wilson. Everyone says that, even with permission, it is really impossible to get the material for building now. I have applied for licensed materials but only as formality because Mr Wilson will start pouring them on to the farm long before the licences get through.

The farm is going really well, and there is no doubt I did the right thing. It is incredibly hard, really rather too hard, but immense fun and a wonderful life. Highman is a miracle —- really so. Pat argued with me about making him foreman and thought he wouldn't be good enough, but he now thinks he is one of the best men he has ever known.

He is so nice and easy to get on with, and never obstructive or trying to get out of things, and no inferiority complex. It is immense luck having him and one should be very grateful. Then Cyril Wheeldon has blossomed so much since I had the farm. I gave him a rise and I had to give him responsibility because there was no-one else and he has risen like a bird to it.

Then I have a girl tractor-driver which is a thing Carling would never have, and between them and me the two tractors never stop even at meal-times and if it only won't rain we shall finish the drilling earlier than Carling ever did, with 30 acres more than he had. But I am afraid it will rain tonight. It looks and feels like it.

The cowman I have engaged and who helped at the sale is a super-man, and he seemed most frightfully nice and awfully unassuming. If I get the cottages built in time to get him it really will be a good team. He had a really nice wife and four children tho' he is only 28. I have a lot to make me content and, instead of hurrying the week on I am always trying to hold it back, as I can't get enough done. You will love it, either as a job or as a background to life.

15 October, 1942

You never can imagine how pretty this house is. It is quite incredible that such a dingy place can be so completely transformed, and I myself am staggered. It is absolutely different from the Wood House and of course not nearly so luxurious, but honestly I think it is every bit as pretty. Anni said that it was like a house that had pernicious anaemia and was suddenly cured.

I never seem to mention the war and the truth is I don't know very much about it. I know that Stalingrad is still holding and somewhere or other deep down I remember to give thanks for that, but otherwise I know nothing.

The Battle of Stalingrad began on September 13, 1942; the first Battle of Alamein had been fought on September 2 so there was reason for some optimism. The Americans had come into the war and the first all-American air attack in Europe had been in August.

Still, things are beginning to settle down and I have at last got back to writing regularly to you. One trouble is there are no curtains in my room so I can't sit there at night because of the blackout.

Farmhouse at Gypsy Hall

23 October, 1942

The children are back (*from Much Hadham where they had stayed while Frankie moved house*) and Rose has grown about two inches and is nearly as tall as Thomas. Rose went away with a very strong Warwickshire accent but she has come back enunciating every syllable like an elocution class in an extremely refined and affected way.

They are very sweet and I am very pleased to have them back. Think what a lovely little family we shall be when at last you do get back. The background of the farm makes it all so much more whole, somehow — something for everyone to do and to concentrate on.

When I was in London I had dinner with Buck *(de la Warr)*. I made some remark about the war, and he said, "O, let's face it, we've won the war now". Apparently this is what people think. They think there is a long way to go, but the fact that they couldn't break the Russian resistance this year has broken the Germans and won us the war. Rather good isn't it? Even if they will be thinking something quite different in a week or two. Perhaps we can hope you'll be here for the 1944 harvest even if not for the 1943.

25 October, 1942

I have been asked by the BBC if I will do a five minute question and answer broadcast to America sometime in the near future. An American farmer asks questions and you answer. It is a trifle nerve-making as you don't know beforehand what the questions will be and you have to be careful not to say the wrong thing. The other thing is that Mary Griggs of the Farmers' Weekly has asked me if she may tell the M.o.I that I will do a 1000 word article to be syndicated in America on first woman war time farmer.

26 October, 1942

I want to start discussing what school Thomas should go to. I think he ought to go when he's 7 unless the war is over by then — which is not likely now. He can't get educated here and, unless you're back by then I think it would really be better for him.

I am going to London today to broadcast to America tomorrow. I do think I'm silly about broadcasting — I always say yes and there is no point.

Now I must tell you about Rose this morning. She really was so sweet. We went up together to pull up pea plants for the cows. She worked very hard but she began to get bored and she kept saying "I don't really like pulling peas. Of course I know it wins the war but it makes my hands so cold"; or "Thomas is so naughty. He won't do anything he doesn't want to and although pea-picking is beastly it does win the war." Don't you think it's heavenly?

2 November, 1942

The BBC was quite an experience tho' really quite pointless as usual I took an instantaneous dislike to them all and realised it would be difficult to get into good form of a conventional kind with this crowd. First there was Lady Clarke, wife of Sir Kenneth --- a loathsome bitch who seriously believes that the whole nation is healthier because the war has stopped them eating five course dinners. Then there was a man called Brockington from the M.o.I. He was a sort of imitation of Castlerosse, Brendan Bracken and a few others mixed up. Knowledgeable and slightly showing off with a dry humour which he fancied too much and no interest of any sort in me. There was the question master, a Canadian of an American ingenuity and earnestness. The fourth performer, an 18 year old boy-scout, who has recently toured America, of a precociousness and mature poise only usually seen in film stars and broadcasters, was not present at lunch. I hated them all, and disagreed with everything they thought and said. However I refused to be got down. After lunch we went to the studio where we went thro' the sort of form.

There were eight questions, all dull, and I was given two to make the first answer. This meant being prepared with an answer to start the ball rolling. After we had done this we were put on to New York. For about five minutes you talk to your opposite numbers in New York without being on record. This is supposed to warm you up but of course it does the opposite as there is nothing to talk about and nothing could be more nerve-making.

There were only three on the other side beside their question master. These were Miss Elsa Maxwell, whom you have doubtless met, a man called Dalmage who is the head of the Canadian press in New York and another odious 18 year old. My two questions were "How was the harvest" and "What have you eaten to-day". Then there was a question to be answered by the M.o.I. gent about the effect of our increased arable acreage on Canadian wheat exports after the war. This was no 7 on the list and no affair of mine. However when we actually went on record, Dalmage opened up by asking it first and quite directly to me. I had therefore not only to answer it but to do so shortly and pass the ball to the M.o.I. gent who had pages written out he was determined to spout, and I had to do this sufficiently well so as not give away the unspontaneousness of the arrangement. I did this alright.

We were given whisky to binge us up. Once we got going it wasn't really so awfully frightening. One had to listen carefully to the other side in order to answer and one's attention was sufficiently concentrated to make one forget one's nerves. I think I was alright, tho' I repeated myself a bit and was once unable to finish a sentence. I sat next to Lady Clark, and when the broadcast was over the M.o.I. said "I'd like you two ladies to know that the last time I was on this programme was with J B Priestley and Leslie Howard and in my opinion this was an infinitely better and more interesting broadcast". However this doesn't necessarily mean much, as apparently Priestley had let himself go on India and Howard had backed him up and M.o.I. hadn't liked it at all.

Elsa Maxwell suddenly burst into a eulogy of Noel Coward's new film for no reason at all as it had nothing to do with any of the questions. Afterwards Mary Adams, who was our producer, spoke to New York and said it would have to be cut and New York said O no it couldn't because she was doing a column and had promised them some publicity if they would allow her to spout this piece. Aren't Americans wonderful? Anyway it was all quite fun and rather an experience to be speaking to New York etc but it leaves you cold really and I don't know why I do it because you can't do well and you never get a good enough subject. No-one is cross with you but no-one thinks you're wonderful and wants to take you on a yearly contract.

11 November, 1942

I've had a lot of letters from you worrying about my health and overworking. Well, I'm not anymore. I was for a short period but now things are settling down and going more smoothly and I'm not milking anymore, and I very often take a morning in bed till about 8 o'clock.

Now about the children. Before we were up here I used to be fairly careful about them getting in the men's way. So they never had much fun on the farm, and didn't get many tractor rides etc. Now I never bother about them and in spite of the bog of mud they are having a splendid time. They have bought a rabbit which they feed and clean out without being prompted, which is unusual in children, and they go everywhere with the men and the girls. They always go out into the fields when there is a job like mangold pulling. Today the men were threshing.

Thomas was there all afternoon. The first time I saw him he had got Highman's penknife and was cutting string to tie round the sacks. Later I saw Highman pushing a sack round to the granary on a sack lifter. Thomas was following. On the way back Highman walked in front and Thomas pushed the sacklifter — terrific straining to get it thro' the mud. Then at 4 o'clock Rose came to ask Nanny if it was tea-time. Nan said, "Not quite" — Rose said, "Well, I'm going to the haystack — that one in the corner by the cows. You'll know where to find me 'cos you'll see a ladder." All very good, don't you think?

The following letter is replying to a letter that Jack wrote in October.

The dates are all over the place in the following section, but this is mostly because although Jack was answering her letters, Frankie often did not get the answers for a month or so, and then might get several all together. There was no proper letter and response, or question and answer.

13 November, 1942
The news is awfully exciting. It's just beginning really to sink in to people in England. It took a long time to percolate thro' the crust of cynicism and disbelief which had formed as a result of the last two years. People in the streets are whooping with joy, and when one stops to speak to anyone they all say it's the beginning of the end, and it will be over this time next year. I don't allow myself to dwell on all these possibilities because I had such a bad time after the fall of Greece and Crete that I don't suppose I shall ever believe too much in anything again until peace is actually declared. But even I believe it really is the beginning of the end.

November 10. Churchill speaks: "This is not the end. It is not even the beginning of the end. But it is, perhaps, the end of the beginning."

Lieutenant General Montgomery is knighted and made a full General.

November 13: British Eighth Army recaptures Tobruk.

Later in the month the Red Army begins to succeed in defeating the Germans at Stalingrad on the eastern boundary of Europe.

Jack with Lt Colonel Maston, USPGSC, meeting Russian officers

Jack in a meeting with Russians. He is 2nd left, wearing glasses

He labelled another copy of this photograph as follows: Head of the table, facing the photographer: General Korolev; with their backs to us: Colonel Doronin and interpreter Robbins; the 3 at the left end of table: Sinclair(UKCC), Jack,

Maston (USPGSC); at right hand end of table: Hart(TN) and with pipe Clotz(US).Portraits of Lenin and Stalin hanging on the wall.

I had a terrific post this morning. All about your work and the compliments from the Russian general and the American. I am interested in all the details and all about the horrible Hayward and all that. It's rather fun your being such friends with some of the Russians and your description of yourself as a "stores for Russia maniac". You are quite right to be because God knows they've won the war for us.

Jack had written in July. He was now working in PAIForce (Persia and Iran Force)

12 July, 1942   I've also made good contact with the UKCC. They've got a new transport man called Hayward. Oddly enough I met him in a bar in Baghdad and we both criticized the way the Russians had been handled and both said how much better we would do it ourselves. Now here we are trying to do it, which is amusing.

Extracts from Wikipedia: The crisis of midsummer 1942 had demonstrated that, until rail capacity in the Corridor could be vastly improved, the only hope of dealing with mounting backlogs of cargo at the ports was to strengthen the existing British motor transport system, as operated by the United Kingdom Commercial Corporation and British military trucking units.

The Persian   Corridor was   a   supply   route into Soviet Azerbaijan through Iran   by   which   British   aid   and American Lend-Lease supplies were transferred to the Soviet Union during World War II.

This Persian Route became the only viable, all-weather route to be developed to supply Soviet needs.

190

18 October, 1942

I had a good and bad day yesterday. In the morning I got a call from Sheridan, the new American adviser to the Persian Food Ministry. He said "I had an interview with the Minister of State yesterday and I told him you were quite the most helpful and useful person I'd met yet in Tehran, and he made a note of it and said it was the kind of thing he liked to know." Then a sweet American colonel, who often blows in to see me, was discussing our people in general, and said the people he'd been most impressed with were McCrudden and me. Of course he's quite right, but it's nice to say so. So I had rather a successful morning. But the afternoon was a very difficult interview with the oil company who are on the verge of a row with the Russians and a long and maddening one with Hayward, who's in the middle of a blood feud with Krasnov. I've got to try and get it stopped, as it's really too stupid. But it's the hell of a business and I came away feeling half the size I felt at lunch.

20 October, 1942

I was thinking, how completely one has changed, from an ordinary Movements officer to a stores for Russia maniac. What I like about it is that I am fully extended and know I'm wasting nothing of energy or brain, in fact haven't enough of either, to do the best possible.

1 November, 1942 – Operation Supercharge (Allies break Axis lines at El Alamein). 8 November, 1942 – Operation Torch begins (U.S. invasion of North Africa). Soon after this the Russians begin to drive back the German army from Moscow.

14 November, 1942

Pat and I went to Reading yesterday, expecting to come back empty-handed. As far as pedigree stock is concerned we did. But we actually bought 3 cows. Pat is a really good judge of stock and he will always spot a cheap cow like the plain one yesterday. Without him I shouldn't have the slightest chance of getting out of the rather nasty financial position I am in at the moment.

William Davis was here yesterday and said that the wheat on the front field was better than any he had seen on the clays which are all being very funny this year. He was also pleased with the leys. He said the one in the field where the mangolds were grown last year was better than anything they've got at Dodwell. It's much more fun when things are admired now than it used to be. One feels entitled to the compliments instead of inadvertently in a fraudulent position.

16 November, 1942

What do you think about Darlan and all that?

wiki: **Jean Louis Xavier François Darlan** *was a French Admiral and political figure. After France capitulated to Nazi Germany in 1940, Darlan served in the pro-German Vichy regime, becoming its deputy leader for a time. When the Allies invaded French North Africa in they recognized him as head of French North Africa, and he ordered French forces to cooperate with the Allies.*

19 November, 1942

The farm goes reasonably well, but the peas put us behind with the mangolds and the mangolds put us behind with the muck-carting and God knows when we shall catch up. Metcalfe the new cowman is obviously a very good stockman and nice and reliable, but he isn't used to this type of machine yet and I am not tremendously impressed yet with his powers of organisation. But it is too early to judge.

I was going thro' a drawer yesterday and found some letters of mine during the last weeks you were in France (*after Dunkirk*). They were all incredible and I wouldn't have believed them except they were in my own handwriting, but there was one which was without exception the most awful letter I have ever read. Sweat poured down my back and even tho' it was your property and not mine I burnt it. I would have liked to have burnt them all but I thought you might be cross. I think I must have altered. I can't imagine, under any stress of emotion, writing those letters today. But I suppose it was the most awful time of my life.

20 November, 1942

Yesterday Thomas was sitting on a stool in the milking shed and a cow called Jane came in and stood in front of him. She is actually the only really first class cow we've got. T. said, "Mummy, is that one of your best cows?" He didn't know her name so I asked him what made him think she was one of our best cows. He said, "O, I was going by her bag!" How about that for a 6 year old budding farmer?

I've taken to wearing my battle-dress. It is dark green and the trousers don't fit too well owing to men's waists being so different. But I love it. I can get two jerseys under the coat and it is a perfect outfit for farm work. I'm going to apply for a permit to have another so that this can sometimes be cleaned and if I can get one I shall wear nothing else all the winter.

Metcalfe is not going to be a success I fear. He is doing that business of veiled hints that he isn't going to like the job on account of things which he knew about before he even took it —- such as the bail.

'Bail' means the milking parlour arrangements – quite modern at that time.

Not Jane, but Ethel, with the best bag of them all

I am being patient up to now, but next time he starts it I'm going to say "Now make up your mind whether you want the job or not because, if you don't, there are plenty who will with the house and the money you're getting". Then he will either leave or shut up. But either way I don't care. I have quite made up my mind that Carling is the last man who is going to bully me.

I got a very sweet letter card today — the one which said you were beginning to feel the war badly as you can no longer get fresh caviare. I wonder how great a change you would find in England?

9 November, 1942

I asked Doronin, our no 2 Russian after the General, to come and see *The Great Dictator*. He and Vorobei and Parachonski the interpreter came. We got a kilo of caviare for a pound (it's obtainable again now) and two bottles of whisky, which we gave them before the film. Afterwards Doronin insisted on a restaurant. As we'd eaten basically nothing but caviare this seemed a good idea. A lot more vodka, beer, food as required — I must say they have great presence with the lower orders — the old regime must have been superb if the new one is as good as this. He paid the bill without looking at it, with a thousand Real note, all splendidly in the old manner. Then the band stopped by about 11, as there's a curfew at midnight. Doronin called them all back and made them play Russian songs for ½ an hour, and then never tipped them. An amusing evening, but what impressed me was the way everyone treated them like old Russian princes.

22 November, 1942
Reggie has gone bear-shooting with the Russians. He's off somewhere in the mountains. He'll love it and it'll do him good. I'm also very pleased for the glory of it, as there's no other British officer in any walk of life on those sort of terms.

 27 November, 1942
    You are very pleased about the news. So am I. But I take it differently with immense wood-touching and no letting up of the cloud of pessimism. My university students who were here in the summer said that no person or animal ever arrived on the farm without having to melt the cloud of pessimism with which they were immediately surrounded. "I've bought a new cow —- I paid an awful lot but I don't suppose she'll be any good." "I've got three university students to help with the harvest but I expect they'll be an awful nuisance" etc. Was I always like that or is it the effect of the war?

This house is really so lovely. When I look up from my letter the room is really gracious. I do hope you will like it. Of course lamplight is awfully pretty.

I saw in the paper that Thomas Beecham *(the conductor)* was getting a divorce. Now I hear that Emerald *(Cunard)* has come back to London. I don't know whether the two things are connected.

29 November, 1942

As I write this the news is unbelievably good. The Russians have encircled the Germans at Stalingrad and according to Nora's interpretation of the 7 o'clock news are on the offensive somewhere else.

November 19, 1942 – Soviet counter-offensive at Stalingrad begins.

And the French have sunk the fleet at Toulon. It would have been better if they had sailed it away. But one can't grumble. And what is so wonderful is the way that when you get some power everything begins to tumble in without a fight. It happened for the Germans and it happened for the Japs and now it seems to have begun to happen for us.

So maybe you will be home for Christmas 1943. Darling, I do hope so. I miss you as much as ever, if in a different way. I no longer think of you all the time and in every circumstance with an ache because I have now lost the habit of expecting you to be here. But I always think "Jack would like that" or "I wonder what Jack would think." That is a bore. I am no longer always absolutely sure what you would think. It is time we got together again. But, whenever it is, it will be all right when we do. I shall soon find out what you think and I am sure I will like it. That is the great thing about us.

Have a happy Christmas my darling love and get tight with the Russians or Christopher Sykes, but think of us. I am staying here this year and Jan and Dave are coming to stay and Anni and Haschi for the day so if you get this letter you will be able to imagine us.

The Gropius house was finished in 1937. In 1939 the war broke out. When Frankie moved to a farm the army requisitioned but never used it. Frankie and Jack finally had to sell it to help pay for a new and larger farm in Gloucestershire. It is now a listed building but at the time was regarded with distaste by most of their friends and general opinion. The house was a bit like their politics – wonderful but out of tune with the majority of their friends.

The Wood House, by Walter Gropius, today

1 December, 1942
I told you I have to pay £126 in back tax on the Wood House rent and that Burgis said this could be saved if we mortgaged it instead of the farm. I therefore wrote to Ball *(the bank manager)* asking him to get it valued. I got a very cheeky letter back saying he understood the house was modern and would not be easy to dispose of and he didn't think the bank would like the present position disturbed. I wrote and said would he please say whether the bank was prepared to lend money on it or not as, if not, I would arrange a loan either with another bank or a building

197

society. He came off it at the run and said there must have been a misunderstanding and of course they would and did I want it valued at once? I love sucks-ing bank managers, but I am disappointed in Mr Ball. He should know me well enough by now not to try such baby stuff.

I had a lovely letter this morning telling how grand the Russians are in restaurants. I do think that's good. I rather envy you your society. Up till now I have been the one who saw reasonably amazing people. Now I never see anyone at all while you are surrounded with vodka and caviare and Christopher Sykes and Russians and high Embassy society. I hope you aren't going to come home with expensive tastes because by the time I have bought about six cows we shall only be able to afford water.

5 December, 1942

The cows are doing well under Metcalfe and we are averaging 2 ½ gallons a head which is a thing we've never done before.

The children are interesting at this moment. They are not good-looking, and they are rough and unmannerly and make lamentable jokes and then roll with laughter and are rather unmanageable and tiresome. They use a lot of slang. Thomas says "Blow me" about everything. They both use Warwickshire dialect as an endearment. If they are talking to the cats or dogs (we have a new terrier pup called Bubbles and a drove of kittens from three different cats) they always talk in strong Warwickshire. They are learning to ride and Rose (just 5) will soon be good. She and Sheila (the student) and I rode all round the farm this morning with Rose on the leading rein. She can't rise to the trot yet but she manages the pony well and has no fear at all.

The news is not so good. I wonder if we are going to make a balls of it in Tunisia?

9 December, 1942

Two very busy days. We went (Pat and me) to a sale near Bicester in the morning (of bullocks). We only managed to buy 7 but ran into a dealer who said he had 10 so we went to see them and bought them. Then there is a sale of pedigree Ayrshires in the next village, but Pat can't go so I've got to bid for myself (if at all as prices will probably go above my limit while I'm trying to catch the auctioneer's eye). So we tore on from the dealers so that Pat could see the cows and mark which I was to bid for.

Then today I first of all received Mr Slater who we sell our milk to. It was a wonderful bit of luck his choosing today because we have constant trouble about churns. When he arrived I said, "Come here — I want to show you something". And I took him into the dairy and showed him gallons of milk standing in pails. He said, "What's the matter with it?" I said, "Only one thing. We haven't got a churn to put it in". That took the wind out of his sails, particularly as he had come over to get me to sign the new contract. I refused to sign it. I said I'd sign in a week's time if there was some real improvement in the meantime. By lunch time ten brand new churns arrived. In two years I've never seen a new churn before and I had no idea what they looked like.

10 December, 1942

I went up to 100 guineas for a pedigree cow and up to 85 for a non-pedigree and I bid for a lot of others but I bought nothing. Rather disheartening. Whenever you see a cow you would like to own you know she will fetch £300 at least. Hannah was there. She bought two cows, but she has now got to the stage where she thinks £150 is cheap. But it will pay her because, being Mrs Hudson, everyone will rush to buy when she starts selling and she is collecting a very very good herd. But if I ever succeed in getting a reasonably good herd I shall have done something. But the question is, will I? I hope all this cow talk doesn't bore you. It is the burning question with me at the moment and I haven't any other news to relieve it with.

Hannah Hudson was wife of the Minister of Agriculture.

Here is a specimen of your children's conversation. T. "Mummy, can I have honey on my cake?" M. "No." (I then apparently lapsed into a dream.) R. "Why don't you have honey on your cake, Thomas?" T. "Mummy said I couldn't". R. "Well, why don't you just take it?" T. "Cos <u>Mummy said I couldn't</u>." R. "Well, what can she do to you? She can't kill you, can she?"

I had a close friend at this time, the cowman's daughter, who was aged about 11 or possibly more. She probably only played with me because there was no one else. She taught me wonderful phrases, like 'Gotchyer eye full?' if someone looked at you on the bus. (I never actually went on the bus). She probably taught me to say 'She can't kill you can she?' I was an eager pupil.

12: 1942-3

Scarlet fever and impetigo

12 December, 1942

Stapes rang up at lunchtime and suggested they came over. It's the first time he's been here since 1941. He said a) I am a very good ley farmer and b) he thought they ought to hold one of their neighbours' days at Gypsy Hall, and c) that all my leys except one were excellent. The wheat is also beginning to look extremely well so the whole thing was quite fun. The only pity is that I have no cows to graze the leys. I <u>do</u> wish I could buy some cows. Metcalfe is doing so well with the present ones and all the yields are going up and up. If only I had more cows I should really be making some money.

How awful the Darlan thing is! The Statesman has some trenchant things to say. "The attempt to co-operate with Darlan is as morally pleasant and looks like being as militarily satisfactory as Munich". I think the whole thing is shocking and disgusting.

17 December, 1942

I met a group of Free French pilots the other night. They are very sad people, homeless, familyless, with no very great pride in their small group and no very great faith in their leader, yet glad they aren't Vichy. They get little love from us or the Americans, and now that we're officially approving of the arch-traitor Darlan they feel pretty shattered. They struck me as empty, lonely and sad.

 20 December, 1942

A bad week. I got to London on Wednesday. On Friday a message came to say that the children were ill and I ought to go home. I dashed straight back to the flat to find a wire from Nora saying the children had got measles or scarlet fever. I caught the first train and got home at 7 to find that it was Rose not Thomas and that the doctor said he would wait till the next day to give a final diagnosis. I rang him up and he said it was 6 to 4 on scarlet fever. Dr McWhinney came the next morning and confirmed scarlet fever. He thought, too, that she ought to go to the fever hospital. He said I could be forced to send her unless she could be adequately isolated.

It was particularly important that someone with scarlet fever should be kept in isolation because of the milking cows. Pre-antibiotic scarlet fever was an often fatal disease. Charles Darwin lost two of his children to scarlet fever.

I knew all the time that there wasn't a hope because that couldn't be done here for all sorts of reasons. Rose (aged just 5) herself was really wonderful and tremendously endearing. During the time I had been away she was apparently really ill and they say she never once cried or made a murmur. Once when Thomas went to see her she told him to go away. Yesterday I went into her room and said, "Now, look here, Rosebuddy, you're going to go to a sort of school. It's not really a school and you won't do lessons but there will be lots of other little girls and boys and you'll have a lot of fun. And anyway it will be good practice for school and you'll be able to tell Thomas all about it."

She didn't say anything and she looked quite inscrutable. She looked as tho' she was suspending judgment but prepared to wait and see. She never did say anything about it but when the nurse came she went off with her in the ambulance without a murmur. I called yesterday afternoon and telephoned this morning and both times they said she was perfectly happy and playing with the other children. I must say I am glad we have brought them up to be self-reliant. She takes this sort of thing in her stride and of course that takes 3/4 of the horror out of it.

I was, as I usually am in a real crisis, quite alright and actually I didn't really worry. One could hardly make a fuss with Rose herself behaving with such admirable composure. She's a tough one and I was proud of her. The shortest period for the disease is 28 days and Dr McWhinney says it might go on for two months.

21 December, 1942

Since I wrote, Thomas has turned out to have impetigo. I must say! Three weeks of the village school and scarlet fever and impetigo! I went to see Rose today. You stand in a garden and look and shout thro' a closed window. When I first looked she was sitting up in bed and fairly tucking into her tea. Then they wheeled the bed over to the window. Her face lit up when she saw me. She looked perfectly well except that her face was covered with impetigo. She was very slummy, her hair all over her face and dirty pyjamas.

At one moment the nurse brought her tea over, and in the cup was very weak tea. Rose pointed to it and in a voice of complete triumph said, "We 'ave tea 'ere". I said I'd tell Thomas. I think she really is absolutely happy. She is a great little girl and I think you will be really fond of her.

23 December, 1942

I do feel we have been separated too long — you say this too, and ask about changes. I think I have changed. When I dress myself up and do my hair and face, I think I look about the same. Anyway I always get a few compliments when I go to London. But on ordinary days I can look very old, thin and lined. Of course my clothes, a very filthy battle dress or some faded dungarees, don't help. Then my habits have changed quite a bit. I often think how amused you would be if you could see how dirty I often am.

You see, if you get up at 6 in the dark and in a hurry and the water is cold, there isn't anyone living who would wash after about the first three mornings. And I just don't. I always have a bath at night if the water is alright and it usually is but occasionally a ball-cock on some distant trough goes wrong and the water runs out all day and there is no water in the house at night. I have been known to go without a real wash for three or four days. I occasionally smell — either of sweat or sour milk — but not for too long.

Now would you believe any of that? As to whether I have changed in character I simply don't know. It will be interesting to see what you think. But surely I must have. I have done so much and suffered a lot, both on your account and in all the sordid ways of coping with Carling etc. Thank God that last is over. Anyway, I'd like a nice holiday. I'd like you to be there and I'd like the sea and the sun, Runton would do, *(the holiday house which Jack and his sisters had inherited from his mother)* and I'd like a lot of cocktails and lobsters and nothing at all to do. That's a long way off, I fear. I do resent getting older during the war. I wonder whether I shall be able to face having any more children. It's not the having them. It's the nappies and the nannies and the nurses and the scarlet fevers.

25 December, 1942

I am whooping with joy about Admiral Darlan. I think it is the best news for ages because, whatever is right and whatever is wrong, I'm sure he is better dead. I do hope a Frenchman did it.

27 December, 1942

I went to see Rose this afternoon and it was a good thing I did as apparently she was expecting me. There were a lot of people all shouting thro' the window and I couldn't find the nurse. But I could see her (Rose) thro' a crack. She was fidgeting about and presently she got firmly up and sat on the end of the bed where she could see the window better. When she was pushed over she looked well and the impetigo was much better. She said she had a big bit of chocolate and some "gooms" for Christmas and she ate them all in one day and she had a weelbarrer from Daddy. She was still quite happy and she knows the form. She said she had to stay in bed for another week and then she would get up in a blanket. She said, "We have two baths a week."

I remember the hospital and the wheelbarrow for Christmas. I remember being by the window and seeing my mother and brother but not being able to think of anything to say to them. When an awkward silence fell into the rather artificial conversation I remember rather wishing they would go away. How shocking is that?

I am disappointed that, tho' it was a Frenchman who shot Darlan it was the wrong kind of Frenchman.

30 December, 1942

I am worried about the children. I can't take their catching all these awful illnesses but also they are completely uneducated. But as day schools and governesses are out the only possible alternative is boarding school. Do you feel it is out of all possibility? I think a lot of parents have sent very young children owing to the insuperable difficulties created by the war. Nanny is very keen I should send them. Thomas will have to go I think next autumn for the sake of education, and I think when he goes Rose might just as well go too as she would be lonely here.

I of course am against it myself. But I am also against scarlet fever and impetigo and a total lack of education and there doesn't seem to be any middle course. I wish you would think about it and let me know what you think.

They have a wonderful life here in many ways but in others not so good. I am always busy and often tired and cross. So that, tho' they have plenty of fun, they also have a very rough and ready life and their accents and general outlook on life are really rather too terrible. I wish I sometimes had days with nothing to do and more time for the children.

 23 December, 1942

What is such fun for me is, that no-one's <u>wife</u> has done anything at all. Coney, Barbara, all my colleagues' wives, they're just wives doing a bit of war-work. But you've done two very remarkable things, farming on your own successfully, and writing and speaking about it in such a way that you've become "an interesting person", someone whom strangers are interested to look at and perhaps speak to, to see what she's like and so on.

 3 January, 1943

Whether as a result of a cable saying "Together this year", I don't know, but I am feeling rather better. I feel for the first time for years that it is possible that I will one day see you again. I never actually doubted this but it always seemed something that was so far away in the future as to be unimaginable. Now I feel it is somewhere near, and I think about it quite a lot. I hope the feeling isn't too spurious.

Jack's first home leave was in April 1944, having left England in November 1940.

Thomas is endlessly spinning out a slight temperature, and Rose, tho' apparently getting on well, no longer looks well. Apparently she did cry a lot after I left last Thursday and it is difficult to know whether to go and see her or not. I think it upsets her if one does, but she is old enough to know about the visiting days and to expect one. O dear, I wish it was over.

Evening

This house gives me real pleasure. I think one of the reasons I am feeling good is that, in pursuit of my rest cure, I have been sitting for the last few days in the larger of my two sitting-rooms, the first one with the telephone in it. The other is furnished as an office. This room is really beautiful, I think the most beautiful we have ever had. Tho' it may not strike you so at first sight as it owes some of its beauty to a sort of pleasant graciousness which grows on you. It makes me happy.

I thought I'd tell you as I have spent money on this house, which is so to speak down the drain because a) we shan't live here forever, and b) I doubt if it really adds anything to the commercial value of the farm. But if one buys happiness with money, it is probably worth spending it, don't you think? When you come back you must do something about the garden.

12 January, 1943

Pat is over here today. He is down the fields with Highman. He really is good and useful. I find that, after a week, too many things have accumulated which are in a mess and which I don't know how to deal with. Then he comes over and spends a day straightening them out and everything goes on again for a week. I could manage without him, but I shouldn't manage well.

Anni and I sat up all night talking about the children and decided they ought to go to a boarding school but come home at weekends. Nora is developing more and more strongly that desire to get them down which so many grown-ups have in their attitude to children. It doesn't matter what they do, it's wrong for her. Then Thomas is so eager to make aeroplanes etc and I'm no good at it. He wants more opportunity that he is getting here. So I am going to see Mr Perkins, the Director of Education we went to see together, and, if I can find the right school, I shall send them. Nanny writes asking if Rose could go to her in Brighton when she is better. I have a damn good mind to send her. It is just that they do still get raids. But after all Nanny is still there after 3 ½ years and the air is so good and she ought to go somewhere. What do you think?

20 January, 1943
Goodness only knows when I last wrote to you. There are several reasons. First of all I had a fit of depression. And if I am depressed enough I get in a mood where I can't do anything. I don't eat at night or write letters or do anything. That lasted about two days I think. Then since then I have been really hard worked again. We were threshing. Most of the jobs are hard, pitching and moving bales of straw and making a rick and weighing and moving the sacks etc., hard beastly jobs which tear the guts out of you.

Building a rick

Then there are two supposedly fairly skilled jobs, cutting the bands off the sheaves and chucking them onto the opening of the drum (the skill here is simply a question of intelligent timing), and the actual feeding of the drum, which is thinning the sheaves out a little and pushing them into the drum.

These two jobs are fairly hard in the sense that you can never take a rest, as you can on the other jobs, but they are infinitely less heavy and slightly more amusing. Carling always had two men doing this, and when he worked himself he fed the drum. All the girls sweated round on the rick. I got on to the fact that the cutting of the bands was probably dead easy and directly Carling went I put a girl on to it.

Conkers, the deaf and dumb, has always done it and does it fearfully badly in fits and starts, but it is his only claim to fame so he sulks and flies into a passion if anyone else does it. The other day I had the idea that I'd do it myself, so when Pat came over I made him come up and teach me how.

As usual it turned out there was practically no skill in it at all, but I don't do it as well as a good man — because it does need slightly stronger wrists. But I do it better than Conk. So I did it triumphantly all day, feeling very much like the boss. And with three girls on the box it releases two men for the tough jobs. So that was quite fun but hard work.

 19 January, 1943

Just heard the early morning news — colossal! Relief of Leningrad, massacre at Stalingrad, 40 miles advance against Rommel, 600 bombers over Berlin. I'm full of optimism.

 26 January, 1943

I got no letters for three weeks and then thirty airgraphs.

Next, Rose is home. She is in bed as she still has kidney trouble. When she first got here she was very quiet and flat and I thought she was really rather ill. Jan, however, maintained she was playing the heavy invalid. She hardly spoke all day. That night when she and Thomas were in bed, we stood outside the door and listened while, in a completely different tone of voice, she gave T. the lowdown on the hospital. She was exactly like an old village woman. She said things like "She was a greedy pig. She took our sweets and apples and hid them under her bedclothes. And after all, apples aren't rationed." I couldn't take it, I giggled too much, but Jan listened for hours. She is full of technical expressions. Jan sent her a paper doll and asked if she had brought it home. "Of course not. You can't stove paper." Stove = sterile. Then I asked if she liked Dr Fife. " 'e was alright, 'e was the one that signed me off." "What do you mean?" "You know, signed me chart."

But the children aren't quite right. They are being neglected. Thomas can't read and Rose is too common. It's not only her accent, it's her whole attitude to life and the sort of things she says. You see, I'm too busy. I can't help it. Having started on this, I have to do it properly and it doesn't leave enough time for the children. I think they will have to go to boarding school if only for a short time, to get them started. Thomas badly needs more opportunity.

29 January, 1943

I find life very hard. I'm not referring particularly to the last few days which were physically hard in a way no one could stick for very long, but to life on the farm generally. There are so many difficulties and worries. Everyone has to be driven or cajoled. Then I worry about the children. And I never have any fun. I don't envy you your Christmas parties, but look how often you get drunk! Now I never get drunk; you can't get anything to get drunk on and I should love to get really drunk just now and then.

I'm not telling you all this just to complain, but when you come home you may find a lot to criticise or feel reproachful about. I want you to know that I find life hard, dreary and at the same time difficult, so that you will be forgiving and not too critical. There are a lot of things on the farm I really love. Tho' I don't think one could truthfully say I bit off more than I could chew, I find the chewing fairly tough. And I sometimes think you think too much of what I have done or do and begin to picture me as a much more successful and brilliant person than I really am. I've been meaning to tell you for some time not to be impressed by things like broadcasts.

Price the cowman with a young bull. It is manipulated and controlled by a ring through the nose

I have lost my watch you gave me. I was carrying a forkful of silage down at Broadlow when a bloody great bullock charged playfully at me in his attempt to get at the silage and his horn grazed right down my arm and wrist. I didn't realise it at the time, but he must have skimmed off my watch, and, of course, when I did find out and go back to look, the straw was all trampled and trodden.

This is an example of Frankie's natural courage, in spite of her nervous temperament. Most people are nervous of bullocks – young male cattle usually kept for fattening for meat – as they are not seriously aggressive, but pushy and over curious. She wasn't frightened at all. Nor was she frightened of the large aggressive pigs, or the gentle but huge carthorses. One of the tales of our childhood was how, when a bull got loose inside its pen and attacked the cowman, none of the men watching dared enter but Frankie went straight in and secured the bull and the cowman's safety.

1 February, 1943

Pat came over with two old farmer birds to go shooting, and Thomas insisted on going with them with his bow and arrow. He got soaked to the skin and trudged right round the farm on the heaviest day that I have known since I have been here, but he never drew breath once and enjoyed himself no end. I'm sure he wouldn't be such a cissy if only he had a man in his life. He so seldom gets an example of how men behave and he is tough enough if he is interested.

Frankie was starting to find Thomas difficult. Not because he was badly behaved, but because he was nervous and temperamental, often given to tears. Their relationship suffered because of this, and he probably felt the lack of a father's presence more than I did.

2 February, 1943

I have temporarily started to try to teach Thomas myself. It is only a question of putting his lessons into the category of things which have <u>got</u> to be done during the day.

The Russian news continues to be almost incredible and even I have started to be moved by it.

February 2, 1943 – Germans surrender at Stalingrad in the first big defeat of Hitler's armies.

This means quite a lot, because I long ago gave up taking any interest in the progress of the war. At some point which I don't remember the whole thing became for me simply a period of time to be got through and what happened during that time relatively unimportant. I think it is the German propaganda which has got me this time. It is so extraordinary to hear Goebbels and Goring talking like we did in 1940.

8 February, 1943

I managed Thomas's lesson alright and I think I shall in fact manage it most days, as I am now determined he shall learn to read and so I am quite keen on teaching him.

The hard thing on this farm is this. Highman, who is almost without exception the nicest man I have ever met, has absolutely no drive at all. Nor can he manage men. Therefore I have not only to supply the drive but also to be constantly on the alert to circumvent Highman circumventing me out of sheer good nature. For instance, Metcalfe is a lazy bugger and always trying to get other people do his jobs. At one time he had the whole farm staff dancing round twenty miserable cows on at least two days a week. Then I put my foot down and said no member of the farm staff was to do anything for him without my permission.

Nevertheless, I can't stop Highman. He has Nanny's quality of always doing himself anything he thinks needs doing. But it is no good in a foreman. I will go out in the afternoon leaving Highman to mend a drill I want to use the next day. When I get back I'll find he hasn't touched the drill because Metcalfe's calves were so badly in need of litter. Then my whole week's programme is buggered up. Then Oakley and the land girls all take life too easily because he lets them.

Lately I have had to start working in the fields with them as the only means of getting anything like the right amount of work out of them. It makes life very much harder than it ought to be, but on the other hand Highman has so many wonderful qualities and is so loyal and conscientious and hard working that one has to forgive him. Cyril Wheeldon, too, is a wonderful boy.

10 February, 1943

I had a letter from Daddy this morning. I sent him my book by hand of Mary Grigg. He says "Mary Grigg brought me your book. When I had finished reading it I was convinced that your mother had one night gone for a walk with a man of letters. You appear to be on terms of assurance with words I never heard of, Mr Webster helped me very much. Your talk on the radio pleased a great many people. You even convinced one lady that the English were not all superior. She was a friend of Willie Wiseman. Of course Elsa Maxwell talks about it and in the course of the next few weeks she will be telling them stories of how she found you starving, realized your gifts, had you educated and introduced to Jack. But your book was excellent, charmingly written and very sympathetic. I enjoyed it very much and I congratulate you."

I have written you all this because I thought it might amuse you. But for goodness sake don't take it too seriously. By the time the few trite remarks I made on the broadcast had been cut for record there was nothing that could seriously have impressed anyone. The whole thing is because a) I am Daddy's daughter and b) Elsa Maxwell found this out by a smart bit of detective work and therefore somehow takes credit.

14 February, 1943

I am surprised how good a man Compton Mackenzie is. I have been reading some of his books. They are, I think, quite important books. All that part about Ireland and our behaviour, and the scene in Greece during a Turkish invasion.

It convinces me more than anything has done that it is no use saying "It can't happen here" about anything. Apparently, from no more evil characteristic than the desire not to see or believe anything unpleasant (which we know to be a real characteristic), the whole English race allowed their statesmen, from no more devilish motive than the ordinary desire to preserve the Coalition Government, to behave with a violence and inhumanity in Ireland (and to condone the same violence in Greece), which can only be compared with some of the later demonstrations of the Nazis. But for Munich one might not be inclined to believe Mackenzie, but having seen the Tories willing to throw half Europe to the flames in order to preserve the Tory party, it isn't difficult to believe that an earlier group of statesmen were prepared to see half Ireland and half Greece massacred to save the coalition Government.

In what a very unattractive way the history of statesmen repeats itself. However, it gives me an explanation of the behaviour of the German race which I have for long been looking for. As far as I can see the only difference between the Germans and the English is this. The Germans like regimentation. So if you want to be bestial do it in uniform. The English like peace. So if you want to be bestial make sure first that they have nice gardens to go to sleep in. And I wonder if, before God, it is a lesser crime to sleep than to march. It makes me very depressed and defeatist about the future.

Darling, I hope that you are all that I think you are. Because only so can life ever really get right again after the misery of these years. However, I'm sure that you are so it will be all right.

Thomas is a funny one. He is still such a cissy in many ways, but in others so very manly. Yesterday he decided to go shooting by himself. So he took his bow and arrow and, as far as I could make out, walked pretty well right round the farm. On his way home a cockerel chased him and cockerels can be quite nasty. But he turned round and beat it with his arrow. Every morning he comes into my room to brush his hair with two brushes I gave him. I wish he could read, and I wish you could see him. I wonder if we shall ever have any more children?

20 February, 1943

Today is our anniversary. Perhaps next year we shall be together.

I have found a school for Thomas and I think a good one. It's at Henley in Arden and he can go as a day boy, if we can get him there. He starts on Monday and Rose is going to Nanny for six weeks on Friday, so peace will reign for a bit.

22 February, 1943

Thomas is a funny little boy. Yesterday we went for a walk round the farm and I told him the right way to trap rats was to find out where they went to drink and set the traps there. Later we saw the print of a rat by a puddle by a rick. T. immediately made up his mind to become a rat-catcher. For a solid hour he talked of nothing else. I said he could have some traps I bought for the house, which are the ordinary kind you set with cheese, and not the proper kind, but I thought would do. So after lunch he set off.

So about 2.30 he came into me with his eyes bunged up with weeping and his nose running etc. I said, "Poor little boy, did it catch your fingers?" "No", he said, "But I can't get it down to the rick." I said alright, I'd go with him, and we would set it when we got there. He stopped crying immediately and reverted to his former eagerness. But the odd thing is that he knows quite well that the chances of his catching a rat are very low but he doesn't mind that a bit. He says "I'll tell you what. I'll go and look tomorrow and if there's nothing there I'll leave it one more night and if there's nothing there I'll know it's no good." Yet he is so excited about it that, although today is his first day for going to school, his first words this morning were "Mummy, do you think there'll be a rat?"

Later. Thomas came back from school and in answer to "Did you like it" said, "Yes, all except one part" "Which part was that?" "Well, at eleven we have a cup of milk, and a

217

bun with currants in it." "Well, what didn't you like about that?" "Well, all the boys came scattering round me." "What do you mean?" "Well, they all said what's your name and where do you live and a lot of silly questions." All this delivered in a completely matter of fact tone and apparently he had answered all the questions but just didn't like it much.

23 February, 1943

The most difficult situation has arisen. I sent Rose for convalescence to Brighton last week because she was ready to go and Nanny was ready to have her, and my letter to you might have taken six weeks to arrive. This morning I got your cable. My first reaction was to bring her straight back. Of course people here have grown into a careless point of view. Peggy, for instance, has taken her children to London for six weeks. I shall now leave her about three weeks instead of six and then fetch her back as I shall now fuss all the time she is away.

*Old Nan lived in Brighton in a house that my grandmother had provided for her when she retired. We spent many happy holidays there as children. The term **Brighton Blitz** refers to German air raids on the British town of Brighton during World War II. The beaches were closed at 5.00pm on 2 July 1940 and were mined and guarded with barbed wire. Both the Palace Pier and West Pier had sections of their decking removed to prevent their use as landing stages in a possible enemy invasion. The town was declared no longer to be a "safe area" and 30,000 people were evacuated. Brighton was attacked from the air in 56 recorded bombings between July 1940 and February 1944.*

Thomas ready for school

Thomas is sweet about his school which he loves. This morning he told me there was one boy who was best at reading and that he (Thomas) was second best. I asked who said so and he replied "the boy". However it quite convinced Thomas. He looks terribly sweet in his cap. I must take a photograph for you.

I'm tired and have got a roaring cold and two of my best heifers have had bull calves and Highman took three days to do one day's threshing so I must go to bed.

12 March, 1943

I've been tractoring. I must tell you what I was doing because it is highly significant. I was harrowing some winter oats, which is a normal thing to do in the spring (tho' not often as early as this; we are having a wonderful spell of weather, which may break to-night, which would be a disaster) but in this case was also to prepare a seed bed for grass seeds which Highman was broadcasting behind me. Now the significant part is we were doing it on that field with a bank where I think some bullocks were when you first saw the farm, and which was the first turf we ploughed up when we came here. So for the first time the circle is completed and after three white crops the field will go back to grass.

Thomas is mad with excitement about a broody hen and some duck eggs which he has bought off me for the handsome sum of 5/- to be paid when he has sold the ducklings. A good deal for him if they hatch.

19 March, 1943

Pat was here this morning and I said to him "You know, I think, after about two more seasons with you, I'll be quite a good farmer." He said, "I think you'll be a very good farmer. I think you are a good farmer now." I said, "Do you really?" He said, "Yes. I was talking about you yesterday and I said, "It's a curious thing. She knows exactly what to do. She only lacks confidence to do it without getting her opinion backed." This was terrific praise from Pat who is north country and blunt and also thinks I'm too conceited already and so never gives me a good word. Rather exciting, isn't it?

26 March, 1943

I've had rather a beautiful day, tho' as I am exhausted and both my eyes are entirely enclosed with dust, it wouldn't be many people's idea of pleasure. I've been feeding the drum for two solid days and halfway thro' the first I got the hang of it. The man feeding the drum is the most important because he sets the pace for those behind, feeding him, and for those in front of him dealing with straw and sacks. It has always been done here by Oakley the deaf and dumb, who is quite incredibly bad and our threshing standards are about half as good as they ought to be. Since Carling left I have tried every possible combination to get the drum better fed, but never got it any faster and always produced endless rows with Oakley. Then I suddenly realised that, if you made practically no effort but let the suction do the work and only kept it going smoothly, so the drum didn't get bunged and the suction ceased to work, you went at double the pace.

I can now truthfully say that, tho' I'm not near the class of those who do it well, I could give every man on this farm a ten sack start and beat him. So I am immoderately proud of myself. Also it is the vantage point for giving black looks to people who are not working hard and therefore the right place for the boss.

Of course I am a fearful prefect by nature, and I remind myself of when I was at school. Sheila is a tremendously hard worker, and I am very apt to keep changing her to any place which is holding us up, thereby speeding it up and administering an indirect reproof to whoever she changes with. Whenever I do it, I think of myself when, as an intolerant, pompous and humourless captain of games, I used to say to whoever was my Sheila in a furious voice, "Change with so and so and see if you can put some guts into the left wing". It's very bad for my character and gives me too much sense of leadership and power of the wrong, black-look kind.

27 March, 1943

Nora is very often vile to Thomas in the sort of viciously sadistic way grownups so often get away with. Thomas hates porridge, and so Nora, if she were allowed to, would stuff it down his throat every day. But as we have plenty of cereals which are just as good for him I won't allow it. This morning T. said, "Am I going to have cereals?" "No," said Nora in a firm voice, "Porridge this morning." T. immediately made face like crying which is, of course, naughty of him.

Thomas and Rose sitting at the dining room table

"Why?" I asked, in an even firmer voice, "Are we out of cereals?" "No," said Nora, "it was only a joke. But he can't take a joke. Look at him." I said that if it was a joke it was a poor one and had quite escaped me as well as Thomas. Later, Sheila came in and Nora was rude to her so, with that, I bawled her out flat. So now we shall have sweet temper for a bit.

But this business with Thomas makes me furious. It is not absolutely constant but is very frequent, and is one of the reasons I find it necessary to send him to board at school during the week next term. She doesn't do it with Rose, and this is supposed to be because Rose is her favourite. The real reason is that Rose is much less vulnerable and therefore less sport. However, Nora gets as good as she gives from me and has been snivelling all day so perhaps that will teach her to leave him alone for a bit.

He went down to the threshing to help catch the rats at the bottom of the rick. I wasn't there but they said, in spite of being very frightened, he stood his ground and walloped the rats when they appeared. He said to me, "Mummy,

Bubbles (the pup) has been very brave. She chased a rat. I think you ought to share her with me, as I taught her to catch mice." He always pronounces "very" as "vurry". Now I am listening to Yehudi Menuhin's concert.

30 March, 1943

I had a letter explaining how you felt about Rose which I understand and agree with. *(This was anxiety about air raids on Brighton, where nanny lived)*. I don't think I would have done it if Nanny herself hadn't suggested it. Anni thought you probably didn't feel strongly about it so I sent the wire, since when I didn't have a moment's peace and spent the whole time composing what I was going to say to you if Rose was killed. So I sent for her and I'm glad I did. As Mrs Saunders *(neighbour in Kent)* then wrote and invited them, it all solved itself quite easily and they went to Shipbourne.

1 April, 1943

Two days threshing in a very high wind has reduced me to a pulp. I no longer think it's any fun at all to feed the drum. Actually, threshing is hell. All country women know they must treat their men carefully when they come in after a day's threshing, so you can imagine what it does to us. With a wind it is particularly vile and so dirty. I had to wear goggles to protect my eyes and where my clothes ended there is a high water mark of absolute black. After the war I'm going to be a lady farmer and ride round on a cob saying "How's it going, Highman?"

The women of England aren't starred enough, at least only as a force like the ATS. One hears so much about the Russian women but I bet they don't work any harder than most of the girls on this farm or in a factory. Only, English girls do it without a philosophy and only if they are driven and with an awful lot of chatter and giggling so nobody notices much.

7 April, 1943

You are in Picture Post this week. Leonora told me on the telephone but I haven't seen it yet.

See photographs of Jack with Russians, printed on 13 November, 1942

Then I got a letter from Mrs Saunders saying Rose had seen it and had jumped up and down saying "That's my Daddy, that's my Daddy." She knows quite well what you look like from constant practice in spotting you in photographs. She's with Leonora for a day or two till they join Peter at Thetford. Leonora put her on the telephone and, heavily prompted by Leonora, she said, "I'm going to stay up till midnight tonight, and what are you going to do about that?"

13: 1943

Social Life and the Italian Campaign

21 April, 1943

This farm is sensational — everyone thinks so. But the hedges aren't laid and it is foully and desolately untidy. The grass is so terrific now. Too terrific. I simply don't know how to manage it. But I'm dogged with bad luck with the cows. We now have a terrific go of Staphyloccus mastitis which is dreadfully difficult to get rid of and absolutely wrecks the milk yield. So God only knows when we are going to make any money. I mind a lot about money as it is the ultimate test of my success or failure, but probably you wouldn't mind quite so much, if the farm is slap up.

I saw Tortor who is what I believe is technically known as "browned off" (or is that out of date already?).The poor old girl has been in the bloody ATS for 5 years and she should be given a high policy job at the War Office. But owing a) to jealousy and b) her inability to control her sense of humour and c) that she is as unorthodox as you are, (which can always be highly dangerous) she has been passed over, graded badly on a course for senior officers and told to proceed to Southend. When I got there, she was in the last stages of despair. She said, "I've been saying all day please God make me humble. He hasn't yet but I expect He will." It was too pathetic. She is quite extraordinarily gallant because she has been very ill and could get invalided out any day she wanted to, but she conceived it her duty to stay. Southend with the ATS! Think of it! She sent you very much love, and so do I.

Victoria Gilmour (TorTor)

10 May, 1943

Thomas went to boarding school on Tuesday, and came back for his first weekend on Saturday. When he got off the bus he looked completely changed. He was wearing a tie (of which he was inordinately proud), and his cap and mackintosh, which may account for most of it. But his face seemed thinner and much more grown up. Everyone noticed this. I asked him if it was fun, and he said, in a completely grown up way "I don't hate it but I don't like it."

Then at lunch I asked him if he had had his honey. He said, "Only once, and I haven't had any sweets at all." And then he nearly cried, but he didn't, he controlled it. It was the controlling that got me.

He maintained this completely reasonable attitude throughout the whole weekend until he went to bed last night when he returned to being a baby and boo-oooed like mad and said, "I don't want to go to school, I hate it, I hate it." I promised him that if he was good and went to school without any fuss I'd give him a breeding pig and then he could pay me for the feeding stuffs after he had sold the litter and start to save to buy a heifer. He went to sleep then and this morning he was perfectly collected and talked a lot about his pig and went off without a murmur, except he said with a grin "I hope we miss the bus." I think the truth is he really likes it alright and when he has had time to settle down he'll love it.

He wears this awful tie and is called Donaldson and my dear he is a completely grown up school boy and you haven't seen him since he was a baby. However my lovely fat one returns today with Nanny and that will create a little warmth and happiness. She has maintained a perfectly firm attitude the whole time she has been there, Mrs Saunders says. She has in fact been very happy but has never once admitted it, and she said to Winifred "Mummy had no right to send me here after I got back from Brighton."

Later: Rose arrived, very tall and looking very well, and with a much improved speaking voice. She is immensely affectionate and overjoyed to see us. She had brought us all presents and for herself some bath salts and half a bottle of very nasty scent. She has now scented up the bathroom till it smells like an old brothel. She refers to Webb as "my Webb" and she tells me the garden at the Wood House is very nice indeed.

PS Nanny says Rose stood up in the railway carriage and with the rather extreme gestures both our children use, then addressed her as follows:-

"The Germans will be beaten in December. The Japs will still go on but that won't matter to us and my Daddy will come home." Nanny says one RAF officer laughed so much he nearly fell out of his seat.

Bell box in the kitchen of The Wood House

I have some memories of this trip, and it was my only visit to the Wood House at a conscious age (5) until I saw it again in 2015. So, a gap of over 70 years during which time it had in my mind the status of a mythical, magical place often referred to with love by my parents. All I really remembered from the visit was that the lavatories were dirty inside as they so often are in empty houses, having been used by some passerby and not cleaned. I was astonished when I saw it for real last year, and particularly amazed by the impression of wealth it gave me about the pre-war life of my parents.

During and after the war we always lived in small farmhouses without things like dining rooms. We were always pressed for cash, while this seemed palatial. In the kitchen there was a box with a list of bells to rooms, with day nursery, night nursery, various bedrooms and finally, Mrs D's bedroom. That was my parents' bedroom, still on the list 80 years after the house was built. It drove home the understanding of the complete change in life-style that the war and Frankie's decision to farm had made for them.

8 May, 1943
Mary Dunn has been here and I said to her something about not wanting to see anyone. She said she thought it was from lack of confidence. She said, "I saw all sorts of people I knew in London. In the old days I would have bounced up to them and slapped them on the back even tho' I didn't know them well. But I just turned my head and pretended not to see them." Now if that is what it does to Mary please imagine what it does to me. The isolated life plays hell with your nerves, imagination and character.

21 May, 1943
Highman has got mumps, so I am left with only imbeciles, girls and a boy of 18.

Meg

229

23 May, 1943

I've got a trained sheepdog, a bitch. I wonder if you can have any idea what a pleasure this could be. I have been trying to get one for seven months (it's ridiculous not to have one with all this stock), but they are terribly difficult to come by. This one — Meg — has saved me about ten miles walking in the two days she's been here.

Herding sheep with Meg, the sheepdog

Normally, when we move the sheep or round them up it takes me and at least two others swotting round every corner of the field and yelling strange war cries and then running like hell to head off lots that have doubled back etc. Now I go by myself and stand by the gate and Meg does the rest.

Apart from the work she does there is a great pleasure in it. As a rule I get so much of the grind of farming and so little of these sort of things which are the pleasures. She is a very pretty bitch and one's affection for a working dog is always of a quite different order from that for ordinary dogs.

25 May, 1943

I met Bill Whitney who had lately seen Daddy in New York. He said he was in great form but he thought he was broke. "I dined with him twice and both times the fact that I paid

was gratefully received. Keep a cottage for him on your estate. That's how he'll end." I can't tell you what this does for me. I said, "I'd rather he had died" and then had to spend the rest of the evening explaining it away. He has always been the one who paid, but Bill said he didn't seem to mind and was happy
so I may be wrong.

I'm absolutely dotty about Meg. I must send you a photograph of the dogs and cats at GH. There are seldom less than ten cats of various ages and four dogs round the kitchen door.

Meg and Frankie

I'm getting abnormally lazy. I'm always complaining about the amount of work, but the truth is that for five or six weks I haven't done anything except mess around. I think I have to some extent worked myself out. Priestley once said that women liked to work very hard in short spasms and it should be arranged that they could. I think he's right. Personally I can't sustain the effort. Another reason is, this farm is impossible on present labour. One knows that whatever one does it will beat you in the end so one gives up the effort.

17 June, 1943

Mary brought a very odd American and we had a terrific party. He knows everything in the world, including what's wrong with England and the English. Rather intelligent in some ways, and distinctly amusing. I think he is a case of arrested development, as he does and says exactly what he feels, like a child. One night we decided to have a party, so we put the cob in the float and went to Aston Cantlow, the next village, with a very good pub. We didn't do much when we got there except drink enough to be very gay and bring home enough whisky to make three eggnogs.

On our way home we overtook Donne, who is an old man and rather a character who works on the farm. He was nicely drunk and we gave him a lift. He looked ruminatively at the cob and said, "It's a good thing she isn't a kicker." I asked why, and he said, "You've got the traces underneath the breeching." I said, "It's all right, Donne. We shouldn't know even if we were sober", which at the time seemed a spirited and dignified answer. Then when we got to the hill near GH Donne said we'd better walk. I said, "There are two ways of getting up a hill. One is to walk and the other is to gallop. I'm going to gallop." So we galloped up the hill and Donne took off his cap and waved it in the air yelling, "That's the way, Madam, that's the way, Madam."

Mary laughed so much she fell off the seat which is a plank from underneath us. I rose to my feet and continued to gallop cursing Mary for not being able to hold her drink. At which she giggled all the more. And that's how we arrived at GH.

Thomas in our float, or trap

So my reputation is either enhanced as a good sport or else it is gone for good and I shall remain forever as hopeless drunkard. I don't care which because one must have some fun, but it is a bore always having to have it under the nose of this very curious neighbourhood. When we got home we made the egg nogs and then danced alternately with Peter *(the odd American – see above)*. It suited us because he is a wonderful dancer, and neither of us could have managed more than every other dance.

1 July, 1943

I went to a ploughing demonstration last night where there were some of the more intelligent farmers. One of them said to me, "Mrs Donaldson, what do you do about your correspondence?" I said, "I reserve a room specially to keep it in." This went quite well, so I said, "As a matter of fact I've found a new method. When I get a difficult one from the War Committee or the Income Tax I don't even try to answer it, and then, after a bit, I begin to get letters asking for an answer. I wait till I've had about three of these and then I write and say 'I cannot trace your letter of December 5th. If you will let me know what it was about I will deal with it'. This usually finishes the matter because they haven't any files or records either." About three of the others had got on to that one, too, and said they did it regularly. It shows you what it is all coming to.

3 July, 1943

We seem to have been carrying hay forever. Like many other great agricultural secrets the moment when hay is fit seems to me to be pretty easy to determine. I've been dreading hay for eight months because I knew nothing about it whatever, Carling having been very secretive about it and I thought I wouldn't know what to do. The first two fields Pat had to come racing round to advise but now at the end of the three weeks I should be prepared to back my judgment against anyone around here except Pat.

I'm very worried about Thomas. When he comes home at weekends he is so odious that no words can describe it. He starts off when he gets out of the car adopting a boxer's attitude and proceeds to punch the nearest child at intervals of ten minutes through the day. If by chance they punch him back, which Rose immediately does, he dissolves into tears. He is rude and rough in manners and is thoroughly disliked by everyone except me. I think he is suffering from having had to behave like that at school to keep up with the others, from expecting us to be impressed and from the difficulty of readjusting, both ways from and to school. I'm going to write to the headmaster, saying it is not a complaint but a comment, and I want his views.

The letters show Frankie's gradually deteriorating relationship with Thomas. I remember his being horrible to me when he got home from school and when I had not yet achieved the status of going to school. We got on better when more mature, but it was one of the few sad elements of our family life, that he was uneasy in his relationships especially with Frankie. She had

234

adored him as a small child and felt that his difficult behaviour was one of the consequences of war, and the lack of a father figure. Jack's calm temperament would certainly have helped and she was so stressed and overworked on the farm that she was perhaps a little impatient with him. The problem was that their temperaments were very different.

8 July, 1943

Last Sunday the children wanted me to take them bathing, and I wouldn't, because I wanted to try a cob in the horse rake. It seemed to me important at the time but I thought afterwards that it was really awful the way I sacrifice everything to the farm. Because it's just which you think the more important, to try the cob or to take the children, and obviously I thought the cob.

10 July, 1943

I got a cable this morning which arrived with the first news of our latest venture, which merely said you were alright. *(July 9 An invasion of Sicily begins)* As soon as things are a little more obvious perhaps you will be able to let me know a little more about your job.

10 July, 1943 HQ. Movement Control 7N. 8th Army

The news is out on the wireless this morning, so you now know as much as I do. I'm sitting in Frank's tent, setting off for the party *(Sicily)* in about ½ hour. Nice to be seen off by Frank *(Margesson)*.

17 July, 1943

This is the first letter from Europe — quite an occasion. I won't say where I am but if you don't know you must be stupider even than the censors. It was wonderful steaming into sight of land on the morning of the second day, and seeing ships and craft and everyone unloading like mad, pouring an army into Europe. And all as quiet and peaceful as a Sunday morning at Runton. There were interruptions later on, of course, and before, but not at that particular moment, and it was quite an emotional experience. The first two days after landing were very exciting, rushing round trying to get railways and things going.

Jack wrote a month later when 'the party' as he referred to war events, battles etc, was over.

4 August, 1943

I can now tell you something of the past bit of history. The two months in Cairo were hell, as they were planning and planning and making preparations for the party, while conditions kept changing so that every arrangement had to be amended and amended again. The planning was done in England, N. Africa and Cairo, which made it more difficult. It was a dreadfully trying and tiring job. But great fun to see it actually happen. It was a triumphant and unqualified success, even tho' there wasn't much opposition.

18 August, 1943

I see now from orders I'm allowed to tell you I'm in Sicily, and came here from Malta. We came over from Malta in a very fast minelayer, and we picked up the crew of a Flying Fortress on the way, and were at the same time attacked, very briefly, by a Boche plane. Quite exciting for about four minutes, then over — no more thrills. The concentration of the invasion fleet was one of the most extraordinary feats of naval warfare.

We saw most of the ships, coming from our side, on the way out, and they met the others coming from elsewhere perfectly to time, drew up in position for assault and then assaulted all in some unbelievable way without the Boche knowing what it was all about. And the final assault achieved surprise, a thing no-one had thought possible. I left Malta the day after the assault, but hung about here for twenty four hours before we could get off. It was all fairly exciting, and extremely successful. I feel things are on the move all the world over.

*Operation Mincemeat ensured that the invasion of Sicily surprised the Germans. This was later fictionalised by Duff Cooper, written up by Ewen Montagu (*The Man Who Never Was)* and Ben Macintyre (Operation Mincemeat)*

 16 July, 1943
        I'm lying in bed at Nancy Hare's. For the first time since the war began I'm formally taking a week's holiday. I'd got to the point of staleness and fatigue where I really had no interest left in anything. As I left I got two letters, one from Bos and one from Malcolm Messer and Mary Day, who have just married each other, both saying they wanted to see me.

        Yesterday I had lunch with Peter Chance *(an army contact of Jack's)* and last night I went to Love for Love, a Congreve comedy very bawdy and very good, with John Gielgud, Yvonne Arnaud, Leon Quartemaine, Leslie Banks and lots of others, settings by Rex Whistler. I find going to the theatre a greater stimulus than almost anything else.

        Today I'm lunching with Peggy and dining with Bos, and tomorrow, which is Saturday, I'm going to Fisher's Gate *(the de la Warrs)* for the weekend. I'm really enjoying it.

18 July, 1943
The De la Warrs still have no news of Harry but they both still hope he will turn up, and take it with excessive calm and courage.

Harry Sackville posted missing. Later: Hon Thomas Henry Jordan Sackville RAFVR, missing presumed killed on air operations.

21 July, 1943

I should like to discuss with you the whole question of wartime standards and morality. Almost everyone I know is in it. It isn't only that they have young men, altho' they do, it's that they no longer think anything of any of those things anymore. P has had five in the last year, M no longer counts, Mb has two going on at once at the moment, and so on. By the time you have wished a fond farewell to your husband and then to your first lover and then to your second I suppose the whole thing begins to lose any value it ever had. I think it's partly because nobody stays long enough to become a steady. The men are just as bad, at least all those who, before the war, were potentially a little dangerous, but would have behaved with reasonable propriety, now don't bother about anything. A is reported to be rather miserable and certainly has cause to be if she takes it that way. Does it or does it not matter? I think there are heaps of people not doing it — like Bos's wife Stella and me — but the atmosphere is all the other way.

24 July, 1943

I have taken on a new man to put in Highman's old cottage. He has cross eyes, drinks, has a wife that drinks, five children and a potty sister-in-law (one room down and two up!). It seems a fairly large chance to take, but as he was the only person who answered the advert I had to take him. He is turning out well. He knows his job and having so much to pay for before he <u>can</u> drink he is a tiger for overtime. Last week he drew £2.17/11 in overtime.

It's extraordinary how much difference even one goodish man can make to the work of the farm. I also have a new girl who is doing secretarial work. Seems very efficient. Too earnest but willing to be fagged on every point as only the real secretary is. There is this about farming. You use all your money once and then you borrow two thirds and use it all again and have as many cars, hirelings, secretaries, pony-carts etc as you can jolly well get. I work hard but am surrounded with what in the ordinary way would be luxuries we could never afford.

25 July, 1943

A beautiful tin of boiled sweets from Groppie *(famous restaurant in Cairo)* arrived just in time as we are right out and Mrs Wheeldon hasn't got any except on coupon. Thomas is much improved and Nelson *(the headmaster)* seems to have done him good. He is always sweet when he is alone with me. Of the two he is the more obvious product of his heredity. He has my conscientiousness and respect for the law, and your reasonableness and possibly your brain, tho' not a spark of originality. Rose is really nobody's business. Neither of us have that peculiar and in some ways rather attractive sullenness and both of us are much more straightforward than she is. Also I don't think either of us is so tough.

26 July, 1943

Yesterday Mussolini resigned so I think that deserves a letter. It's really the beginning of retribution. I wonder if Hitler feels awfully good and I wonder what he and Mussolini met for. I suppose now one can really count the weeks until Italy is out of the war. What does a resigned dictator do? He can't take a house in the country, can he? I take it Switzerland won't be mad keen to have him.

Mussolini was reported by the BBC July 25 to have resigned. It was later said that he was in fact voted out of office.

Things are about to change here a lot, too. I have a really efficient secretary and you have no idea what that means. I spend my time saying telephone to that or answer that or make a note of that and it makes life possible instead of absolutely unendurable. The cottages are ready and so, having advertised "two exceptionally good houses", which is the only bait which attracts anyone nowadays, I have had two answers for a cowman, either of which might do, and so many for the tractor driver's job that we have had to shortlist them.

I think I'm definitely going to write another book, probably not till harvest is over, but I've just seen how to do it and I think it might really be good. (It became *Four Years Harvest*)

Then I'm having 100 acres of wheat cut by a combine, provided the Government dryer is ready in time, and, if this goes all right, not only shall we shorten the harvest but we shall have practically no threshing next winter, which makes the whole difference to the rest of the work. I think in about six months this place will be fit for you to come back to, but whether we shall have any money to live on by then is another matter.

Combine harvester cutting corn at Gypsy Hall

27 July, 1943

I got a letter this morning posted on the 17th. I was pleased — it was almost like the first letter when you first got to Cairo. It is rather exciting and it must be fun for you. According to newspaper accounts you will be getting kisses from all the Italian women and wine from all the Italian men. Also it gives me the feeling that you are much nearer home. Geoff Poole is there, a PRO with the press people. You might look out for him if only because he is married to my sister Mab, tho' why that should be a reason I'm not sure. Phil Dunne is also there, liaison between English and Canadian Commandoes I think. I wish I was there too — it must be far more fun than stooking oats under a hot sun which is how I spent this afternoon.

I wonder if you will have got any of my letters, as I have addressed them all to 12th Army.

I think Jack used 12ᵗʰ Army as a code for 8ᵗʰ Army as he wasn't allowed to tell her where he was. If so, she did not understand. The 12ᵗʰ Army was actually a German army.

You say you won't write much but you'll try to be regular. I don't want to be a bore, but it just does make the whole difference to my life to hear from you, even if it's short and scrappy, and as soon as you can I want to hear details. I

241

think the really wonderful thing about Mussolini is that that sort of thing <u>can</u> happen.

28 July, 1943

I got a letter of the 10th today, having got the 17th yesterday. On July 15th Peter Chance said to me "Aren't you glad that Jack isn't in so and so and so and so?" I said, "Am I not?" and all the time that's exactly where you were.

We made a profit, so the books work out, of £650 last year. That means that, even after everything claimed, we've got to pay nearly £300 in income tax. Damn it.

Then the cottages. I'm told they ought to have cost £1,000. They will have cost about £1,500. It is my builder friend, Mr Garlick, who tells me they ought only to have cost £1,000, so I shall try to fight it, but the Ministry of Agriculture seems to be paying as much and more. They are really good and today I engaged a cowman who, unless he is a liar, is the top. Among his previous jobs he was five years at Balmoral. I chose him out of some twelve applications, and the real attraction is the cottage. I'm going to take a photograph of the cottages to send you. They are absolutely square and not much more unpleasant than any ordinary factory.

Every time I think about old Musso I wonder what you are thinking!

31 July, 1943
Here I'm in a mess. I have arranged for 100 acres to be cut by a combine. The Ministry of Agriculture is erecting a drier and storage place in Stratford and that was where my grain was going to be dried. Believe it or not, and it's quite easy to believe it, it's not going to be ready for the harvest. So now I'm left running round in circles trying to find something else. And I can't. God, I'm getting bored with it.

The trouble is I'm like you. I could go away from here and face a new set of problems with enthusiasm, but I'm bored stiff with these same old ones. However, I still have a conviction that somehow or other it will straighten itself out. The first field of wheat is due to be cut on Tuesday. If nothing happens over the week-end I shall go into every office on Monday and burst into tears and sit there having hysterics until somebody does something.

Rob Hudson *(Minister of Agriculture)* told me that Woolton *(Minister of Food)* had agreed to take over the lot

Loading corn straight into sacks in the field. No need for threshing.

as it is his Ministry which is responsible for the drier. But none of his local officials know anything about that. So I may have to wire Rob, and if that doesn't do any good I shall take a match and fire the lot and go and pack parcels for the Red Cross.

9 August, 1943

The Thomas situation is much improved and I am not worrying about it anymore. I worry much more about the children because you're not here.

The combining of the wheat is working away and is really the most miraculous thing. Not only is everything done in one but it means that, as the combine leaves the field, the plough can go in. So that next year's drilling ought to be completed three or four weeks earlier than it otherwise would.

It seems to change the whole business of farming from the hell of a nuisance to a pleasure. At the moment we all have a slightly guilty feeling as tho' we ought to be doing an awful lot of work we are not doing. I have been so disconcerted by the whole thing, particularly as with it have arrived one extra man and a secretary, that it all seems too good to be true and I have even started to write a book. I really believe that next winter I shall get some hedges laid and the buildings tidied up. So it will be ready to sell in the spring if you come home and we should decide to do so.

19 August, 1943

The cows are a mess, and I can't produce clean milk. After two years of chivvying cowmen it turns out it's the cooling. The water is not cold enough and never will be. I shall sooner or later lose my licences. As I've bought all these cows TT that will involve a lot of money. I'm going to write to the War Committee and tell them that, as I am unable to produce clean milk I intend to sell the herd and go in for rearing. Milk is priority no 1 and they have powers to stop me doing that but, as they are also making a drive for clean milk, they will be a trifle in a cleft stick. My new cowman is an argumentative bugger who thinks he knows everything. A year ago he would have got me down completely and ruled the roost because I knew less and was so keen and green and eager. Now I am not bothered. I just tell him to shut up and give his views when asked, and at the end of the month I shall have to sack him and begin again. People who know everything are always a hopeless proposition.

Landgirl writing milk records on the board

20 August, 1943

The milk situation is awful. We have no water owing to the drought and we can't cool. Regularly it is returned as sour. Luckily we have very few cows in milk at the moment so it's only nine or ten gallons, but it is a bad situation and lowering to everyone's morale. And it's not likely to let up for at least six weeks.

21 August, 1943

When the new cowman annoyed me this morning I was automatically, and without feeling, as tough as it's possible to be. We got straight into whether we suited each other and whether he'd better go or stay — he, of course, started that. I said he could do what he damn pleased, but if he stayed he'd do things the way I wanted them done.

The war has stuck again, hasn't it? I'm worried about the Russians. For the last six months I've taken the view that our plans must be good ones because Stalin had stopped asking for a second front and therefore must know what we intend to do and be satisfied with it. But perhaps by the time you get this, something will have been done which will satisfy them. If not it will be another three years before you've worked out your service abroad and by then you'll have to come and get me out of Bedlam.

What annoys me is not being able to take up my bed and walk. That is the only panacea I've ever had for a rut of depression. Break loose, start again and see everyone in hell. But I can't do it. So this letter goes from Wilmcote to the place the censors still think is a secret to bring you nothing but gloom and depression.

30 August, 1943

I think the news is awful. Talk, talk, talk, and nothing done. And I am terrified by the withdrawal of Litvinoff which when it happened before was the beginning of the end. But then I have an awful temperament. I think I ought really to join Claude Cockburn on The Week. I know no one but he and I who can consistently see nothing but bad in what appears to everyone else to be good. I wish you'd come home my honey. Then perhaps I'd change my ways.

21 August 1943: Moscow announced that the U.S.S.R. had withdrawn Maxim Litvinoff as ambassador to the United States and named Andrei Gromyko to succeed him. There was speculation that this might be an expression of Stalin's

displeasure over the failure of the Allies to meet the Soviet
appeal for a second front in Europe.

Darling I'm so awfully sorry about dreadful letters last week.
I don't suppose I'm like that really at all. So you must always
think of me as I used to be and not worry about what I'm
like now because I shall be all right when you get back. And
I'm sorry I haven't more guts. I should have. But I've had a
bad time I think. With the one exception of the fact that
I've got the children, which is a pretty big exception, I think
I've had a much worse time than you. Because Teheran and
all that does keep the time moving and the juices rising
whereas this has really been one long endurance test.

So forgive it all and love me as I love you which is as
much as anyone could.

5 September 1943

I've completely recovered my spirits and feel all right again.
I don't myself understand exactly what happens during the
very bad phases.

I don't think I've ever described to you the formidable
nature of GH meals. At the moment we have Win, who
either has a worm or something psychologically wrong
which turns her mind to food. I've never seen anyone eat
like it.

Then there's Nora, who is rude and rough and by turns
sulky or out to entertain with dull stories about what she
said to the butcher. Then there are the two children who
quarrel incessantly and usually make scenes about their
food. My method of enduring all this is to withdraw from it.
I'm told I very often have to be addressed three times
before I even hear it. This doesn't seem to me to be a
hysterical defence but a perfectly good rational one, and if I
didn't do it I could not stand it at all.

We've been burning stubble which is both frightening
and exciting and I never wish to be in a forest fire.

15 September, 1943

I don't know where you are. You should be in Sicily but perhaps you are in Italy. I always find it disconcerting to write to you when I don't know where you are, and I'm not getting any letters from you so there is nothing to answer.

17 September, 1943

I think I'd better tell you about the cows. You know that the milk yields are always disappointing and the reason we don't make more profit is that. About a year ago I changed my vet and acquired a first class live wire called Gold. Soon after he came here we started a new kind of mastitis. This is a virulent disease and not enough is known about it. Most vets and cowmen do nothing much. The more progressive dose with sulphanilamide which is M & B.

Alan Brookes, the current owner of Gypsy Hall wrote that "Gold the vet was Norman Gold from Redditch, an iconic vet in his own day and the only vet that I have known being driven around by a chauffer in a big black car. He looked rather like Captain Mainwaring in Dad's Army."

Gold is like the Peckham doctors in that he takes tests to find out what things are. Ordinary mastitis is a streptoccus, but there is another kind, which most vets have never heard of, which is a staphiloccus (*staphylococcus*). Sulphanilamide won't touch this and it is much more difficult to cure and there is no prophylactic. Ours is a stapholoccus and we have it in a chronic but not in an acute form and we lately tested every cow in the herd. Only three were without a positive reaction. Gold admits himself beat. He doesn't know what the original source is. He thinks, and we agree, that we have probably had it from the beginning. It is more prevalent on the Warwickshire clays than anywhere else, and he thinks it may be the hard water. This theory would account for our consistently poor yields. Jolly, isn't it?

21 September, 1943

You've been away so long that I find it difficult to write to you now. You seem so awfully remote working twelve or fourteen hours a day on something we none of us know about that I can't believe it would be of much interest to you either.

The cow situation is horrifying and also frightening. It could bust us. I wrote to you about the mastitis. It's getting worse and worse. Before a cow calves, you steam her up with a lot of food so that she will be fit to milk. I keep doing that and, as I'm milking myself, I take immense trouble feeding ahead of her yield etc to get her to milk well; a lot of good cows have calved lately and so I get them up to 4 ½ – 5 ½ gallons, and then the mastitis starts and, within a week, they are down to 2 gallons. It really is the most depressing thing that has ever happened to me and hangs like a cloud of depression round my head all day.

We have been producing about 40 gallons a day for weeks. Every time a new cow calves we get it up a few gallons and then it immediately returns to 40. We should be sending away at least 60. On top of this all the cows' records are going to hell. And there's nothing in the world we can do about it except grin and bear it.

Thomas goes back to school today. I do hope he will settle down and improve a bit.

September 24, 1943

I've been up at 6 for a fortnight doing the milking. The only way I can cope with that is by going to bed at 8. But last night I had to take a sugar-beet plough over to Pat's. Pat took Meg away from me. It's quite justifiable. He got her in the first place and he has never quite given her to me and he has far more sheep than I have. But I was furious, even if it is absolutely justifiable.

I agree with all you say about the farm and I also agree with what you don't say which is that you would be disappointed if I did chuck it up. But if you like to have it there and if you want to be able to come back to it then that is sufficient point. I think you've earned it so I'll carry on and see you get it.

1 October, 1943

I had lunch with Phil today. He told me all about you; also that it was you who got him here because he had only permission from Bob *(Laycock)* to hitch-hike if he could. I was rather surprised because I didn't know you had control of all forms of movement including that one. Phil was very sweet about you, tho' he didn't like driving with you because you would keep the laws about passing.

He said, "Jack's so nice. Everybody notices it. They all said to me 'Fancy you having such a nice friend' ". He said you wouldn't talk politics because a) you were too tired to talk about them (and we agreed you must be very tired) and b) it wasn't worth arguing with him anyway. How about your being back for the 5th Christmas of the war?

5 October, 1943

The new cowman, who is not a grand chap and could conceivably be some good, arrived. In another week or so, when I'm quite sure he's doing what he should, I shall stay in bed in the morning and live the life of a lady and perhaps even find time to write proper letters to you.

Darling, don't your socks ever shrink? If so, <u>do please</u> send them home to me, I haven't any socks to wear under gumboots and I can't endure the idea of using coupons to buy some because they wear out so quickly. I have managed for two winters on your old shrunken socks, but now they are all used up.

6 October, 1943 Two Rose stories:

I got up at 6 this morning not to milk but to load up 20 bullocks which we have failed to fatten owing to prolonged drought and are sending to a sale at Tenbury. I came into the house at 7 and found Rose up and dressed. This is against the law, so I said she was very naughty but as she was there she could come and help get the bullocks in. I made her stand at the entrance of a road down which I didn't want the bullocks to go, and told her to jump about and yell at them when they came. This she did and that's about all there is to that story except that the sight of 25 bullocks all stopping with their heads down to look at Rose *(aged 5)* hopping up and down, and them turning away and going down the proper road is one of those things I shall never forget.

The other story is that Lucy at lunch was talking about demobilization when Rose suddenly said, "When I go out to meet my Daddy I shall take a photograph". Someone asked why and Rose said, "So that I shall recognise him of course". Aren't you entranced by the picture of Rose anxiously comparing you with a photograph?

8 October, 1943
People are beginning to get home. It's a pity none of them is you. I haven't heard for a while. Perhaps you are on the move.

 Jack had written: September 26, 1943
I was dining with Gerry Wellesley *(uncle of the then Duke of Wellington)*, who's the chief Amgot (Civil Affairs) officer here, and I took Humphrey along. Humphrey asked him if he's seen his nephew the duke, whom H. knows. I piped up that Phil Dunne had told me he was killed at Salerno, thinking of course that Gerry would know. His eyes opened very wide, and he said, "What" very slowly three times, and I thought "Oh, God, I've dropped a frightful brick he must have worshipped him and this is the first he's heard of it." But it soon became apparent that the

251

paralyzing effect was produced by the fact that, if true, Gerry would succeed to the title! Quite an effective little scene, and rather an unusual one. I think it is true *(yes, it was)* as he was in a commando, and Phil told me as a fact, so I was the first to create a duke, as it were! I like old Gerry. He's fun and independent and goes his own way, fairly left wing in an aristocratic way, and intelligent and cultured. Fun to find running East Sicily, anyway, and fun to make a duke out of.

Duke Of Wellington Killed In Italy

LONDON, Sunday (AAP).—The Duke of Wellington, great-great-grandson of the Iron Duke, was killed in action in Italy while serving as a commando. He was with a raiding party which landed in North-east Sicily during the invasion.

He also fought earlier in the Abyssinian campaign. He was not married and will be succeeded by his uncle, Major Lord Gerland Wellesley, who is now a Flight Lieut. in the R.A.F.

15 October, 1943

The Duke of Wellington story is extraordinary, especially as it turned out to be true.

I'm waiting for the vet, who is bringing with him the president of the Veterinary Research Council. Such are the proportions and interest of our outbreak of mastitis that this gentleman has come all the way from London to have a look at it.

Later.

Quite interesting. I always enjoy giving very exact information on case histories to research workers and occasionally pointing out to them logical conclusions which they hadn't noticed themselves. They both agreed that nothing but superlative management of the bail would get us out of the mess we're in, so my winter is well mapped out as I shall have to spend most of the time making sure of the superlative management.

'Bail' is the word for the indoor milking shed/parlour which had separate partitions for each cow to stand in and be milked, and fed at the same time.

Frankie had always been a perfectionist and had an extraordinary ratio of success in nearly everything she had turned her hand to in the past. Now she had managed to find a vet good enough to help her tackle her dairy problems, had taken on the milking herself until she was sure that the problems – which no cowman had been diligent or able enough to solve – were under control. Later she won milk records for the county and the farm was graded A. In her letters we hear more of her depression and struggle, but it was all to a purpose and a triumphant ending. I remember that at Christmas that year we had to wait till after 5pm for our presents as that was when she came in from the milking.

19 October, 1943

I have had further thoughts on the farm. Philip said, and I thought he was right, that the one thing we must keep was the independence represented by private money, and advanced that as a reason for selling the farm. But I think it might be a reason for not selling it. If we sold we should have about £15,000 more or less which invested at 3 ½ % would yield about £450, ie. 2 ½ d for people brought up as we have been. But the farm is a house and cars and food and telephone and dogs and ponies and a lot of work and thundering great overdraft but still a very independent and grand way of life compared with £450.

I believe, in spite of mastitis and all that, we are going to make pretty good profits now. Now we only need the independence for the first year or two till things and you have settled down and decided what you are going to do. So it seems to me that, even if we sold rather badly after the first year or two, we should still have had independence during the period we needed it most. Also, I am now getting the benefit of the cottages and of having been strong-minded with employees I didn't like. The new cowman is good and nice and so is the new tractor driver. With Highman they form an almost perfect team. That's taken 3 ½ years — it seems a pity to throw it all away.

On Sunday Johnnie Miller rang up. He was in London for two or three days on his way to India. He was sick as muck that he would have to stay and fight the Japs and therefore everyone else would get home before him and get

Jack, Johnnie & Madeline Miller, Frankie at Serge Chermayev's house

all the good jobs. Again, the farm preserves us from all that.

The Millers were close friends and also friends of Serge Chermayeff, a Russian born British architect. They may have been influential in introducing Jack to Walter Gropius.

26 October, 1943

I went to London to see Johnnie. It was rather depressing. He was taking it well but simply hating it. Barbara Kenyon told me that once he got really down and just sat the whole of one evening saying "Jesus Christ, think of me in the Indian army!" He told me Geoffrey is there. Now, Jack, you've got to avoid it at any price. It's no good your thinking that, if you go to India, I'll be waiting for you when you get back because I won't. There's a limit to everything and India's my limit. I stayed in Barbara Kenyon's flat with him on his last night, and all his luggage had gone and at 7.30 in the morning he got up and went — walked away down the road like the end of a Charlie Chaplin film. It was horrid. Let me repeat, don't on any account get into that. Far better to be in prison in England.

26 October, 1943

I've written to Faber's and told them to send *"The Living Soil"* and *"Alternative to Death"* direct to you. I've already got them but I can't spare them. You must read them. *The Living Soil* is excellent and rather frightening. It is written by Lady Eve Balfour.

Lady Eve Balfour (1899-1990) was an English farmer, educator, organic farming pioneer, and a founding figure in the organic movement.

She is a friend of Dod and Pete and Dick *(The Peckham doctors and Dick de la Mare)*. It's about health and very pro composting. The compost people have always said that, on a long-term view, artificials did harm to the soil, but I always thought they said it in an arrogant and cranky way without evidence. Now this book produces evidence of a pretty frightening kind. I use artificials with great liberality and I feel a bit shaken.

I have therefore for the first time in my life written a fan letter. I said could I come down and see her and discuss certain points with her? She lives in Norfolk or Suffolk so it would involve staying the night. This is very courageous of me as I hate meeting strangers and travelling and I don't in the least want to be convinced about compost and fertilizers because it will only involve being on the wrong side again (people like us always are) and much more trouble and less profit. But I feel you would want me to do this. So please read the book with great care even if you are busy and far away because all sorts of things could arise from it. It's all about health in its widest implications — wider even than the PHC stuff (*Peckham Health Centre*), any way more basic, and one would need to be a farmer to do anything about it at all. So if it's right and I make a small beginning you would have to take it on.

Jack had been heavily involved in the Peckham Health Centre in the 30s. I think the contact with Eve Balfour and the Soil Association came from there. This was the beginning of serious organic farming in Britain. Mary Langman, from the Peckham Health Centre, founded Whole Food with a shop in Baker Street after the war.

Then, the whole focus was on food production, to produce enough to keep England independent in the war. After the war Jack decided to experiment, and devoted one field on their new farm in Gloucestershire to organic practices. The crops were so spindly and thin in comparison with the fields that had artificial fertilisers that he used to conduct parties and friends around the farm and then visit "Eve's field" and have a good laugh. In the long run opinion has gone the other way, and probably practice has improved so that organic farming can produce better results than in the 1940s.

Peckham Health Centre 1935, described by Walter Gropius as 'an oasis of glass in a desert of brick'.

31 October, 1943

Things are going much better. We have, temporarily at least, cleared up the mastitis and are sending away a reasonable quantity of milk. I think, barring accidents, we shall make a good profit this year.

The more I think about Humphrey getting home the more I think you'll have to put your foot down and insist on coming, otherwise you'll be the last person left and then you'll never get home. I'm disgusted with the speed of our advance. Everyone said, when the Russians reached the Dnieper, they'd need six months to reorganize. They took exactly four days. Whereas we always have excuses for taking six months when we're expected to take four days. Johnnie *(Miller)* thinks, if we don't get on a bit, the Russians will pull up snorting on the cliffs of Dover and leave Churchill and Roosevelt to think that one out.

3 November, 1943

I've just had a letter from you asking about the men's wages and milk production. As you ought to know about these I'm answering at once before I forget. Please also get the names and occupations so that I don't always have to remind you. The minimum wage is £3 for men and 45/- for women.

Highman used to get £4 plus cottage plus overtime but he never put in any overtime for things like messing about after stock etc so I changed it. The milking people get overtime for anything unconnected with milking but not for Saturday and Sunday milking so they don't really get as much as they appear to in relation to the rest.

Highman (foreman) £4.10.0 + cottage but no overtime ever.

Price (cowman) £4.10.0. + cottage.

Walden (tractor driver) £3.10.0 + cottage.

Wheeldon, Cyril (tractor driver etc, under 21 and therefore only entitled to 45/-) £3.0.0.

Oakley (deaf and dumb and fearful nuisance) £3.0.0.

Peggy Brooke (land girl) £2.5.0. + cottage.

Joan Hosie (cowshed) £2.10.0.

Yvonne (cowshed) £2.10.0.

Win Lewis (secretary etc) £2.10.0.

Anne Oliver (ex-university student only here because I'm too weak to sack quite good worker) £2.5.0.

I think the landgirls at Gypsy Hall all got free accommodation, often with our family.

I read out to Pat the wages list as given to you and he says I must be dotty and I've got to sack at least two girls and the two half-time women. I'm not dead sure he's right. I've got work for them up to Christmas and again in May onwards. Is it really right to sack people who are good and have taken a lot of getting together when it means employing gang labour in the summer months if you do. Any way I don't really know who to sack. I'll finish this tomorrow. Goodnight my love.

You will see from all this three things. One, there is nothing to be ashamed of in wages paid and general standards of employment. And in reference to this I should say that everyone at present on the farm considers themselves to have a good job and is really happy. Two, I can no longer complain of a shortage of labour. In fact I have too much and will sooner or later have to get rid of some of the women. Nevertheless, only the first four named are at all skilled so there is still a slight (only slight) lack of skilled labour. Three, I have a nice little cheque to cash once a week. On the other hand, I no longer have to get land girls in gangs for threshing, mangold pulling etc so it evens up a bit.

Two points – one, there is about to be an increase of minimum wages from £3 to £3.5.0 and from 45/- to 48/- so everyone including those getting higher wages will go up in this proportion. Two, the standards of pay are pretty high in relation to most farmers but not particularly high in relation to the money makers. I know people who pay their cowmen as much as £6 and most foremen get at least £4.10.0 if not more.

I want to see you <u>soon</u> and I really can't wait much longer.

3 November, 1943

I'm having an awfully pleasant and really Shipbourne time. On Friday I met Peter and Anthony (*Mildmay*) and Leonora in London and we dined at the Bagatelle. That's that place at the back of Devonshire House where we used occasionally to go when we were getting engaged. We were all fearfully pleased to see each other and Peter and Anthony are very rich now and make a great point of spending money when on leave. We had cocktails at 8/- each and champagne at £5.10.0 a bottle. It is rather extraordinary isn't it. It must work out at about 2/6 a sip.

Peter & Jack had been school   as had Frankie & Leonora who
friends   was married to Peter

I got very quickly into roaring form and I said to Peter "This is the first time I've been in good form for two years" and he said, "I don't believe it. I think you've been practising every day". And we all thought all our jokes were wonderful and so on. And it was awfully lucky it went that way because apparently Peter and Anthony have to put up with a shade of sourness from wives whose husbands have been away a long time. For instance with Peter in the chair at a meeting at Shipbourne Mrs Joynson gets up and says "Wouldn't it be better as <u>nearly all</u> the people it concerns are <u>overseas</u> to leave the matter until they come home" about some piffling thing that no one cares about any way. And Peter had said, "The test of Frankie is whether she's sour or not". And of course by nature I am awfully sour but I don't really keep it up and I do get nice and drunk. So it all worked out very well and was a very typical evening with only one thing missing and that of course was quite an important thing. I'll go on on another.

7 November, 1943

Fairlawne   Last night we went up to Thelma's *(Peter's sister, Thelma Cazalet-Keir)* which was another frightfully typical evening only we missed you more than we always do because we needed you so badly. Quentin Hogg *(Frankie spells it Quentin all through although it was actually spelt Quintin.)* was there and you must know that he considers himself, and I think perhaps in fairness one ought to say is also considered by a lot of people, the young leading light of the Conservative Party. There is a group who call themselves the Tory Reform Committee and has forty members. When I tell you that Hinch is the chairman you will get how low is the tide and also how Hinch is proceeding according to plan. Thelma is a member and Quentin Hogg is the young hopeful and they have produced a manifesto and appear to be taken quite seriously.

Quentin Hogg held the floor and had against him Leonora, Thelma and Dorothy Dickson.

Dorothy Dickson, an American-born musical comedy performer who captivated British audiences in the 1920s. Although her career had faded considerably by the 1940's, Miss Dickson re-emerged as a founder of the London Stage Door Canteen, which entertained thousands of Allied troops during World War II.

In the room were also David Keir, *(husband of Peter Cazalet's sister Thelma Cazalet Keir)* Peter and I but for a variety of reasons we three stayed out of the argument. Now before I go any further I must make it clear that I do know Q.H. is supposed to be brilliant and I believe supposed to be by people like you. Nevertheless I think he's one of the stupidest people I've ever met in my life. I don't deny his brain (though he didn't show much of it) but one has to have more than a brilliant brain to avoid being stupid.

He did everything wrong. One, he constituted himself the referee of the argument and gave himself all the points whether he had made them or not. Two, he was rude to Leonora and treated her like you used to tread Irene Ward *(Conservative politician)* which was not only an error in taste but a fundamental misjudgement. Three, he underrated everyone in the room so badly that he didn't even try to make sense. Four, he used that political trick of scoring points by bringing in bits of knowledge which no one else had and therefore couldn't say were true or untrue.

I mean he used the fact that he is up in the arguments to score debating points and not in order to make himself clear. Five, he talked very much too fast and too much and switched the subject slightly every time anyone looked like making a point. Six, he used that despicable trick of making people define what they meant about things which he really understood. Like "What do you mean by Christian principles?" Seven, he announced at the end that everyone in the room had a confused brain and didn't know how to argue. Three of us hadn't opened our mouths. Everyone knew the only person who could really have dealt with him was you and in my opinion you would have done it very nicely.

In your absence Peter put him in his place once very beautifully with great dignity and made me realise an Etonian education is a great thing and David was frightfully cute about three times. Dorothy Dickson was there and has lately been entertaining the 8th Army and has gone off her nut as a result. No one ever told her about what men get like when they haven't seen any woman for years and so she took it all quite seriously and then she sat next to Eisenhower and so of course she knows all about the war. She was too pretentious for words and really rather pathetic but what is wonderful is knowing that Leonora and Peter won't miss a trick either. One the way home I just said, "you baffle me Thelma" which was a quote and we all yelled and that began it and we haven't really stopped yet. And it is fun after four years of land girls etc. Only darling it is stupid that you aren't here. Do make sure that you are next time.

7 November, 1943 Fairlawne No 2:

I've nearly finished all the exciting bits but Peter will tell you some more. O by the way I forgot Peter's joke which was awfully good. Quentin Hogg was telling about his experiences in Libya and someone asked about prisoners or something and Q.H. said, "Well I got one man with a hole in his bottom", and Peter said sotto voce as it were "There's nothing unusual about that." Perhaps I haven't made it sound as good as it was but it was good and we all thought it was wonderful.

Later.

All Thelma's party came to lunch and Quentin Hogg was very chastened and polite and had a political conversation with me on very controlled lines at lunch and sucked up quite a lot to Leonora. So we think he had got onto himself a bit.

I've just been talking to Peter about the farm. He started off about how you wouldn't want to farm and you'd be wasted and so I told him all the reasons why people thought it would be economically wise to sell now and Leonora thought that would be lovely and we'd be just in time to come and live here when Peter goes to do the second front. But then I explained my new theory of the farm giving independence to decide what you want to do after the war and the same amount of money not giving it and so on and Peter was rather won round to that and any way saw the point.

14 November, 1943

I'm still faintly worried about T. You see I know I am rather a neglectful mother but I simply haven't been able to help it. You can't run 400 acres under extreme difficulties and be a wonderful mother at the same time. That's all there is to that and you must never really blame me for any failures. In a way, once I got launched on this I was driven by it and we both agreed I should be launched.

After I'd finished the letter I've just written to you I started talking to T. I asked him if he thought it would be more fun to be a day boy and explained it would mean missing cricket and football etc. So shall I do that next term? Why the hell don't you arrange to get back before that and see for yourself.

17 November, 1943

I've bought a new dog. I haven't seen it yet but it's a good ratter and Bubbles has turned out to be such a hopeless cissy and sits by the fire but she's wonderfully bred for ratting and I think if she was with a dog who was some good it might hot her up. Its name is Bonzo and it's a sort of Border.

I wonder if you'll ever really get together with my dogs. You couldn't fail to love Meg whose charm is obvious but Bubbles charm is of an obscure kind and consists in being pretty hopeless and very disobedient but wagging her whole bottom with her tail while trying to get away with doing what you're telling her not to. Bonzo I don't know about and I may have to give him to Pat after a month or so as I closed quickly on a deal Pat rather wanted to do and as he gave me both Meg and Bubbles I really owe him a present. Meg is going to have puppies and I think I'll let Bubbles marry Bonzo so if you don't feel really fatherly to any of the present ones you must get back in time to choose a puppy and begin from the beginning. It never rains now.

Our fox terrier Bubbles playing in the straw. One of her puppies slept in my bed at night.

Frankie adored dogs and had always had some. Pat had refused to give Meg to her, but one day when she got out of the car on arriving home after a trip to Pat's farm, a sheepish looking Meg crawled out from under the seat. She had stowed away in Frankie's car. Pat gave in at this point and Meg lived with and was loved by us for the rest of her life. She is an important memory for all three children, including Kate who was born in 1945.

18 November, 1943

I'm just one shade off actual tears all day today. You know we haven't had any hot water since July. Some days we just have cold water. It's frozen quite hard four nights running and its freezing now. The house has no heating of any sort and only the boiler for the bath kept it liveable in last year. The mental and physical struggle to get out of bed and either carry water or wash in cold every morning is my effort for the day and I haven't any guts left for the rest. I'm late getting the mangolds in and they get frozen every night which means they won't keep and there's no one here who's even kind and I can see nothing but gloom and misery and I just don't think I can take much more.

I got the new dog Bonzo this morning. He's quite nice with a little grown-up personality but quite dull and I don't think he will rival Meg and Bubbles in my affections.

You know don't you that we always have hordes of cats. They are apt to die on us because we make them live exclusively off rats and mice and I've just discovered that as the sole item of a diet these are fairly poisonous. But as they breed like mad we generally manage to keep the supply up. This afternoon I counted nine round the kitchen door. Some of them are very pretty and though I always pretend I keep them to keep the rats down I really keep them for you because you always loved cats and I think you would love to have hordes of them round the door. They all have the most dreadfully unoriginal names as they are named by the children. Fluff and Tibby and Fatty and Smoky are the only ones I can remember – O and Gina. Gina reversed the ordinary procedure by turning out to be a male. He's very self-possessed and a great rabbiter. He is often to be seen miles away from the farm snooping about.

Today I took Rose with me and we passed a lorry carrying sugar beet to the station. "Gosh" she said, "they're late with their sugar beet." I thought you would have been proud and amused. There now I feel a trifle better but I haven't any more to say so I'll finish this tomorrow.

21 November, 1943

First of all Tom Mosley. *(Oswald Mosley, leader of the British Union of Fascists).* He has been let out and his wife because he is ill and with that the country that remained unmoved by Spain, Munich, Darlan, the fate of the International

Brigades and the fate of the Jews has risen as a man to show what democracy is about by signing protests in an attempt to get him put back again. Now I think that's very seriously distressing and I want to know what you think.

You see, I see it like this. Mosley was always a joke and everyone knew it, in spite of the fact that he did annoy a few Communists by marching through the City and beating them up at meetings. There was only one moment when he ever aspired to be anything more than a joke and that was when a German invasion was feared. Then he was put in gaol and quite right too. Now he is ill and in any case has no organisation and is no longer a menace. So he is let out. And in any country which believes "IT COULDN'T HAPPEN HERE" quite right too.

But not at all. There's the biggest and most united dust up I ever remember about anything. They say it's because he's a fascist and we're fighting fascism and at the best he's a symbol of what we're fighting. And so on and so forth. And I don't believe a word of it. I think it just shows that we're a lot of dirty little sadists like everyone else. And also of course that it's a damn dangerous thing to have a title if you are ever going to put yourself in reach of the law or the mob. But I may be wrong about all this and influenced by the fact that I know he's an utterly broken man and though I never knew him and disliked her intensely, I don't like the idea of those sort of people being in prison. i.e. when it comes to it I'm just a soft and broken renegade from their class. So I want to know what you think. Personally I'm really shocked. I think the only excuse for the English brand of complacent tolerance is if it's tolerant about people being let out as well as about them being shut up. But I've been reading more Arthur Koestler – this account of prison in Spain (Dialogue with Death) – and I've got a thing against prisons so I may be all wrong. So far not one single person or paper has come out on my side any way.

Second thing – tea's ready. I'll go on after. Second thing is about your coming home. I think about it most of the time and I've just worked out one that will keep me watching the pot boil all winter. You see I've always assumed I'd hear first by cable and then it would be a few weeks if not months. But if you can't cable it means you'd write and if everything happened in a hurry you might walk in one day ahead of the letter or at any rate you might telephone from Liverpool of something. So now every time the telephone rings I shall pretend it might be you.

14: 1943

Plans for the Farm and a second book

26 November, 1943
I don't know whether I've told you but on the recommendations of the War Agricultural Committee the electric light people are now prepared to put electric light and power on and are getting out a scheme now. It would be a very real advantage on the farm quite apart from any amenities it may provide in the house. My inclination is to go on spending but that's because I'm a spendthrift by nature and can't bear not to do improvements. What do you feel about it?

(This letter was received about a month later than it was written in answer to Frankie's of 13 August 1943 above)
13 September, 1943   I have been so immensely proud of what you've done, and every one I've told about it has been so full of praise and envy, and often even said they wished their own wives had the guts to do the same. So you can feel that, to the ordinary chap I meet out here, what you have done has been almost a wish-fulfilment of his own ambitions.

Everyone wants a farm after the war to go back to, and we're the only ones I know who've had the courage and brains, energy and determination, not only to get one but to make a success of it ... and write a first-class book into the bargain. I suppose I've lent the book to some 50 people, and several have read it independently. I've never had it back without the most sincere and genuine compliments, and I feel separtely proud each time. When you gloom about life, because I feel the gloom so deeply myself I realize it's worse in every single aspect for you. You've done something truly remarkable and widely recognised as such, so if you <u>can</u> keep it up till I get back, it will be all the more so. If you can't, it will in no way detract from the fact behind you and you can, with a perfectly clear conscience, stop the whole thing and find another temporary solution.

I can only give you my absolute confidence in whatever you do. I recommend more holidays and a bit of gaiety if you can find it, and some company if you can get it. People sometimes help to pull one out of introspection and depression. What you've endured is three times longer than anything you've got to endure in the future, so keep on, darling.

27 November, 1943

My darling Jack you are everything in the world I want in a husband and even at the distance of – I never know how far it is – you succeed in giving some ballast to my irresponsible and wavering mind. And I agree with every word you say. You see the thing is that apart from all the grumbles etc I like farming. I like it better than golf and tennis and riding and parties and everything I've ever enjoyed all rolled into one. I'm pretty sure that must be true or I wouldn't be here now. Yesterday for instance was vile – sleet and wind. I've got a semi-broken cob which I'm not prepared to trust to land girls. So I took her out myself to take mangolds down to some heifers. I came in feeling good at a net cost of nothing. And I like that. The part I hate is the loneliness and dullness at night. If you were here I'd love it all.

Then about the farm. I'm really so awfully pleased about your attitude. You see I absolutely hate this place and it's cold and gloomy, and wet and muddy and boring to an extreme. But for 3 ½ years I've sweated at it and every penny I've ever earned I've put back into it and now I've got two good cottages and a wonderful staff of frightfully nice men – not one of them is less nice than Webb – and the cows are doing well for the first time and I made well over £2,000 in wheat alone this year. It is probably hard to understand quite what a success this is.

As a result, in spite of the fact that my overdraft isn't any smaller and so on and so forth, and the net result is that I don't really want to part with it – at least not until I've got the hedges laid and the yard concreted and forty thousand other things it will take me at least five years to do. I need it to be perfect before we sell it.

But when you come back I'll want to do whatever you want to do. Only I think in my secret heart I'll always want a farm otherwise I'll feel jealous and out of it every time I see a haystack. But that I'm sure we could arrange without your necessarily having to farm too if you decide you don't want to.

Darling <u>do</u> come home soon. I'm bored with this.

27 November, 1943
I've let myself in for a mess. I wrote to Lady Eve Balfour after I read her book and asked to go down and I'm afraid I wrote in the spirit of a possible disciple. She wrote a charming letter back and there's no way out but in the meantime Stapes and Pat between them have quietly demolished every point I thought any good at all. So I've either got to go as a fraud or as an arguer which wasn't the point at all and I'm no good at that sort of situation – and feel generally horrified. I wish you were here to go with me.

2 December, 1943
I want to give you another lecture about the farm. My life has changed a lot lately. I've stopped doing any work. I don't

mean by that I do nothing, just that I do not physically labour much any more. There are always heaps of things to go and look at and see are all right and I walk round among the men or I use Meg to move sheep or cattle etc. But I never do any hard, physical work. That is what is meant by work, on a farm. I shall have to of course in the summer but now I just don't. Also I don't go out before breakfast. I just take the attitude that Highman can run the farm until breakfast time and if I want anything special done I tell him the night before.

It's quite all right because in the winter they've nearly all got a routine job to do before breakfast – milking, feeding, carting mangolds etc. the result of this new way of behaving is simply extraordinary and I realise fully now what a strain the last year has been. First I look five years younger and much prettier. Then I'm never bad tempered and seldom depressed. And I'm so wonderful with the children. I read to them and play with them and never bite their heads off. And lastly I am so comparatively happy.

For the first time for about three years I really love the farm. I walk round it feeling good and really liking it and I get real pleasure out of small things like that the cows are really milking extraordinarily well (which isn't a small thing) and that last night we mated Bubbles to Bonzo. It's a bad cross because he is a Border and she a white smooth terrier and very small but I couldn't hear of a terrier dog and he is a very good ratter and rabbiter.

We spent hours thinking of names for her puppies. They have to be B's and all the best ones have been taken by Bubb who bred Bubbles. Finally we decided on Bantam, Bramble, Beastly and Belinda. If you can think of any better ones you can let me know as there's 9 weeks to go. The names want to suggest a rather cocky and courageous little dog.

Frankie also privately gave the puppies names of several b-swear-words as a joke but these had to be given up when the puppies found homes. My puppy was called Biscuit and slept with me in my bed every night until Jack came home from the war. He was very shocked and talked me into giving her away. I remember Frankie being angry when she discovered what he had done. Dogs were always important to her.

4 December, 1943

Here is the lecture I promised you two days ago. If your cows in milk are averaging less than 2 gallons a head you are doing damn badly. If they're doing 3 you've reached the meccas of the milk producers' dreams. Darling I think we're about to start making money. If I could add at all I could tell you how. ...

4 December, 1943

I've been explaining why I think we've made money here. Of course Price *(the cowman)* has a lot to do with it but it doesn't matter how it's done as long as it is. Of course I suppose I get more kick out of all this because I've always had so much trouble with the cows and I always found it more difficult to get high yields than someone who kicked off fairly well as a lot of people do. But any way I'm as proud as a turkey cock and I nearly embrace Price every time I see him and I really do think there's reason to suppose I've at last broken the back of it and things should go now.

I therefore – now that you've decided we won't sell the farm – propose to spend some more money on it. I want to put in electric light if at all possible, I want to do whatever is necessary to improve the water supply and I want to do something about the roads and the yard. I don't know whether we can afford to do all these this year or not but they would make it a possible place to live in and they wouldn't have actually to be paid for before the spring or summer when we shall be nearer next harvest. So I hope to get general approval from you.

One reason I want to do all these things is I want it to be nice for you. I want you to be able to bring your friends down a reasonable drive through a reasonable yard into a comfortable house. And I want you to be able to show them fields with the hedges laid (not that they'd notice or care but still) etc. etc. You've never been here in the winter so you've no idea how God awful it is at the moment.

Dick wrote. He will send you some books and still wants me to write another. A cow kicked me on the nose this afternoon. She actually got me with her hock. It didn't bleed much but is completely bunged up and I can't breathe so I must assume a position where I don't have to bend my head over. So I'll stop. Do come soon and help spend the money.

11 December, 1943

According to an article I have just read the place where you are *(Italy)* gets bombed pretty regularly. You never said anything about it? Is it true and how badly? Please let me know at once.

Thomas came home today with a large parcel. I asked him what it was when he got off the bus. "Ah" he said, "you wait till we get home". I said, "Is it a surprise?" He was very mysterious and said it was jolly lucky because it was only because he was a weekly boarder and therefore able to get things home easily that he'd been able to bring it. When he got home he started undoing the parcel. There was miles and miles of newspaper and then out came what looked like a bit of plasticine.

I said, "O it's plasticine." "It's not," he said indignantly, "It's clay." He then brought out a lot of pieces and they looked exactly the same – like a piece of plasticine that had been held in a closed hand. "That's a shepherd," he said, "He's kneeling. And that's another one standing up. And that's Jesus only he's got a bit squashed. And that's Mary only her head's got knocked off." Is it funny on paper? It was really very funny at the time and we nearly killed ourselves not laughing because he was so pleased and would have been so hurt.

12 December, 1943
I've told the Times to send you a copy of "Scum of the Earth" by Arthur Koestler which I am just reading. I think you liked "Darkness at Noon" which I sent you and this is just as good. It recalls things which one ought to recall — how the war really began on the day Stalin signed the non-aggression pact with Hitler, and how the democracies had nothing to fight for but only things to fight against. It recalls to me how I felt about a lot of things before I got too bored with the world to have much feeling about it.

I think I've at last got an adequate farm staff. The two new men are both good, and the work of the farm could be quite pleasant now if only I could get rid of this mastitis which spoils everything. We've got an exceptionally good crop of potatoes.

Thomas is a problem. He kicked up hell about going back to school this morning and had to be lifted on to the bus by Highman, who had taken him as I was in bed with my cold. He's so thin and got no teeth, and I don't know whether he's unhappy or just tiresome and I don't know what the hell to do with him. I feel so strongly he needs you. He and the mastitis are about equal sources of discouragement.

15 December, 1943
Hudson *(Rob Hudson the Minister of Agriculture)* has let the farmers down by raising the minimum agricultural workers' wage and not adjusting prices to meet it which he has always promised to do. There is a first class boiling row going on and N.F.U. branches screaming for his resignation and so on but apart from this I think that what with that and the Government's refusal to announce a post-war plan

confidence in agriculture is really very seriously shaken at the moment.

Today I had to go and give evidence for the Ministry of Food against my ex-cowman, McClegg. It was rather interesting. I hated going and was a shade nervous. Then the police came over and started talking to me and asked me whether I knew if there was anything against him. I said, "I should be damned surprised if there isn't". Because he really is an outsize in bad hats and had put up as a defence that it was his wife who had done it and not him. So they asked me if I'd missed anything and I said no and they said, "Are you absolutely sure?"

I said, "No one on a farm can be sure. All farm workers are so fearfully careless one loses things all the time." So they said, "Well someone and we think it's him is advertising some horse clippers and we thought they might be stolen." So then I absolutely roared with laughter because I've been cursing Highman and Cyril for a fortnight because they couldn't find some cow clippers and it had never crossed my mind that they had been pinched. So it looks as though I may have to trail off to Campden again some day soon and it also looks as though Mr McClegg may, through no real intention of mine, rue the day he started shitting about on G.H.

Sim *(Feversham)* is home and so are 100's more. They're pouring in. All except you. You really must do something.

I think Jack wanted to come home as much as she wanted him to, but his personality was such that he would never dream of asking for a favour or wangling an advantage. Only when she became demonstrably ill did he ask for compassionate leave and came home briefly.

19 December, 1943

I want to get on with my book. The thing is it's not very good but it's now turning out to be reasonably easy. For ages it would not take a concrete shape chapter by chapter.

Now suddenly I can see it as a whole and having delayed it so long it turns out there's so much material it almost writes itself. This being so I want to rush through it in about 6 weeks before I change my mind again.

21 December, 1943

My darling – Nora has pneumonia which is a bit of a thing. I don't know whether she's very bad or not. Doctors are awful nowadays. They won't come at all unless you telephone before nine – and how anyone with pneumonia living in a house where the two other inhabitants have flu can telephone before 9, I don't know. The doctor came once, said she had acute flu, went away leaving a prescription which there was no one to get made up and never came back again. The sister who lives with her *(Mrs Higley)* said to me on the third day of this "She's very ill and she sees things on the wall" but apparently thought it unnecessary to do anything about that.

I rang up the doctor and said I was sure she had pneumonia and if he didn't come at once I thought he was taking a very grave responsibility on himself. He came at once and got her into a hospital within a couple of hours. But it would be interesting to know what would have happened if Nora hadn't been working for me. At what point I mean would Mrs Hig have done something drastic?

Before the introduction of antibacterials, pneumonia had a chance of being lethal. Medicines used to treat Churchill on 2 occasion, were made by the British firm of May and Baker. The tablets were simply known as 'M&B' at about this time. Churchill is quoted as saying: "Dear Nurse, pray remember that man cannot live by M & B alone". His doctors, Lord Moran and Dr Bedford, were also referred to as M & B. 'M&B' was certainly a familiar phrase in my childhood.

I forgot to tell you I've ordered the electric light. It will cost exactly £500 – that is £330 to get it here and the rest for the wiring etc. I think it's worth it and I think you would too if you'd lived in this cold and bathless house for long. One gets up to stone cold water in an ice cold house every morning and all day one wears two thick sweaters and very often a battle dress coat on top of that. It will be useful too on the farm and will add a lot of value to it – at least £500.

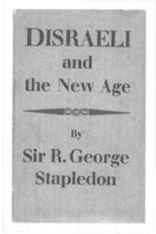

I'm reading a book Stapes has written called Disraeli and the New Age. He takes things Disraeli said and elaborates them to fit today. It is a trifle serious that I find myself disagreeing with practically every word either he or Disraeli says. I can see that Disraeli was a very great Tory but I don't like Tories any better for being great.

15: 1943-4

Irving Berlin

24 December, 1943
There have been three boxes of sweets lately and the last arrived today – which was very well timed.

Darling I had such fun the day before yesterday. Irving Berlin's Army Show was in Birmingham. It's the only thing I've really wanted to see for years. It was only two weeks in London and impossible to get in. So I wrote four weeks ago for seats in Birmingham. The theatre didn't even bother to answer. I had promised to take Pat and when we didn't get seats we decided to go just the same and go to a cinema and do our Xmas shopping.

I saw Irving cross the hall at the Queen's where we had lunch. I hadn't seen him for 17 years but he was always a heavenly little man so I wrote him a note. He was divine. He's one of the most modest and loveable people I've ever met. Any way without any fuss or bother or throwing himself about he put practically the whole American Army on to getting two seats and then in the middle of the show it seemed we'd got into some that were sold and he came through the pass door himself to settle the argument.

In the Twenties Frankie had accompanied her father everywhere, mingling with stars like Fred Astaire, Irving Berlin and the Gershwins.

The show is really good – really fast American revue as only Americans can do. I think it's going overseas. I'm going to try and see Irving in London before he goes and if he's

279

going near you I'll ask him to do the same for you as he did for me. The wonderful thing was that the one thing he loves and can't get is eggs. So the next day I sent a Land Army girl in with all I could muster – which was only 16 but not so bad. The G.H. Christmas news is the boiler's burst so we shall never get a bath again. Win thinks we're being tested out for saints.

Irving Berlin's travelling wartime show.

14 January, 1944

Every now and then you ask me a question about something which I have forgotten or avoided writing about for the reason that it is too long and dull on paper. Such a one is your question about Common Wealth.

The Common Wealth was a new and alternative political party, leaning to the left rather than the right. It was started by Sir Richard Acland, a rich Exmoor landowner who left his land to the National Trust, with a stated wish that they should continue to allow hunting over the estate. This wish was not observed.

Obviously this is a thing which we would examine together but also it is something which I cannot reach conclusions about myself. I think that to some extent I deliberately refrain from thought on political questions partly because I am ultimately more prepared to follow you than anything else and partly because I have an instinct that any of our political conclusions should be formed together and not separately.

Having said that I personally think Common Wealth worthy of respect for its aims and principles though probably tactically rather woolly and made up of people who are mostly slightly intellectually discredited. Certainly the Tories aren't frightened of Sir Richard Acland. I think they despise him and are morally probably wrong but in effect probably right. The fact that Common Wealth occasionally win a bye-election I think only means that people are angered and bored by the political truce and that Labour is slowly cutting its own throat.

It's a lovely day and I've been round the farm with the dogs. You have no idea how lovely this life is when it is lovely – satisfactory in every way.

16 January, 1944

I'm immensely excited at the moment about my book – that is about the actual writing of it. I must discuss it with you because you are the only person who understands that to say what you think about yourself is not necessarily conceited.

First of all it turns out I've been absolutely right in putting it off so long. For two reasons. First, there is now so much material the damn thing writes itself. Second, one cannot write if one is being harried from pillar to post. At least I can't. I can't just settle down in the evening. It's not that I need so much time to think it's that I must have some basis of ease of body and mind before anything happens at all. Then it seems to pour out. And this is the first time for years that I can reasonably live like that. I've got the farm deliberately slightly overstaffed – land girls – and as there is no terrible urgency about anything at the moment – thanks to the combine and a breakdown of the crawler tractor which necessitated the ploughing being done on contract – I'm leaving the management of the farm to Highman – who I may say is blossoming under the treatment.

Nanny is here now and Win has turned out to be a treasure above all price and so with old naggy Nora away there's peace in the house, for the first time that I can ever remember. And the book just flows. But this is what I particularly want to say to you because it's so interesting. In as far as I can do it at all it's a gift. You remember how surprised you were when you read A to F and how you especially commented on the facility and economy of phrase. Well I thought that out a good bit. But this time I haven't had the time.

I sit down with a good idea of the material I'm going to use but no idea of anything else and what is so extraordinary is that I then tap out – not fumblingly and with corrections but straight on to the typewriter – incredibly explicit sentences turned exactly right and full of words I hardly knew I knew. And I am as surprised as anyone else could possibly be. Of course I hope it's true and not just me that thinks so. I wish you were here, though I shouldn't do it at all if you were. So often one achieves a sort of glow while writing which is misleading and later one finds it isn't so good at all.

I am interested in the farm too. You see I'm sure we're making money now but as I spend it all on capital works we don't know it or notice it. But one day the capital works must stop and alongside that they ought also to produce more income. Suppose that some day the question became not "Are we going to sell the farm?" but "Can we afford to sell the farm?" How very queer that would be. In the meantime I have two cars, a secretary, men to do any odd jobs, Nanny and two half-time women in the house. And in the ordinary way it would take a hell of a lot of money to earn that. And I'm temporarily (I'm sure only temporarily) in danger of becoming conceited.

Four Years harvest, published by Fabers

19 January, 1944

My beloved – I am working like a maniac on my book. It's funny how things come out. I am doing a chapter on ley farming and I meant merely to say in fairly temperate words that the ley lets one down in July and August in this district. Owing to a rather good bit of quite unintended descriptive writing I've given an absolutely damning picture of what actually happens. And yet every word I've said is true and not really overstated – in fact the descriptiveness arose out of the strength of my feelings last summer. So what do I do now? As an artist (so to speak – I don't really claim to be one) I am horrified at the idea of cutting it. As a friend of Stapes and what is more important as an advocate of the ley I'm a trifle horrified at the idea of letting it stand.

I shall in fact let it stand for the moment because I find that my artistic feelings can stand mutilation quite calmly once I get at a sufficient distance from the work. But I do find that there is some truth in what writers often say – that you don't completely control your own output. It leads off by itself in the most surprising way and if you wrote the same chapter on a different day you might get quite different results.

I've taken a day off from the book. I've got Bonzo back because he would eat Pat's ducks. Pat didn't seem to think it would matter if he ate mine. So now I've got Meg, Bonzo, Bubbles who is about to have puppies and a loaned greyhound bitch called Minta who killed Tinker Rouser Edward Stubbins (kitten) with one crack of her alligator jaws and so is not too popular.

I remember clearly the murder of the kitten. It caused a considerable scene. Frankie sent the greyhound home almost immediately.

I wish you could see the children right now. They are at the best they have ever been, although T. Sometimes annoys Highman by being bossy with the men. One queer thing is that you don't know Highman who is about the most loving, genial, loveable, faithful, hardworking, loyal and heavenly employee you're ever likely to have.

21 January, 1944

Thomas went off to school today. You will be relieved to hear that he was quite pleased to go. Rose had to have a treat because I wouldn't take her with us and T. said to Nanny "I don't really mind if you give her two treats if you can think of them because I know I shall have lots of fun".

I was thinking last night about the nightmare quality life always has. I was in bed. I was very comfortable and the light was still on and the room is very pretty and yet there was something wrong and I had a very well known sense of unease. And it was simply that you weren't there. And I am always haunted by this feeling so that I can practically never say I am happy. Do you think the time has now come when you can push to get home in the sort of way you never would have before? Almost everyone who gets home has I find and is quite honest about it.

16: 1944

Thoughts on Marriage

23 January, 1944

I haven't any news except that the cows reach fresh heights every day. This morning 27 cows produced 90 ½ gallons of milk which is 3 1/3 gallon average. One cow has done 68 lbs another 57 and one heifer did 51 this morning. I wish these things meant more to you because it is one of the major triumphs of my life. To think that only about 3 or 4 months ago Pat seriously advised me and I actually considered selling the heifers. You know if it goes on it's going to make our fortune.

This month's milk cheque will be about £350; next month we have 8 or 10 more good cows to calve and this time next year about 20 heifers to enter. Goodness only knows what it might not mean. I am seriously thinking of trying to work out a scheme which gives Price a direct interest and benefit from the milk. I don't think it would be wise to introduce it until he has been here about a year but he is really a gold mine to us and I think he should be a gold mine to himself – partly because I think he should be and partly because I am afraid when these yields get known some kind friends might make an effort to pinch him and I'd like him to be on such clover that they wouldn't have a chance.

Darling I haven't any other news and my eyes ache excruciatingly. It will be nice to have electric light. One can't see at all by these lamps and has to have them so close they burn the skin off one's face and make one feel perpetually as though one was starting a cold.

27 January, 1944

I am coming to the conclusion that there aren't so many marriages like ours as we thought there were and we should thank God on our knees every night for each other (it's odd not believing in God). I often think when I look around me that I can only see one thing as great as your faith and love for me and that is my faith and love for you. That of course isn't true and I do know quite a lot of others but I know now that no one can be sure who hasn't stood the test of four years separation.

Of course it all comes of marrying someone who amuses and interests you more than anyone else, whose views you respect more than anyone else's and who makes you breathe more easily when he's around. Because then you could never accept anyone else in his place. And it's still so like losing a leg "She does so remarkably well considering she's only got one leg."

My parents love for each other never wavered, even in a time like the war, which put a strain on so many marriages. It is impossible to be sure, but my impression is that they were neither of them ever unfaithful to each other during almost 60 years of marriage and nearly 6 years of wartime separation save only a few short leaves.

29 January, 1944

Pat bought me 45 in-lamb ewes which I am excited about because I love having sheep. They make a reason for a walk and keep my old Meg in trim. I am longing for you to see Meg. She gets more real love from me than any dog I've ever had and more love than most people around here. She's so absolutely pretty and so clever and so affectionate and knowing. She's only got one vice. She regularly bites the postman. I pretended at first that he must be wrong in thinking so but you can't go on with that forever when he's obviously not. So now I have to keep her shut up till he's been.

Frankie and Meg herding sheep

Nanny is here and we talk interminably about you. I make her repeat everything over and over again and I'm jealous of every second I missed. My darling do you know you get 300 miles free petrol when you first come home. We'll take it on the Ford and use it on the Minx and you'll be glad I'm so extravagant. And we'll do thing like this. We'll take the children to bathe in the bathing pool and leave the car in the park and every informer within five miles will rush and tell the police and when they appear on their motor bikes you'll produce your leave ticket. And the children's spines will curl with fear and they'll think you're too wonderful to escape the police.

Jack also met Denis Healey about this time.

27 February, 1944

I met Denis Healey, the most intelligent officer we've got (double first at Oxford, job as a don if he wants it after the war, very young and amusing). *(Jack also got a double first, at Cambridge)*

288

Denis and Edna Healey 1946

He is great fun. He's got the same sorts of interests as I have, and a much better brain and is much better read and is also ten years younger, and I find conversation with him stimulating.

Denis and Edna came to stay at Gypsy Hall after the war, and Denis, who was talented at nearly everything, drew a very good likeness of me.

Drawing of Rose aged 8, by Denis Healey.

 **20 February, 1944**

How many years ago was it? I think 8, and I think it's our ninth wedding-day, of which we've spent five together and four apart. No, it's our tenth, so that makes five apart. Jolly, isn't it?

16 March, 1944

Reggie came back after lunch and he came up and said, "I think I've fixed you up alright — I should say about the 1st of April."

22 March, 1944

Well, darling, it's happened. I was in the office late last night at 7.30, when the duty officer brought in a signal from the Brigadier N.A. saying the War Office had asked for me and in view of his conversation with Reggie he had agreed, so please be prepared to release me on receipt of authority from the Military Secretary.

Jack came home for his first leave April 1944 and then spent a short time in England at the War Office.

On 16 May 1944 Frankie's great friend Leonora Cazalet died. There is a gap in letters.

D-Day (6 June 1944) was approaching. Jack had a short leave in the first week of June, before posting back to Europe.

8 June, 1944

I was a shade gloomy coming down in the train. The main point is that this is such a heavenly place because even when you arrive back feeling thoroughly gloomy and anxious you are nearly always plunged into such activity and excitement that your mind is completely occupied. And it's much better than the sort of superficial occupation which people or a less enthralling job provides. And that of course makes for independence.

You think I'm dependent but you've really no idea what a compliment it is that I'm dependent on you. There isn't anyone else and never could be that I would give up G.H. for. Haymaking is a most awful time – full of anxiety and I hate it. But I can never describe the satisfaction each time one knows one has got one field safely in. It was lovely in London. Darling please write as soon as you can and as often for a week or two. When the thing settles a bit I shall stop worrying about you but just at first it is rather a beastly one. Darling be good and careful and write when you can.

10 June, 1944

I haven't much news and the wind is high so if by chance you are leaving today you will probably at the best be sick. So I'm thinking of you.

The other thing is there's quite a run on "advance extracts" from the book. You remember Scott Robertson. Well now the Farmers' Weekly have written saying they've heard about it and can they have exclusive rights on advance extracts and will send to take photographs.

I wonder where and how you are. I think when I know I shall leave off fussing – not that I am really fussing badly now, just a faint undertone of unrest.

 ## 14 June, 1944

Two rather nice things. Pat brought two old farmers here yesterday. One was called Davis and Pat said, "Do you know Mrs Donaldson?" and he said, "Well yes we heard her speak the other day". The use of the word we instead of I was friendly somehow. Then Pat has a farmhand called Perce. He read it in the Leamington Courier and thinks it the most wonderful thing that ever happened. He made Hans the refugee go through it paragraph by paragraph and kept saying "Fancy her saying that" "Fancy her knowing that". I think it's absolutely sweet and I'm really pleased about it in a way I never am when quite good people like my books etc.

18 June, 1944

I haven't heard a word from you yet, which I'm disappointed about. Also I want to know about the French. What about these girl snipers who are in love with Germans and damn the British? Is the whole occupied story untrue propaganda? Or is it only in this province do you think? Or isn't it really true at all except in isolated cases? Any way don't trust any women until you're sure they haven't a gun hidden anywhere.

23 June, 1944

So far all very well. I'm sitting in the sun on deck off the invasion coast, very peaceful and happy. More shipping around us than I've ever seen in one place in my life, and than anyone else has, I expect. We spent two days in a marshalling camp and finally got on board Sunday morning. It's unbelievable to sit here all day in this mass of shipping and never hear a gun fired. I think Monty has got his "firm base" alright. Our last two months have been a very wonderful foretaste of what is to come.

17: 1944
Flying Bombs

 3 July, 1944
London and the South, by the way, dislike the flying bomb a whole lot more than you would ever guess from the news. I've now met at least 6 people, some of them like Barbara Kenyon and Mab who slept peacefully through the blitz, and everyone agrees that this is unbearably horrid. It's the 24 hrs out of 24 that gets them down plus the inhumanity of the thing. They don't sleep much and they are getting thoroughly strained. I don't mean by that that anyone regards it as a serious weapon – just very nasty.

A flying bomb is a manned or unmanned aerial vehicle or aircraft carrying a large explosive warhead, a precursor to contemporary cruise missiles. In contrast to a bomber aircraft, which is intended to release bombs and then return to its base for re-use, a flying bomb crashes into its target and is therefore itself destroyed in its attack. It was usually called a doodlebug, or a buzz bomb.

After the invasion of Europe by the Allies, these weapons were also employed against targets on the mainland of Europe, mainly Britain and Belgium. The V-terror-bombing killed approximately 18,000 people, mostly civilians. The cities London, Antwerp and Liège were the main targets

5 July 1944

My darling – I got your letter of the 1st promising more Camemberts. Of course they are wanted. The first two weren't ripe and I wanted to keep them but Dave said they were already past their best – that is not unripe but drying up – and would get worst from keeping. Anyway now having heard from you I will keep the next ones until they seem ripe. The others were very good and much nicer than anything we have had for a long time. Also if you don't mind, it is a very nice thing to be able to give away occasionally.

Dr Anni Noll

Jan and Dave are staying for a fortnight and then Anni and Haschi are coming. Although they don't say so, I owe this unusually prolonged visit to the flying bombs. The thing is I really rather hate people staying in the house for more than a couple of days. You see what happens is that I am out all day on one thing or another and so when I come in for meals or in the evening naturally I have to entertain them. But I don't want to. I want to read. Also I would quite like to write a bit too at the moment.

All conversations are so basically dull – flying bombs, how long can the Germans hold out, are the French pleased or cross to be liberated, does Anni really love Haschi or is it that she doesn't and has to make up for not? Who knows and in the final analysis who bloody well cares? It may be that I don't have amusing enough people to stay but I get more and more to prefer not having any people at all. Not that I'm not fond of Jan and Dave. I really am.

I went to see Thomas this afternoon. You know he's got chicken pox. He was quite all right, no temperature and very good spirits, but he looked pale and had dark marks under his eyes. The matron said he looked worse than the others had done and I think one has to admit that if he is at all ill his heart does show itself. Not that there is any worry. He is quite all right, it just takes more out of him. He was quite sweet. He said, "Is this rain really a bit much?" And I said, "Well, you see I've still got one field of hay out". and he said, "You haven't. Well I've been going round telling everyone that you'd got all yours in". He obviously felt very much let down.

7 July, 1944

I got letters from you in which you said you saw a flying bomb going for the German lines. This is interesting because here there is a theory that if they are hit in the right place it turns them completely round and that our pilots are beginning to get the hang of doing this. But I don't know whether there is really anything in it. People are making a pretty good fuss about it.

I think it must be pretty bad because people like Peggy who have never taken much notice of the blitz think it's pretty awful. Peggy goes to London, but she said, "I shouldn't go if I hadn't got a good reason".

11 July, 1944

I've bought you a gun I think. £70. Pat says it's a dream. It's my *'Four Years Harvest'* present. Rose has got chicken pox so I've got Thomas home too for a week. He looked pale and thin and I felt sad for him being at school so long.

Darling, I'm absolutely staggered by your categorical instructions about the flying bomb. What makes you take that line. You always agreed one should go up during the blitz and this is obviously a joke compared to that whatever people say. I won't go up till I hear from you again but I have a coat and skirt I want to fit and I want to get some electric light fittings etc., and I don't agree with your instructions at all. So let me know when you've thought them over. I enclose letters from T. The thing he has learned is the deaf and dumb language. He was awfully pleased with your letter and recited your views on possible German collapse to everyone.

15 July, 1944

On Tuesday I decided to go and see old Robertson Scott about the article. Then on Wednesday Thompson came down to take more photographs and insisted on going over to Peggy's where was John Hare for dinner. Then Thursday I had a hangover all morning and a lot of farm work to do and then in the middle of the morning Nora lost her temper and walked out.

First Robertson Scott *(founder and editor of The Countryman magazine).* He was very charming and I think I quite misjudged him when he came here. There was no trouble at all about the article and by cutting here and there and changing a few things I think we succeeded in making it a very decent article, considering it wasn't originally written in that form. Cripps *(John Cripps, son of Sir Stafford and later editor of The Countryman)* was there and Mrs R.S. and they were all exceedingly nice. R.S. is very ingenious and rather sweet about his views. He says of someone "O he believes in nationalisation" as anyone else might say "O but he is a very nice fellow" and he talks always in that rather innocent way. When I left he gave me the clenched fist. I think you would be rather amused though possibly only for a short time.

There was a row with Nora who then said she was leaving. Mrs Hig came the next morning and said, "Nora is very sorry and she would like to come back" and I said, "Well I'm not going to have her back".

Anyway I saw her this afternoon and I was very nice and just said, "We've been together too long Nora. You are always best when you don't know people too well." And she said, "I know. I can't help it. It's too much for me. It just comes out and then I'm sorry afterwards", which is the absolute truth. And I said she must always regard us as her friends and come and see the children whenever she wants to and let me know if things really go wrong, etc., etc., but I stayed firm.

We went to Hamlet. There is a Hamlet called John Byron who has made an enormous success. I haven't discovered yet whether it is a national success or only a local one but many people who know about Shakespeare have said he is the best for years. Anyway I enjoyed it as much as anything I have ever been to and I am going again when Anni is here. I was rather bored at going. I always think I don't really like Shakespeare and it is a bit of a pose for me to go. But I was really enchanted and adored every minute of it. The season goes on until nearly the end of September. I wish you might be able to see it.

See Letters to An Actor playing Hamlet, by Christopher Fry.

We went to Summer Fields to look at the school for Thomas. Evans is really a charming man with a very good speaking voice. The atmosphere was good and the boys looked really nice and happy and gay. The matron was the most awful horror but everything else was nice and I think we've done moderately all right. Thomas is definitely to go in January. I talked to Evans about his being badly taught and backward and he took a very strong view about his not being able to read well yet.

Evans said he'd absolutely got to be able to read when he goes there. So I'm going to do at least half an hour's reading with him every day during the holidays. The curious thing is that Rose can really read now. She can read the newspaper to you and she hardly ever makes a mistake even with difficult words. She was rather sweet this morning. I was talking to Thomas and I said I would give him a present when he could really read. And presently I heard Rose stumping about the house saying "It isn't fair. Mummy is going to give Thomas a present when he can read. But I can read now and no one gives me a present."

18 July, 1944

I got a letter from you this morning. I won't go to London if it undermines your feeling of security about me. Probably the thing will stop soon now and then it will be all right to go.

T. has gone back to school but R. is here. She is awfully good and amuses herself all day. I brought some of her lesson books back and she just took them of her own accord and sat working at them. Now she is painting. She makes her own bed every day and peels the potatoes and knows where everything is. This is a very disjointed letter but I'm helping Rose with her arithmetic which she had after all done all wrong. (She dared to argue with me about who knew what 49 from 63 left – she or me). Anyway this is only meant to tell you that I won't go to London and I love you very much and I wish you would come home soon and I haven't any news.

18 July, 1944

All the windows are out of the Wood House but the War Office are dealing with it. Darling I got a letter from the War Office which began "I regret to inform you…." and then went on about the Wood House. Can you imagine?

Not much news. The Nora business is now decided because she has got a job at Stratford Hospital. This suits me down to the ground. We are on the best of terms – she came to tea yesterday.

24 July, 1944

We started cutting oats today on Pat's advice. After they had cut 4 acres I went down and stopped them because I really didn't think they were ripe enough. I don't know whether I am right.

Since that was written Pat has been and said we should go on cutting but he had 2 farmers with him who said we would be better off asleep in bed. So you pay your money and take your choice. I'm in a hurry to get this off now.

26 July, 1944

I got a letter this morning posted by Gerry Duke. You don't give much news about the Russian medal – the Order of the Patriotic War.

1) Is it now official? 2) Can you wear it yet? 3) If not how did you hear about it and can I go round boasting or is it a secret? Personally I think it's the most impressive thing that's yet happened to either of us. I regard it (possibly wrongly) as a passport to Russia if we ever want to visit there after the war. And I also regard it as exclusively chic from an English point of view. I shall always boast of it wherever I go. By the time you are back you won't be in uniform anymore. You will have to take to wearing a white tie and orders for the opera. Actually you are getting quite a little string. Probably there will be something for this current show and if so you will have 4.

I'm awfully disappointed you don't come home at all. I fully believed you would. And I can see now that it's not going to be very likely at any rate during the present phase. And I miss you very much. I miss you now in the everyday things I would like your advice about.

We went again to Hamlet last night. It is really wonderful. I wouldn't mind how often I saw it and I do wish you could see it. 6 Camembert cheeses arrived this morning.

29 July, 1944

We were cutting oats yesterday. I drove the tractor. I haven't driven it with the binder before because I always thought there was some difficulty. However, it's dead easy so I shall do it in future.

Bos rang up the night before last and asked himself and 4 other people to tea yesterday. In the end they didn't arrive here until 8 o'clock so I gave them supper instead of tea. It was jolly good. Pat was here too so there were 7 and they had scrambled eggs, plum tart and cream, cake and ginger biscuits which I had made from Emma's recipe, Camembert cheese and lettuce, beer and coffee.

The Combine is here and is being put together now. It's going to be a God awful nuisance because it's too wide for any of the gates.

3 August, 1944

I wrote today but I forgot to tell you the following rather endearing conversation. I asked Susan (*her niece*) what she was going to do when she grew up and she said she didn't know.

Rose – I do

Me – Do you? What?

R – I'm going to have this farm.

T – No you're not 'cos I am.

Me to T. – Would you like to have it?

T – Yes.

Me to R – Would you?

R – Yes. And I'm going to.

Anni – You'd better marry a farmer Rose. Then you can both have a farm.

R – No. 'Cos this is the best farm.

Me – Why do you think so?

R – It's got pear trees on.

Me – But hundreds of farms have pear trees on.

R – Not great big trees like that one with lots of little pears on. I love lots of little pears.

T – (Who had appeared not to be listening) I'll send you some every summer.

Sometime soon after this I wrote in a children's writing competition for the Farmers' Weekly. It was a story about sitting at the top of a big pear tree and seeing the view all around. I won a prize. I always assumed it was my brilliant writing that did it, but of course it may have been my farming connections.

I'm having the most dreadful time and I don't write to you or get your tobacco or anything. I've got Michael and Susan *(nephew and niece)* here and I'm nearly going mad. Both of them are an eye opener about how good it is to bring children up on a farm. They can't find anything to do here although there are always about 6 children playing in the barn, tractors going in every direction and dogs and cats, etc. They only want to go to the cinema in Stratford

I went last night to the Merchant of Venice with Pat. We have all become Shakespeare fans.

Jack came home for a couple of days on leave.

6 August, 1944 The Berkeley, London W.1.

Just a line to tell you it's not too bad. I was a shade depressed when you left because it's so much worse when a long day stretches before you with nothing to do and a tiresome train journey at the end of it. But I soon cheered up and stayed in bed for a bit and now am downstairs filling in the morning by writing to you and then Peter.

Peter Cazalet's wife and Frankie's great friend, Leonora, had died on 16th May 1944 just as Peter was preparing to leave for France and D-Day operations.

It's now 11.40. I think I shall stay here till lunch then lunch at 1 o'clock and then walk to the Savoy Hotel which has a bookstall to see if I can buy anything to read in the train. The hotel bill was £5 and I suppose my lunch will swallow the rest of the last £. I've just had a long talk with the clerk who agrees with me that in spite of the Government claiming a small rise only in the cost of living owing to their having pegged a few foodstuffs, there is really an inflation of at least 100%. Still that's not very interesting.

Well it's nice not to have any news to tell you because I've so recently seen you. Every minute was lovely and worth at least twice as much exasperation in trains and boredom in hotels and I do hope you felt so too.

10 August, 1944

Bob Kyzer *(army contact)* has just rung up so I know you got back all right. Looks like you'll be in Paris before the end of the month.

P.S. Send as much as you can of that thick chocolate you said you didn't like. When we work late I'm too tired to get supper and a piece of that and a glass of milk vitaminises me until morning.

18: 1944

Good War News

 13 August, 1944
The children have gone to bed and it's cool in this lovely east room and it's the first peace for ages – since in fact supper in bed at the Berkeley. 2 things – one I'll try for the cigarettes but for the first time since 1941 there appears to be a cigarette shortage. Reason – they are all being sent to Normandy. So it looks like you'll have to send them to me. I can't remember what the second thing is. But darling if I fail to do the things you've asked me to, forgive me for a short while because it really is a bit much here. O I know, I'm madly excited about the lunch at the Soviet Embassy.

Isn't the war news wonderful. And by the time you get this it may be even more wonderful. That's what's so exciting. Lovely things happen and there's always the feeling there may be even better round the corner.

War news: **3 July** *The Russian city of Minsk is retaken by the Russians.*

8 July *U.S. taking of the island of Saipan becomes certain.*

25 August *Paris is liberated by Allied French troops.*

16 August, 1944
Frank Sykes sent me his book with a rather sweet inscription: "To Frankie Donaldson whose book I should rather have written."

Frank Sykes, *This Farming Business*, Faber, London, 1944

25 August, 1944

Frank Sykes' book is the best I have yet read on farming. I am reading it now and I shan't send this copy to you because it's got an inscription I'm proud of and I don't want it lost but I'll try and get you another as it will do more for your education than anything else I've read and in my opinion knocks Henderson silly as it deals with things of wider and more general application and implication – not just a special method of making money by working yourself to death.

29 August, 1944

I think I have decided in my own mind in the last week or so what it is I want out of life. I will tell you that first because it explains so many other things.

I want a farm and I want some work. But I never again want to cry from over-exhaustion in the middle of harvest nor do I want to lie awake at night wondering how the devil I am ever going to get us through all the things we have got to get through – even if the lying awake is caused by hysterical over-tiredness as much as by the inherent difficulties. Then I want beautiful and reasonably convenient surroundings – on of course a simple scale – and I want a nice pony to ride and books to read and I want to be able to play the gramophone and write when I feel like it.

In return for this I am prepared to work quite hard but hard in a reasonable way, not hard in a totally unreasonable way, grinding away until I am silly. Then again I'm tired of hearing the children say "Mummy I suppose you wouldn't have the time to take us bathing". and always having to answer "NO". They won't be young and sweet for so much longer and I don't want to spend all their summer holidays turning them out to amuse themselves because I haven't got time to do things with them.

Now in the last years I've not only worked extremely hard but I think if we sold out now I would have made a few thousand pounds. My idea is as follows. If I could get into a more amenable farm I should say to you as follows: this is my contribution. This is our home and I am prepared to work hard enough to see that it provides us with the home, the milk, butter eggs, vegetables, cars, telephone bills, etc. But I'm not prepared to work any harder than that. That is to say if the farm is going to be worked to its ultimate capacity and is not merely to provide a house and a background you are the one who's going to do it because I'm not.

In conclusion two things. I feel I have found out that the proper way to live is on a farm. But I am quite sure that it's no use living on a farm where it's a struggle. But it leaves you, as before and as you ought to be, the breadwinner. So put that in your pipe and smoke it. You'd either have to earn the children's education, etc., etc., on the farm or somewhere else. Because I'm not bloody well going to.

31 August, 1944

I had a very sweet and gay letter from you. I don't exactly take the Friday week line, *(for the end of the war)* but I would if I didn't think that Hitler and co will go on saving their own lives at the expense of thousands of German lives as long as they can. Even allowing for that all, the evidence seems to suggest that it ought to be over before the winter.

Now I've just had a shattering blow and I feel indescribably depressed. I went to the accountants this morning about the accounts. I said, "Have you arrived at any figure yet?" He said, "Yes, but it is looking like a loss". We then went through the various points he was doubtful about but none of my replies made it any better.

It seems as if Frankie was overly depressed at the figures as she had during the year moved house and done a lot of rather expensive decoration and furnishing to the farmhouse, in an effort to make it nice enough for Jack to return to. Like many other people they had been used to much higher standard of living before the war, and as she says, she was not brought up right. Her father once had a competition with Lord Beaverbrook to see who could spend the most money in a week.

Anyway however you look at it I seem to have made a hell of a mess of everything and there's no thumping profit anywhere that the income tax wouldn't take. What shall we do? The point seems to be that if I can't make a profit now when prices are good I never shall. So what? Darling I really am worried sick and I do wish you could get back to discuss it.

Gosh I am depressed because you see our overdraft is so fearfully big and even the harvest which is coming in isn't going to put it nearly right and if I feel that I am doing badly it is really too destroying on top of everything else. Because it simply means I am an ass. And I work terribly hard and am thought to be not an ass and the whole thing is so confidence destroying. I simply don't feel at the moment that I can ever get over the fact that I'm not really doing nearly well enough. You see I've spent too much on the farm itself and there's no way out of that if I'm really not earning the money to do it with. O damn and blast.

I've just had a long talk with Pat and in the way people always do we've succeeded in talking the accounts into looking better. Taking Burgis' later figure of about £400 profit and then saying that in that year we stood £300 worth of bills from the year before.

It's now pitch dark so I must stop. But I'll get a clearer picture soon and let you have it. And in the meantime please don't discuss it with anyone as I am so frightfully crestfallen and I don't want other people to think I'm a dud – at any rate until I am 100% certain I am.

2 September, 1944

Well, then, about here. I have decided to take the risk and I have let Margetts *(the local auctioneer)* know that though I should be glad to hear of any exceptional chance that might arise in the meantime, the farm will be officially for sale in the spring and not now.

What I am perfectly prepared to believe is that I used all the profit on improving the farm.

Well, now as to the farm. It could hardly be gloomier. For weeks now it has rained for a short time every other day so that on the fine days the crops dry out just enough to be fit and we are just going to get going when it rains again and we are boiled again. *(She often said 'boiled' for 'done for' or 'finished'.)*

However, the war is going marvellously and perhaps you will soon be here. It wouldn't be so gloomy if you were. I've always managed to face anything with you about. But it is a trifle harassing on one's own.

03 September, 1944

This is the fifth anniversary of the war and the news is so wonderful one should be very gay.

Also from what today's papers say there must be some chance of your being demobilised quite soon after an armistice in Europe is declared. Also you have the O.B.E. and although I have forgotten to mention it in two letters I am really quite pleased about it and have boasted to everyone. By the way you have become a local hero as your O.B.E. is mentioned in the Stratford Herald as a local honour.

6 September, 1944

I was just going to sit down and write you a long letter when I got your p.c. of the 3rd saying you were going so fast you wouldn't be able to write and you wouldn't get any of my letters.

I envy you enormously. You must be having a most exciting and memorable experience. I wish you had time to write about that.

Jack wrote a long letter listing, in code, the multiple towns that he had passed through on the rapid journey up from Italy through France and into Belgium. It gave an incredible view of the speed of the battle front and re-occupation, but is not given here as the coding makes it difficult to read or understand.

12 September, 1944

Here everything is so inexpressibly bloody that it's not worth writing about. It rains every single day. It is impossible to get the harvest in. Therefore no money comes in while it continually goes out. There are 3 land girls in the house and the ram *(water pump)* has gone wrong so we have no water.

15 September, 1944

I'm in a mood of such extreme fedupness that I would say that I was physically, mentally and spiritually played right out except that I know that if there was any fresh stimulus such as your coming home to help or something quite new happening it wouldn't be true. But you've no idea how utterly wearing and boring farming can be to anyone who has not got the complete Henderson (Farming Ladder) mentality.

At the moment for instance there is the rest of the wheat to combine. That takes Highman and one boy. There is the straw to sweep off behind the combining. That takes a whole gang. There are the potatoes to be got up which takes the biggest gang one can get. There is sugar beet to be lifted – can't start on that anyway for the moment. There is silage to be made which takes a whole gang. There is 70 acres to plough. All these things should really be done before autumn and winter rain make them impossible. In addition there are a thousand and one delaying jobs like weighing sacks and getting them off to the station and grinding for the cows, etc., which also have to be done. One simply never knows how to arrange the work to get the maximum out of everyone for the day.

Of course for anyone with a zest for life all this could be rather fun. But I haven't any zest for life. I hate it. And I'm tired and bored and I want to stay in bed and read a book. And I see no chance of a change for at least 3 months. What was that about you not doing any work for the first 6 months? Just walking about and reading farming stuff? You haven't got a hope my boy. Not even for six days.

I saw Mary Messer of the Farmers Weekly. They are thinking of serialising Four Years' Harvest. But it's not quite decided yet. I'm sending you the Countryman.

I did order your tobacco and cigarettes from Army and Navy Stores but as it doesn't appear to have been sent I'll try and send some more tobacco from Stratford today. The war is wonderful isn't it. But I'm afraid it may settle down to taking rather long over the actual end.

16 September, 1944

I had a letter this morning from a man called C.S. Orwin and as my letters to you lately have been full only of gloom and this is quite pleasant I thought I would write and tell you about it. Orwin is one of those names one knows. He is a pundit of sorts. Anyway he has sent me two pamphlets and a Penguin of his and from the latter I see that he is Director of the Agricultural Economics Research Institute, Oxford and a Fellow and the Estates Bursar of Balliol College. He has also been a lot of other things in his time and prepared the case for the N.F.U. in 1919. He says:

"May I say how much I enjoyed your article in the current issue of the Countryman. It seems to me to face the real position of farming and the issues of reconstruction confronting the industry in a way few of the many people who speak for the industry are prepared to do. The claims of landowners for preferential taxation, the claims of farmers for guaranteed profits but no interference from Whitehall, seem to me to be merely beating the air unless, of course, landlords and farmers want to make their industry parasitic on the rest of the community."

I'm rather pleased because this must mean that the arguments do in fact make some sense. And that is all that matters because one always knows that the ones who want to disagree will disagree whether it makes sense or not.

Darling I do hope you aren't going into Germany. I'm awfully frightened of all those civilian snipers and you alone in a jeep.

21 September, 1944

I feel slightly better than when I last wrote about the farm losses. I still think it's a great blow both to vanity and of course to income. But I think it might be overcome in the future. I am worried about the crop returns in this coming year but on the other hand the milk is good. We are sending 66 or so gallons at the moment as against 36 this time last year.

I've now got a wonderful economy campaign on. I'm going to be rid of all landgirls except Joan by the end of November and have the two little boys in their place at 26/- instead of 48/-. It will mean I shall have to do the pigs and poultry myself but I don't suppose that will hurt me.

Then I'm sorting out all the things we could manage without such as the Ford van and I'm going to sell them. So that though it's all going to be rather hard and poverty stricken again it should be better in the future. And anyway it's no good crying over spilt milk.

The other thing is I've decided not to tell anyone and you must keep to that. You see it's not quite fair. The truth is that we made considerably less profit the year before than I thought and said but we really didn't make a loss this year.

Then quite apart from that we have lived on the fat of the land and charged it up at £1 a week whereas it's probably nearer £5 with all the cream and butter and poultry and the stuff I give away and the fact that all coal, etc., is paid for by the farm. Then I pay myself £80 and although of course I ought to be able to one can't have that £80 both ways.

The other reason why I've decided not to tell is that if you write as I have in the book – the last chapter I mean – you've got to make a profit. Otherwise although it's got nothing in the world to do with your opinions on wider things you're simply written off. O you needn't bother what she says. She made a loss in one of the best years of farming. And I'm not going to have that. Because my takings were higher than any of those gents. It's simply that I was brought up extravagant and they weren't.

Also it isn't as though I had nothing good to show. This farm is out of the class of fertility of anything it has probably known for a century. And I've improved it in every way and made it habitable. And if I had concentrated on being economical I should have left all those things alone and made a profit. So I hope you agree that it's nobody's business but ours.

I had a letter from Peter. I moaned to him about the harvest and so he had a moan back, about the war. He simply hates every minute of it. He minds so dreadfully not only his own discomfort and danger but all the waste and futility. And he loathes the killing - even the killing of the Germans. He says of course everybody does. And he says that even the young officers hate going in anywhere first because they know some have got to get killed. But the point he makes is that it's all waste because we always win in the end.

His description of entering Brussels is really good and I must say a great change after such enlightening remarks as "I had a great reunion with the Racines". Not that I really want to crack at you my sweety even though you do manage to travel right through history and treat it as you might a journey to Southend in 1935. However, I shall keep Peter's letter if only to have one historical document to show my grandchildren.

She didn't, of course. She threw nearly everything away each time they moved house, which was about every 12 years. She had inherited her father's restlessness, though in a less extreme form.

Mr. Dowler rang me up this morning about something else and he said I read your article in the Countryman. I thought he mightn't like it because he is very simple and I thought some of the ideas might be offensive to him. So I said, "It's not very good, but it isn't as I wrote it. They've compressed it and mucked it about". He said, "I think it's absolutely brilliant. And if it's not as good as what you wrote then I should like to see what you wrote".

Then I went to fetch some children from the Stratford Council school to pick potatoes. I was talking to rather a charming master who, however, wasn't making much sense about what I wanted. I said, "Donaldson is my name". There is a slight smile of enlightenment which people give when they suddenly realise who you are and approve of it. He said, "I read your article in the Countryman" and went off at once and arrived back in no time with the children.

I think I love you very much and I'm quite sure you are the nicest person I know but I am so much more dead than alive at the moment that I can't be very certain about anything. However, I thought of something new about you the other day. You always only bring the best out of me.

That's why I like you so much. Almost everyone else brings out other things – things I hate and which humiliate me. When you are here I'm always nice and that makes me feel good.

Frankie was pregnant at this time although she may not have known it yet. This may account for her feeling overwrought. I think the feeling that the war was nearly over also made it all the harder for her to bear it all patiently.

19: 1944

Omnia Vincit Amor

23 September, 1944
Forgive a card, but I've been rushed off my feet for a week in a series of flaps. I got four long letters feeling gloomy about the farm accounts. I hope it's not too bad. I hope Peter has rung you. He was slightly wounded in the arm and flew home today. I saw him for two seconds in the street.

This letter will have taken a week or more to arrive

29 September, 1944
Something nice has happened for the first time for months. Peter's in hospital in Birmingham. I got a letter from him but obviously not realising how near he was. I rang up and spoke to a fearful sister who said I couldn't possibly speak to him because it was her private office line and no business of the patients at all. So I just said, "Could you possibly send a message to say it's Mrs Donaldson and shall I come and see him?" In about 2 seconds Peter was on the line which was what I expected. He is absolutely whooping with joy and we exchanged congratulations for about 5 minutes and then fixed for me to go and spend the afternoon with him on Sunday.

02 October, 1944
I really have had enough. It may be that I simply haven't got enough guts. But you've no idea what it's like here. The

really frightful thing is that we can't get through it all whatever we do and since each thing is about equally important one can't make up one's mind just to sacrifice something and get on with the rest. The men are overworked and from time to time they get a bit fed up. Price is the worst. He just gets bolshie every now and then and I should like to give in to him but I can't because then I should have to do the same for the others and then we should never get anything done. And honestly darling it may be frightfully wrong and I know it's the exact opposite of all I said to you when you were here, but I've had enough. I won't ever do this anymore. So either you've got to be back – back enough to cope – by this time next year or we're going to sell the farm and be out of it by then.

I wish you could come home if even for a few days. I should feel better if I could talk it over with you. But everybody is pretty gloomy about the failure of the Arnheim thing and I think most people are beginning to think of 1945 now.

The Battle of Arnhem was fought in and around the Dutch towns of Arnhem, Oosterbeek, Wolfheze, Driel and the surrounding countryside from 17–26 September 1944, following an airborne landing behind enemy lines. After sweeping through France and Belgium in the summer of 1944, the Allies were poised to enter the Netherlands but the Battle of Arnhem resulted in a German victory.

03 October, 1944

The accounts: Now I don't propose to go on about this so I want to say once what I feel about it. Outside emotional matters it's the biggest knock I've ever had. For the last 2 years I've had a view of myself as a person who was successful in a quite difficult undertaking. My book was written from that point of view, everything I've done or said was from that point of view. And now it simply isn't true. You know even when I'm unreasonably impatient with one of the landgirls and feeling repentant I think "O well it's a great pity but you can't do all I do without being short tempered sometimes". And that's founded on conceit – unjustified. And so on.

One thing – there seems to be a job for you if only in preventing me frittering an £800 profit into £200 loss every year. What I resent is there was no reason to expect it. The first 2 years I was surprised to make a profit and could have understood a loss. But that particular year absolutely everything seemed to be on the up and up and I still can't quite understand it.

I think there are only about 2 ameliorating things to be said. One is I'm glad the production is all right. Two, of course I was brought up wrong. Except that I take this so much more seriously it isn't really any different from the fact that we always overspent our income by about £500 and never could see where or how it was possible to cut.

Frankie's childhood was financially unstable. Her father, at one moment possibly the most successful playwright of his day, was either stinking rich from a recent success or broke after a period of not writing. Three times in her youth the bailiffs arrived to turn them out of the house, but in between they lived like kings. This did not help to develop a rational approach to finances.

The thing I didn't realise was that it wasn't enough to earn as much as another farmer, I'd also got to have the same outlook on expenditure as another farmer.

The truth is that I'm suffering a blow to my inordinate pride. It comes on top of the worst harvest I've yet had. And this afternoon I spent on the tractor only to come in and find that Highman had had the whole of the rest of the gang on threshing and simply from absolutely fatuous organisation had threshed 8 sacks where he ought to have threshed 30. In my present mood it was the last straw and I cried.

12 October, 1944

Tomorrow is the T.T. sale and we've got 8 cows and heifers going so it's rather exciting. We sent 88 gallons from 28 cows this morning. This time last year we sent about 35-40.

On the new economy campaign I've sold the Ford and also the Fordson tractor. It is a saving but it will make my life even more unpleasant and hazardous. No other news except it's now pouring with rain which will bitch us some more. I'll write and tell you about the sale which I'm much looking forward to.

14 October, 1944

I have such an immense longing to read. I've collected about 6 books I want to read and one of them, Social History of England by Trevelyan, which I am reading right now is hotting me up with all sorts of ideas for future reading. I'm not really enjoying it as much as I might because I find it impossible to settle to anything as long as the potatoes are still rotting in the ground.

The reason I hate it all so is that I worry so much. I spend the whole time doing calculations about how many days' work there are and making allowances for rain, etc. None of it does any good and it just makes me miserable. On the other hand, if one hadn't a nervous conscientious temperament one would never make the effort to get through it at all. Anyway as a result I spend the whole day longing to get to the fire and my book and then the evening with half my mind on the wheat, sugar beet or potatoes. I think it's simply hateful and I wish I was born a writer or something else that was leisurely. You must be getting very sick of my letters. Anyway you'll have to put up with it for about 6 more weeks and then I shall suddenly get very enthusiastic again and begin writing to you to tell you farming is the most wonderful thing in the world. You must be getting used to me by now.

28 October, 1944

My Darling – I haven't written for a day or two and this morning I got a letter from you in which you said that you loved me but you were sick of saying so. That's the whole thing about writing at the moment and I think we'll have that one right out because I am just as bad as you are about it. The thing is I love you as much as ever I did and I want you to be here as much. But somehow since you came back then went away again and then the war seemed to be going to end and then seemed not to be, the whole thing has become too much.

I can't go on forever and ever writing to you about everything that happens when nothing at all ever happens and I can't go on writing to tell you I love you when you already know it and I can't go on thinking in living terms of something I've been waiting for five years and isn't here yet. I don't think it alters a thing and I don't worry about it because you so obviously feel the same. Nor does it mean that I am any the less glad to receive your letters or any less disappointed when I don't but it's just that when it comes to writing to you I feel I've said everything there is to be said more often than is good for me and I just have that little tired feeling that one simply can't go on and on forever just writing letters. However, that's the feeling and I do still think it's fairly important not to be too much swayed by it because though it's become intolerable to write letters it still is a great joy to receive them and as I have said a continual disappointment when one doesn't.

So, as I expect you feel exactly the same about that, I will go on writing whenever I have the time and whenever there is anything to say and, even if there isn't either, I will still write pretty often and you must do the same. And that's all there is to be said except that you mustn't worry about finding it rather boring writing to me because we are always pretty mutual and reach the same stage at about the same time and I understand exactly how you feel. And nor do I think it denotes anything basic at all.

I feel we have reached a stage where, because we are so absolutely sure of each other, we can afford to admit that superficially it is impossible to keep up the same exclusive interest in each other's lives when they are not joined and have not been for five years.

You see one reason I know this is true is that if I had the faintest feeling that there was the smallest thing wrong between us that would give me the necessary stimulus to want to write – I should be writing alternate stinkers and apologies at least once a day.

I feel now so very definitely what we've always felt a little, that nothing is any good but the end. I should love to see you on a hurried and unsatisfactory visit of a day or two and I should be very excited and glad and then a little sad when you left, but it isn't what I want.

What I want is for you to be here altogether and to share my life and I'm really not particularly interested in anything else. So until then, because I can't really bear it anymore, I've gone into a sort of black out about the whole thing.

The other thing I feel is that no one understands anything about us but us. And I feel now that we should always understand each other. So if you aren't mad keen to write to me I'm not the least upset by the knowledge that, in theory, you ought to be, because we've gone through five years and we know a hell of a lot which most people will never know but what emerges most strongly from that for me is the belief that, not only because of our love but also because of your rather peculiar character, nothing could ever go wrong between us now.

That last statement is the final analysis of my present feelings which I think are all right and even rather good in a new and slightly tired way. So I may as well leave it at that and not say any more.

20: 1945

In brief

The war dragged on for nearly another year. Frankie, like many other people, suffered from war fatigue and depression. Many letters begged Jack to somehow wangle to get home, as many of their friends already had. The few short leaves were not enough and they were unsettling and almost made matters worse. These later letters have less interesting material and were more occasional.

She had been briefly pregnant but lost the baby in January 1945. Jack came home on compassionate leave from Europe, where he then was. She became pregnant again in March and there was more pressure to get him back. He returned finally in July 1945, about 2 months after VE day, and was at home to support her and take over the farm for the last few months of pregnancy. My sister Kate was born in November.

VE (victory in Europe) day was the 8th May 1945 and VJ (victory in Japan) day was 15th August 1945.

It is important to stress before finishing, that Frankie, and later Jack, were serious professional farmers, dependent on the farm for their entire income and later the costs of sending 3 children to expensive private schools. This was different from the many wives of landed gentry who farmed for the war effort and after, but not with the intensity and rarely with the skill which Frankie achieved. It was always made clear to us that they were NOT 'gentleman farmers'.

21: 1945 onwards

After the War

Jack arrived home after the war. Gypsy Hall Farm was sold and soon we moved to Gloucestershire, to Burden Court Farm, Tresham.

Burden Court Farmhouse in 1948

The farmhouse, though small and with small rooms, was a beautiful Cotswold stone house overlooking in the far distance the Bristol Channel and, in good weather, the blue of the Welsh mountains. They had to sell The Wood House to finance this purchase, which was a great sadness, but inevitable.

Burden Court farm was right on the edge of the Cotswolds, above Wotton-under-edge. The last field on the higher part of the farm was called World's End.

It was about 500 acres and a few years later they rented another 275. This enabled them to make enough income to send Thomas to Eton, me to Cheltenham Ladies College and, later, Kate to Cranborne Chase school. This was no mean feat, and I remember the almost regular conversations at the end of the school holidays, as to which cow would have to be sold to pay the fees. There were 3 of us now, as my sister Kate was born in November 1945.

They farmed successfully together until the early 1970s. Frankie continued to write. Her great success was the Marconi Scandal, followed later by a ground-breaking biography of Edward VIII which won her the Wolfson prize for history. She became an acclaimed writer and wrote continuously until she died. We gave her a Toshiba laptop computer with a half-sized screen and one 3 ½ inch floppy drive and a tiny screen for her 80th birthday in 1987. She wrote 3 books on it, including her edition of the P.G. Wodehouse letters.My sister Kate and I had to be constantly on the telephone sorting out dramas, but she conquered it, as most other things in her life. She would not let Jack learn it because (this was the days before Windows had come to the PC with a graphic interface) she said, "We are not going to keep having arguments about whether it is CTRL this or CTRL that." I heard her showing off to Denis Healey one day because she knew how to do footnotes and he didn't at that time. (It helped having 2 daughters in the trade.)

Jack worked for prison reform and was a governor of Kingswood Approved School near Bristol and later Grendon Underwood prison. He wrote an important report on the subject of prison reform with Frank Pakenham, (Lord Longford); and was Chairman of the National Association for the Care and Resettlement of Offenders. He became a life peer in 1967. He hated the idea of becoming a peer, and refused it at first, but was persuaded by his Labour party friends (Tony Crosland – who was our MP, Roy Jenkins, Denis Healey and others) that the party needed him to help represent them in the Lords. He would have been glad of it without the title and the appearance of privilege, but he settled into it and enjoyed the work and, increasingly, the pleasures of the House of Lords, which are many.

He was a member of the Labour governments of 1974-1979 as under-secretary for Northern Ireland and later Minister for the Arts. When one of my friends said to him, about the Arts, "It must be a change from Northern Ireland", he replied, "The only difference is they don't carry guns."

His passion was always music. In his youth he had started the first Eton Jazz band (The Eton Outcasts) and also played saxophone in the Cambridge Jazz band led by Fred Elizalde.

In later life he was for some 20 years on the board of directors at the Royal Opera House, Covent Garden, where he introduced Walter Legge, and was the liaison director with English National Opera.

Some of Frankie's books expand the story of their life. The wartime books of Approach to Farming and Four Years Harvest were followed by Child of the Twenties, about her youth, Freddy Lonsdale about her father and A Twentieth Century Life in her last years; as well as numerous others on different topics. She died in 1994 and Jack followed her in 1998.

Jack, standing on the left, and the Eton Outcasts

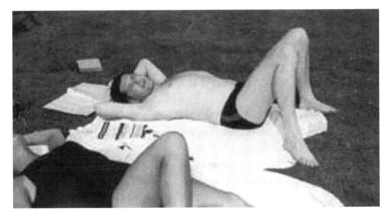

A frequent and popular visitor was Tony Crosland, our MP

Jack & Frankie, 1946, still at Gypsy Hall. Photograph by Denis Healey

Jack and Frankie in their 80s. Photograph by Derry Moore. NPG

Jack destroyed the letters in old age, after he had spent about 3 years two-finger typing them up. I think they did not want them read in full as there would almost certainly have been scandalous or intimate details of friends' and also their own relationship.

I found 2 letters together in a plastic folder. I am sure that these are the first letter she ever wrote to him (before they were married) and the last when she travelled alone to the US to promote her book on P.G. Wodehouse. The first is a one pager. He has labelled it 'Lonsdale'. The other, or last, was long, so I include only an excerpt.

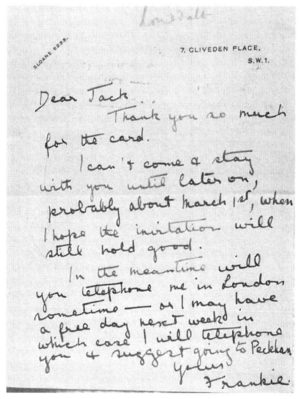

The second letter is labelled 'Donaldson'. She often mentioned Dianitia but I cannot find out who she is. Nor Arlene, whose husband seems to have been interviewing her about the P.G. Wodehouse book.

Darling Jack [Donaldson]

This is a foul hotel although the best in Chicago. Rather like E. Berlin. Room service takes 40 mins to go down. *The Drake* CHICAGO

The first day was typical 3 hr with Arlene! Her husband had decided to interview me. Unusual + I's thought because he was interested. Dianitia said he was U. laid + made I had for me if Arlene kicked him + said crossly 'You never get to the german stuff.' I was nervous + twisted my hands they said afterwards but otherwise O.K. Then to Lippincotts where we

22: Who's Who:

People mentioned in the letters

There are so many people mentioned in these letters that it would be too much interruption to describe them in full as you read. I have compiled a Who's Who here. More information can be found about many of the people mentioned, on the internet.

Initials designate groups as follows:

Family and relations =F

Close friends from before the war. =C

Peckham Health Centre friends, from the 1930s =PHC

The Wood House =WH

Directly connected to the War and the army =W

GH Gypsy Hall Farm =GH

Members of the public, writers, politicians etc =P

People are listed alphabetically by their first names in most cases, as this is how they appear in the text.

- Adrienne Allen, (C) actress
- Amy Moore, (PHC & GH) secretary at Peckham, helped at Gypsy Hall
- Anni and Haschi: (PHC) Anni Noll, a German doctor who had been told she must not treat Jews. One of the Peckham doctors, specialising in the care and treatment of mothers and children. Later she married Haschi Wasserman. She was Frankie's close friend and adviser about children.
- Anthony Eden (P) Foreign Secretary most of the war.
- Anthony Mildmay (Lord Mildmay of Flete), (C) lived with the Cazalets. Later a leading amateur steeple chaser.
- Anthony Shawcross. (F) Jack's brother-in-law
- Aunt Isy (Izzie) Lady Isabel Margesson, (F) Jack's maternal aunt, married to uncle Mag, (Sir Mortimer Margesson) born Lady Isabel Hobart Hampden. (See Margesson family)
- Baba Metcalfe, (C)social figure, friend of Freddy Lonsdale
- Bill Alexander, (PHC +W) a Peckham friend, commander of the International Brigade in Spain
- Billy Rootes. (C) Sir William Rootes of Hillman cars. Frankie was his secretary before she married

- Bob Laycock, (W) married to Angie Dudley Ward (F). Distinguished commando leader and later general.
- Bos, Bosworth Monck, (W+F) war colleague, became a great friend
- Brendan Bracken, (P) Minister of Information, owner of Financial News
- Bryant (GH) – solicitor
- Buck – Earl de la Warr, (F) farmer, politician, friend
- Buddy – Edward Cazalet, (C) son of Leonora and Peter.
- Carling (GH) bailiff/Farm Manager at GH.
- Children of Jack and Frankie: Thomas, Rose and, post-war, Kate. (F)
- Christopher Sykes (P), In June 1940 joined SO1 (later Special Operations Executive [SOE]).
- Clough Williams Ellis (P) architect whose best-known work is Port Meirion
- Clyde Higgs (GH) successful local Warwickshire farmer
- Coney Jarvis (C) wife of Ralph, at Eton with Jack. With Mary Dunn she accompanied Frankie to the Agricultural Institute at the beginning of the war. Coney was also very beautiful, and blonde. Frankie was very beautiful too, in a chic kind of way, perhaps less striking than Coney and Mary, and the three of them must have sent shock waves through Moulton Agricultural Institute when they arrived there at the beginning of the war.
- Constant, (W) an army colleague
- Cyril Wheeldon, son of the village shopkeeper. He started working part-time on the farm when he was about 14.
- Dave (Williamson), (C) husband of Jan
- David Margesson, (F) Jack's first cousin and Baldwin's chief Whip. A conservative MP and then Minister of War. Later Viscount Margesson
- De la Mare (F) Jack's sister Katta married Dick de la Mare, who was Walter de la Mare's son. They had 4 children: Tilly, Giles, Richard and Ben.
- Dedie, (F) Jack's mother's lady's maid.
- Denis Healey, (W, P and later C) who became a friend and political ally after the war. Gave the address at Jack's funeral in 1998.
- Dick de la Mare (F) Jack's brother-in-law
- Dick Watney(C) – old friend of Frankie's

- Dorothy Dickson was an American born London based actress and singer.
- Dorrie Stapledon, (GH) wife of Sir George, or Stapes
- Drs. 'The Drs' (PHC) This referred to Dr Donald Scott Williamson, known as Dod, and Dr Innes Pearse, known as Pete. Together they founded the Peckham Pioneer Health Centre. This experiment in community health attracted Jack as a young man, when he had just become a socialist as a result of the General Strike, and he put half his capital into its development. He then gave up his job as a banker and worked at Peckham instead. Frankie supported him in this, and my brother and I were born under the aegis of the Centre. Such children are known as Peckham babies. Dod's brother Bruce was a heart specialist, and gave advice about my brother Thomas, who was born with a heart condition.
- Duff Cooper (P) Minister of Information in the early part of the war and later British Ambassador in Paris.
- Durling, (WH) builder of the Wood House
- Eddie Sackville West, (C) writer and old friend. Later prominent music critic
- Elsa Maxwell, an American gossip columnist, author, songwriter, and professional hostess
- Emerald Cunard, (C) famous hostess, a friend of Jack
- Emlyn Williams (P) a Welsh dramatist and actor.
- Evelyn Waugh (W + C) was at this time a wartime acquaintance, but later in Gloucestershire became a close friend
- Fisher's Gate, house of Buck, Lord de la Warr
- Francie Margesson, (F) married David Margesson
- Frank Margesson, (F) their son
- Frank Sykes (GH) wrote *This Farming Business,* published by Faber and Faber 1944
- Freddy or Daddy – Frederick Lonsdale (F)
- Garrett, (C) Earl of Drogheda, friend from Eton, worked on Financial News (later head of FT, chairman of Covent Garden Opera). Joan, his wife & Derry, son.
- Gay Margesson, (F) daughter of Francie and David Margesson, married Martin Charteris.
- Geoffrey and Barbara Horn. (C)
- George & Anne Martelli. (C) George was a journalist.
- Gerry Koch de Gooreynd, (C) a business man friend

- Gerry Wellesley, (W) uncle of the Duke of Wellington, then Duke of Wellington himself.
- Gibby and Molly Debenham, (C) who were staying with them when war was declared in 1939 and also when peace was declared in 1945.
- Giles de la Mare, (F) Katta's son, Jack's nephew
- Green, (P) BBC producer
- Gropius, (WH) founder of the Bauhaus school of architecture
- Hall, a cowman (GH)
- Hannah and Rob Hudson. (C + P) Friends from before the war.
- Harry Sackville, (C) Buck de la Warr's son
- Highman, (GH) farm worker and later foreman
- Hinch, Viscount Hinchingbrooke, (C) son of Earl of Sandwich. He was a member of parliament during the war.
- Hudson, Hannah and Rob (C). Rob was Minister of Agriculture
- Humphrey Lomer, (W) Grenadier Guards posted with Jack
- Jan and Dave and Anni and Haschi (PHC + C) spent a lot of time with Frankie during the war.
- Jan Margesson, (F) daughter of Francie and David Margesson
- Jan Williamson, married to Dave, brother of Dod, Dr Scott Williamson. Jan was a painter friend of Jack's from before his marriage and Dave was the brother of Dod, Dr Donald Scott Williamson who ran Peckham Health Ccentre with his wife, Dr Innes Pearce, known as Pete
- Jerry Koch (G Koch de Gooreynd) (W)
- Joe, one of the farm workers (GH)
- John and Nancy Hare (C) – close friends. John became Lord Blakenham
- Johnnie and Madeleine Miller. (C) – Johnnie wrote for a US newspaper
- Jones (GH) bailiff/Farm Manager at GH.
- Julian Sorsbie (C) – a man to whom Jack lent a large sum of money (£5,000) and who failed to repay it. The cash shortage arising from this was a continuing saga although I have cut most of it out..
- Katta, (F) Jack's sister, married to Dick de la Mare, son of Walter de la Mare
- Kitty Sackville, (C) daughter of Buck de la Warr, later m Frank Giles, later editor of the Sunday Times.

- Lady Sandwich (C)– Hinch's mother. May have been a relation of some kind
- Lavendon – Mary Dunn's farm
- Leonora Cazalet. (C) She had been Leonora Wodehouse, and was the adored stepdaughter of P G Wodehouse (one of his books was dedicated to 'Leonora, queen of her species'). Frankie had been at school with her. It was through the Cazalets that my parents met, and their first house, the Wood House, designed by Walter Gropius of Bauhaus fame, was built on land bought from the Cazalets in Kent.
- Lucy Crocker (PHC) (later married Philip Pearce and moved to Ireland where they founded the Shanagarry Pottery). Much loved social worker at Peckham.
- Mab, (F) Frankie's sister. Geoff Poole, her first husband
- Malcolm Messer, (GH) editor of the Farmer's Weekly
- Margesson family: Lady Isabel Hobart Hampden, Aunt Isy, Jack's maternal aunt, married Sir Mortimer Margesson (Uncle Mag) and had David Margesson who was a renowned government chief whip in the 1930s and Secretary of State for War from 1940-42, and later Viscount Margesson. He married Frances Leggett and had 3 children: Gay, Jan and Frank. Gay married Martin Charteris who became Private Secretary to the Queen.
- Margetts (GH) – estate agent
- Marjorie, (GH) a land girl
- Mark Norman, (C)son of Monty Norman, of Bank of England fame
- Mary Coningham (W) – Air Marshal Sir Arthur "Mary" Coningham, KCB, KBE, DSO, MC, DFC, AFC an Australian who had met Frankie and her family at Birchington where they lived at one point. Aged 12, she had been a favourite of his, and he now crops up from time to time with a 'good war'.
- Mary Day (GH) also of Farmers Weekly, married Malcolm Messer
- Mary Dunn (Lady Mary St Clair Erskine, married Philip Dunn). (C) I was brought up to understand that Mary was without rival the most attractive woman of her generation and set. She was not strictly beautiful, but had the kind of charm which is apparent even to small children, and we adored her.
- Mary Langman, (PHC) a Peckham helper and supporter. Later founder of Whole Food
- Maxwell Fry, (WH) architect and friend

- Metcalfe, (GH) cowman at GH
- Miss Strang (GH) – Moulton
- Molly, (F) Jack's sister, married to Anthony Shawcross
- Molly, (GH) governess and looked after children
- Moulton, Northamptonshire Farm Institute
- Mr. Ball, (GH) bank manager
- Mr. Clarke (GH) solicitor
- Mr. Lindsay (GH) – assistant to Mr. Stewart
- Mr. Stewart (GH) – head of the above
- Mrs. Higley, (GH) a villager of Wilmcote who lived opposite and befriended us
- Mrs. Mandelbaum and Freda, (WH) both refugees to whom my parents had given temporary accommodation before the war
- Mrs. Saunders (WH) looked after the cottage at Ivy Hatch where Jack and Frankie lived while the Wood House was being built
- Mummy – Frankie's mother Leslie Lonsdale (F)
- Nanny, Old Nan. (F) Jack's nanny, by then retired, came to stay often to help Frankie. We adored her. She lived in Brighton and we used to go on holiday there to stay with her.
- Nigel Seeley, (C) old friend
- Nora, (GH) sister of Mrs. Higley of Wilmcote. Came to help Frankie and look after us children in the war.
- Oakley/Conkers (GH) farm worker
- Oliver and Maureen Stanley. (C+P) Secretary of State for War in 1940. Close friends of Freddy Lonsdale and Frankie. Both were Frankie's great friends (via her father, Freddy Lonsdale)
- Pattison. (GH+C) Pat, county organiser at first and later close farming adviser to Frankie. He became a longstanding friend of the family.
- Peggy Dunne, (C) another beauty and my godmother. Peggy lived in Warwickshire at a lovely house called Chadshunt, was a great solace to Frankie and bailed her out with money loans when the going got tough. She was married to Phil Dunne who was too right-wing for my parents' taste.
- Peter Cazalet (C) at Eton with Jack and later in life a race horse trainer, including of the Queen Mother's steeple chasers)
- Peter Fleming (C+W)
- Phil Dunne, (C) Peggy's husband . A Commando in the war
- Philip Dunn, (C) Mary's husband.

- Plummy and Ethel (C) – PG Wodehouse and his wife. Ethel was mother of Leonora Cazalet, Jack was one of the last English people to see them in the war. Price, (GH) a cowman at Gypsy Hall. Finally Frankie had found one she could work with and respect.
- Quentin (Quintin) Hogg (P) a conservative MP, who later became Viscount Hailsham, a senior Tory party figure.
- Racine, M and Mme (W) were the station master and his wife at Jack's first posting in Normandy.
- Ralph Jarvis, (C) at Eton with Jack, and best man at their wedding.
- Randolph (P) – Churchill, son of Winston
- Reggie Fellowes, (W) later Brigadier, Jack's CO
- Robertson Scott (P) founded and edited the magazine 'The Countryman'
- Rob Hudson (C) was Minister of Agriculture
- Robin Bolton, (PHC) a doctor at Peckham
- Ronnie Squire, (C)well known actor who had parts in many of Freddy's plays
- Runton: seaside family house shared by Jack with his 2 sisters, near Cromer
- Serge Chermayeff, (C) architect, living in America
- Shawcross (F) Jack's sister Molly married Anthony Shawcross. They had 3 children: Betty, David and Sam
- Shearer, (W) a colleague repatriated for drunkeness
- Shellaker, (W) colleague of Jack in France
- SheShe (C) – Sheran Cazalet, daughter of Peter and Leonora, now Lady Hornby
- Shipbourne Grange, Cazalet house, from where Jack and Frankie were married
- Sir George Stapledon – Stapes – (GH) a grassland expert
- Sir Wm Wiseman. (P) Distinguished writer and friend of Freddy Lonsdale
- Susan, (F) daughter of Frankie's sister Mavis
- The Wheeldons. (GH) Mrs. Wheeldon ran the local village shop in Wilmcote. Her son Cyril later came to work at GH
- Thelma Cazalet-Keir, (C) Peter's sister, married to David Keir
- Tortor - Victoria Gilmour (C) one of Frankie's closest friends.
- Vere Margesson, brother of David.

- Victor Cazalet – (C) brother of Peter, Tory MP later killed in air smash
- Walter Gropius (WH+P) – designed and constructed the Wood House with the help of Maxwell Fry.
- Walter Legge was an English classical record producer, most notably for EMI. His recordings include regarded as classics and reissued by EMI as "Great Recordings of the Century". He married Elisabeth Schwarzkopf, the famous German soprano
- Walters, (GH) agricultural adviser
- Webb, (WH) gardener at the Wood House
- Wells Coates, (GH) architects
- Wilkes, (GH) agricultural adviser
- William Davis, (GH) ? War Committee and worked at Dodwell, ? a war committee farm
- Wogan Phillips (P) Wikipedia: Wogan Philipps, 2nd Baron Milford (25 February 1902 – 30 November 1993) was the only member of the Communist Party of Great Britain ever to sit in the House of Lords.

Index

47849772R00194

Made in the USA
Middletown, DE
04 September 2017